O9-BTN-491

The Case for the Living Wage

HD
4918
.W264
2004

THE CASE FOR THE LIVING WAGE

Jerold L. Waltman

Algora Publishing
New York

KVCC KALAMAZOO VALLEY
COMMUNITY COLLEGE
LIBRARY

JAN 3 0 2006

© 2004 by Algora Publishing.
All Rights Reserved
www.algora.com

No portion of this book (beyond what is permitted by
Sections 107 or 108 of the United States Copyright Act of 1976)
may be reproduced by any process, stored in a retrieval system,
or transmitted in any form, or by any means, without the
express written permission of the publisher.
ISBN: 0-87586-302-7 (softcover)
ISBN: 0-87586-303-5 (hardcover)
ISBN: 0-87586-304-3 (ebook)

Library of Congress Cataloging-in-Publication Data

Waltman, Jerold L., 1945-
  The case for the living wage / Jerold Waltman.
    p. cm.
  ISBN 0-87586-302-7 (softcover : alk. paper) — ISBN 0-87586-303-5 (hardcover : alk. paper) — ISBN 0-87586-304-3 (ebook)
  1. Minimum wage—United States. 2. Minimum wage—Great Britain.
I. Title.

  HD4918.W264 2004
  331.2'3'0973—dc22

                              2004012894

Living Wage: Hardworking cart collector

© Markku Lahdesmaki/CORBIS
 Photographer: Markku Lahdesmaki
 Date Photographed: July 17, 2001

Printed in the United States

Alibris M-00166 1-18-06 $22

Dedicated to the Memory of Monsignor John A. Ryan (1869-1945)

ACKNOWLEDGEMENTS

One of the most pleasant, and humbling, aspects of writing a book is reflecting back on all the help you have received. Perhaps my greatest debt is to the Aubrey Lucas Faculty Development Fund at the University of Southern Mississippi. It provided invaluable resources for travel to Australia and Britain during the early stages of the research. The librarians at the University of Southern Mississippi responded to my continual requests for information with their usual efficiency and good humor. About halfway through this project I moved to Baylor University. No academic could ask for a more congenial and lively environment, nor for a better library staff to work with. A special word of thanks must go to the people in the interlibrary loan department, who tracked down many obscure works. Jenice Langston, the Administrative Assistant in the Department of Political Science, and Paul Deng, my graduate assistant, went far above the call of duty in preparing the figures and tables.

I was graciously hosted during a trip to Australia by Ian Watson, Ron Callus, John Buchanan, Merilyn Bryce, Linda Cowen, and the entire staff of the University of Sydney's Australian Centre for Industrial Relations Research and Training. The holdings in their library were second only to the quality of the conversations I was privileged to have there. I have also accumulated many debts in Britain. Victor Patterson of the Department of Trade and Industry has ably instructed me in many features of the minimum wage. Bharti Patel, Jeff Masters, and Tim Bickerstaffe of the now defunct Low Pay Unit were a continual source of help and encouragement. Deborah Littman of Unison provided both insight and aid at several critical points. Donley Studlar, Executive Secretary of the British Politics Group, helped point me to some polling data.

I am always pleasantly surprised by how much academics are willing to help each other. As but one special example, I e-mailed Martin Evans of the University of Bath, whom I have never met, about some technical data. He wrote an immediate and lengthy response, and pointed me toward some additional information as well.

I also want to thank Martin De Mers of Algora Publishing for his faith in the project, his suggestions for additional material, and his kind patience with my missed delivery dates. The entire editorial staff has shepherded this manuscript through the production phase with remarkable craftsmanship.

The book is better because of all these people. Of course, none of them bears any responsibility for the interpretations I have made of the information and help they have provided.

My wife Diane has listened to many ruminations on the living wage. Her belief in the project never flagged, and I am grateful for her patience during the many times I was preoccupied and/or absent.

A final word about the man to whom the book is dedicated, Monsignor John A. Ryan (1869-1945). His 1906 book The Living Wage: Its Ethical and Economic Aspects was the first to put the case for a living wage. Throughout his distinguished career, he remained committed to it as a necessary centerpiece of any progressive program of economic reform. In a sense, then, this book is a near-centennial tribute to his pioneering efforts. My hope is that if someone publishes a book on the living wage at the beginning of the next century, it will be a historical account of how it was adopted.

TABLE OF CONTENTS

1. INTRODUCTION

In her recent book, Barbara Ehrenreich ably and aptly portrayed the world of the low-paid in the United States.[1] Writing pungently and movingly about working as a waitress and motel housekeeper in Florida, a maid in Maine, and a Wal-Mart "associate" in Minnesota, she has put a human face on the poverty and inequality that now pervade American life despite years of sustained economic prosperity. We meet a waitress named Gail who is on the verge of being homeless because she cannot afford the deposit and first month's rent required to lease an apartment. We share time with Carlie while she manages to enjoy soap operas as she cleans one motel room after another. We cringe at the description of Holly, one of the maids in Maine, who works despite having an injury because she cannot afford to take the time off, and then apologizes to her boss for bothering him with her problem. We are touched by Melissa, a fellow Wal-Mart employee who "calculates in very small units of currency," but who brings Barbara a sandwich when she learns that she is living in a motel without a kitchen.

Polly Toynbee wrote a parallel book for Britain.[2] Her work included stops at a hospital, a school kitchen, a cake-packing firm, a child care center, and a nursing home. We admired but despaired for the fate of Winston, who works as a low-wage porter at a hospital and who will, if everyone else's experience is any indication, never move very far up the wage scale despite his ardent desire to do

1. Barbara Ehrenreich, *Nickel and Dimed: On (Not) Getting By in America* (New York: Metropolitan Books, 2001).
2. Polly Toynbee, *Hard Work: Life in Low Pay Britain* (London: Bloomsbury, 2003).

a good job. He works for one of the many private contractors that now comprise a large chunk of the public sector in Britain and which make their profit by squeezing their workers for all they are worth. We can hardly believe that Maggie keeps such a good attitude as more work is piled on her for only a token amount of extra pay. The pace of the work at the school kitchen she toils in, especially when it comes to serve as a central kitchen for the private firm with contracts for several schools, destroys any possibility of seeing the job as a service to the students. (There could be little more irony, or tragedy, in the fact that the school is named for Clement Attlee.) Then there is Dorcas, who tries her best to care for the elderly under mind-boggling working conditions.

It is not only the poverty and the signs of inequality (maids cleaning mansions) that are wrenching, though they certainly are. It is also the indignities, small and large, to which these people are subjected that are so objectionable. Their time does not matter. Toynbee paints a squalid picture of the conditions under which people must stand around waiting to apply for low-wage jobs at various agencies. At the U.S. maids' agency, the workers must show up early and clean up late, all on their own time. At the Florida restaurant, people must come in on their day off for a mandatory meeting. Their families do not matter. Their health does not matter. They live on the thin edge of utter poverty, and both they and their employers know it. Ehrenreich describes arriving in Maine this way:

> [T]his sudden removal to an unknown state is not all that different from the kinds of dislocations that routinely segment the lives of the truly poor. You lose your job, your car, or your babysitter. Or maybe you lose your home because you've been living with a mother or a sister who throws you out when her boyfriend comes back or because she needs the bed or sofa you've been sleeping on for some other wayward family member. And there you are. (p. 52)

Consequently, these people can talk back or stand up to the often surly managers and supervisors only at great risk. They have, in essence, almost no control over their lives. It is easy to understand how they come to feel isolated in their own country, to feel that somehow they do not belong. A large number of the citizens of the U.S. and Britain are effectively cut off from normal life.

None of this is to deny that some, even (perhaps) many, of the poor are there because of some personal failing or one or more bad decisions: dropping out of school, an unmarried pregnancy, alcohol abuse, and so forth. There is no point in assigning virtues to all the poor that many who are poor plainly do not have, or in depicting them as purely the victims of circumstance. Nevertheless, poverty adds its own independent force to these difficulties and crushingly magnifies their consequences. Furthermore, having not even a bare minimum of economic security reinforces people's sense, on a daily basis, that they are somehow worth less than others. In societies that are built on the inherent value of each individual and that prize political democracy, the debilitated lives led by many of our fellow citizens is something that should not and simply cannot be ignored. The sales of Ehrenreich's and Toynbee's books indicate that many Americans and Britons agree.

We will discover in Chapter 3 that poverty is far more widespread in the United States and Britain than most people think. In short, the people Ehrenreich and Toynbee wrote about are not aberrations. They are numerous, and while many may only be temporarily poor, that does not mitigate their plight. Many of them, moreover, are tragically slated to be there a very long time.

On top of this sad prevalence of poverty, the economic inequality that characterizes contemporary America and Britain is simply astonishing. A few years ago I drove through Breckenridge, Colorado. American prosperity gleamed on every street corner, a picture postcard scene if there ever was one. But right outside town stood a run-down mobile home encampment, peopled undoubtedly by those who serve and clean up after the well-heeled skiers. The contrast could not have been more stark. Stand outside an office building in central London (or one of the theatre and music venues on the South Bank) in the late evening and watch the army of cleaners that come in. Their lives could hardly be more different from those who work in those buildings during the day. Every piece of available statistical data confirms this impression, an ample supply of which will be provided in Chapter 4.

I believe a universal living wage would go some distance toward addressing the twin maladies of poverty and massive inequality. It is, of course, not a panacea; and it is only part of a remedy. Several other policies — chiefly universal public health care (in the U.S.) and humane services for those unable to work — would be necessary to abolish poverty. A variety of regulatory and tax reforms, along with the serious pursuit of full employment, would then be required to close the gaping inequalities. Nonetheless, the universal living wage should be the centerpiece of a revised social policy. Even without a single other policy shift, it would make both the United States and the United Kingdom markedly more egalitarian countries.

A universal living wage is different from the living-wage ordinances enacted by over 90 American local governments since 1994. Most of these apply only to businesses that contract with government[3], and by definition their geographical reach is limited. The universal living wage I am proposing is one set by the national government and applicable to all who work. I would define it as *a wage which would provide someone who works full-time year-round with a decent standard of living as measured by the criteria of the society in which he/she lives.* It would be calculated as an hourly figure and apply to those who work part-time as well as those employed full-time. I will flesh out the details of such a living wage in a subsequent chapter.

The local ordinances have unquestionably made life better for large numbers of low-paid workers, but they are even more important politically. To wit, following a hallowed American tradition, dedicated activists have utilized state and local governments to put the issue of a living wage on the agenda. After a successful coalition of unions, community activists, and religious groups won a living wage in Baltimore in 1994, the movement spread rapidly across the nation. Living wage battles were soon being fought coast to coast; newspapers and magazines were publishing articles on the idea; think tanks were sponsoring symposia; national organizations, particularly the Association of Community Organizations for Reform Now (ACORN), took up the cause.[4] The educational value of these activities has been incalculable.

In Great Britain, the living wage movement is still in its infancy. In East London there is a small but dedicated group working to lay the foundation. Alliances are beginning to be formed with unions and other organizations, but the absence of local governments with statute making authority means the campaign will have to be national. As we will discover, though, that tactic was effective in bringing about Britain's first minimum wage in 1909, and could well be replicated.

Those who advocate a new public policy must demonstrate three things: 1) that it is desirable; 2) that it is practical; and 3) that it will not do more harm than good. The first of these must be grounded in political theory and moral philosophy. No policy can or should stand a chance of being adopted unless it is morally and philosophically defensible. The appropriate queries are 1) Why is the condition it is designed to address a problem? And 2) Why is it important to address that matter through public action? Next, determining the practicality of

---

3. The exceptions are Santa Monica, California and New Orleans. The former's living wage applies to businesses located in the city's tourist district which gross over five million dollars annually (about 40 concerns); New Orleans' ordinance is more sweeping, applying to all businesses within the city.

4. Developments regarding the living wage can be found at the following websites: ACORN: acorn.org/acorn10/livingwage; Universal Living Wage Campaign: universallivingwage. org; and The Annie E. Casey Foundation: makingwageswork. org. The Economic Policy Institute maintains a bibliography of works related to the living wage at its website, epinet. org.

a proposed policy entails a careful and candid analysis of the way things work in practice. Many policies are no doubt desirable but simply impractical. I think a good case could be made, for instance, that everyone should have the opportunity to eat at the same quality restaurants. But the details of policy design and implementation such a law would require make this a completely impractical suggestion. Finally, no policy is without drawbacks. A policy may be both desirable and practical but its side effects overly harmful or even disastrous. In the real world, there are always tradeoffs, and there is no sense in not acknowledging them. A kind of summing up will have to be done, with the projected benefits weighed realistically against the costs.

When the proposed policy is one that has never been tried, items two and three will necessarily be speculative. If other countries have tried the policy, or a close cousin, of course, there are often, indeed usually, important lessons to be learned. A federal system, moreover, sometimes creates similar policy laboratories at the state and local level. If though the policy is a clear departure from previous practice, the argument must rely on whatever threads of knowledge can be gathered. What is important is that opponents must argue the same way. It is not enough for them to say, "That has never been tried" and that close the debate. If that argument carried the day, we would never have any policy innovation at all. It is not unfair that the burden of proof is on those wanting a new policy, and I accept that challenge. But that cuts two ways. If the philosophical discussion demonstrates that a given condition, in this instance poverty and raging economic inequality, are undermining the social fabric, then the cost of doing nothing must be weighed against the risks of trying something novel. In that case, defenders of the status quo should face the burden of proof.

Nor can opponents be allowed to get away with saying "Well, that's nice, but it's utopian because it's contrary to how the world works." We should remember that the idea of mass democracy was once considered absurd, outlandish, and a violation of the natural order. People were "obviously" incapable of governing themselves and needed leaders. So it often is today with what passes for economic theory. We continually hear a Greek chorus standing near the political process chanting "economic reality." But the economy, no less than the political system, is a human creation (a point to be elaborated in Chapter 7). It is not something "natural," like gravity. Consequently, just as the political system was remade along democratic lines, so too the economy can be shaped by human hands. Of course, there are insights that the social sciences, including economics, offer from which we should not shy away; but no way of ordering our economic affairs bears the Almighty's signature. Even, in fact, if some axiom such as the "law of supply and demand" is akin to gravity, we should not forget that we have learned how to fly airplanes.

In Chapters 2 and 3 I will develop the philosophical rationales for a living wage. I will begin by exploring civic republican theory and suggest how its better features are undermined by poverty and economic inequality. Civic republicanism's aim is a society composed of self-governing citizens. Poverty and vast economic inequality are both antithetical to a viable civic republican polity for they undermine the capacity of people to function as citizens. At the same time, civic republicanism legitimates public action — subject to certain limiting conditions — to address social maladies of various descriptions. It does not separate the polity and the economy into watertight spheres subject to different standards of evaluation (or, worse yet, combine the polity and the economy and make economics the measuring rod of both) as modern individualist democratic theory tends to do. A living wage can flow from civic republicanism, then, if it can be shown to be the most sensible policy to fight poverty and inequality.

Next, I will examine a variety of religious traditions. The late medieval just wage theory points directly to a living wage. The church fathers taught that prices of any commodity, but especially labor, could not be just if they were merely set in a market. Though they and later Catholic thinkers fretted about how to set the just wage, the needs of the worker always figured prominently. All four major Western religious traditions — mainstream Protestantism, Judaism, evangelical Christianity, and Roman Catholicism — have something to say about poverty. Judaism and Roman Catholicism combine a societal duty to the poor with a command that everyone should work. A living wage would clearly satisfy both of these teachings. Mainline and evangelical Protestantism have rather different approaches, but both agree that seeking the eradication of poverty is an important Christian duty. As with civic republicanism, if we accept their approach, we must inquire into the workability and practicality of the living wage. Finally, there is a school of Christian thought that emphasizes the equality of all people. If that equality can be held to reach to economic affairs, then inequality should be at the least softened. Again, a living wage can emerge if it can be shown to be the most attractive instrument for doing this

To demonstrate that poverty and economic inequality are serious social problems in the United States and Britain, I provide the necessary data in Chapter 4. Because we increasingly live and work in economically homogenous enclaves, we can easily ignore the scale of poverty. It is too easy to keep it out of mind, and we need to face the reality of it squarely.

My hope is that by the time you finish Chapter 4 you will be convinced by at least one of the philosophical positions discussed and that you will be convinced that there is a need to address poverty and inequality. That still leaves the question of how best to go about it. In Chapter 5, I try to show that the living wage is the best possible policy among the various alternatives on offer. It will help more people at less cost, and at the same time reinforce the political and social values most people desire. It is not perfect, but it is highly desirable.

Chapter 6 is devoted to sketching how a living wage might be structured. I rely primarily on American examples here, but the general propositions are applicable to Britain as well. I will argue that fixing the living wage as a percentage of some objective factor is the best way to proceed.

Few political issues stir up as much white-hot political rhetoric as the minimum wage. I expect, therefore, heavy fire to be directed at my living wage proposal. In fact, the salvos that have been launched at the modest living-wage ordinances adopted by U.S. cities have been intense. I will address, as candidly and dispassionately as I can, the major arguments against a living wage in Chapter 7. Although some will be found to be baseless and others of doubtful validity, I acknowledge that there are difficulties.

Political support is crucial for any proposed policy. Most novel proposals begin with almost no political backing, and then over time, if they are lucky, they attract the necessary support, ordinarily a slow process. What is striking about the living wage is that the public, in both the United States and Britain, *already* supports it. Their support is clear, consistent, and cuts across the population. I am convinced that no politician has yet managed to put the pieces together properly, and that if one does, he or she will easily win public backing.

The next two chapters are more about contemporary politics. Chapter 9 traces the rise and fall of the minimum wage in both countries. It will show that the minimum wage was a central poverty-fighting tool in the early part of the twentieth century. Slowly, however, it gave way to social insurance and public assistance. This was a serious political mistake for advocates of the welfare state, as it decoupled work and the right to be lifted out of poverty. Chapter 10 will take up current welfare reform efforts. In both countries governments have revamped their welfare policies in the last decade. The stress has been on moving people off benefits and into work. However, very little attention, less in the United States even than in Britain, has been devoted to making work pay. Thus, I contend that we have come only halfway to welfare reform. To rebuild the welfare state we should look again to its past, to the living wage.

Australia's pioneering early twentieth century minimum wage legislation had conspicuous living wage overtones. Its federal statute called for a wage that met "the normal needs of the average employee regarded as a human being living in a civilized community." Countless British and American reformers saw this as a model for their own welfare states.

John Ryan's 1906 book *The Living Wage*, for instance, was one of the most widely commented on works of early twentieth century social thought. Its popularity led to its being reissued twice, in 1910 and 1915. Even as late as 1931, Barbara Armstrong, a noted scholar and policy adviser, tellingly entitled her treatise on ways to address poverty *Insuring the Essentials: Minimum Wage Plus Social Insurance*. Even the New Deal, we should recall, turned first to minimum wages, established as part of the 1933 National Recovery Administration, before they undertook the reforms that became the Social Security Act of 1935.[5] In Great Britain, the infant Labor Party offered a living wage as the bedrock of its social policy proposals. At its 1918 party conference, a resolution was adopted calling for a minimum wage that would "ensure every adult worker of either gender a statutory base line of wages not less than enough to provide all the requirements of a full development of body, mind, and character." An important 1919 party document explicitly called for a national living wage as a major priority.[6]

Where welfare state advocates went astray was in abandoning the living wage in favor of public expenditure policies. This was unfortunate philosophically and, as I shall argue at greater length later on, politically disastrous. Non-insurance based cash transfer policies, especially, brought a legion of difficulties in their train, and they provided too easy a target for the enemies of the welfare state. What we need now is a revived interest in a universal living wage, whether based on civic republican demands for equal citizenship or one of the religious formulations. It should occupy pride of place in a rejuvenated welfare state. My hope is that this book will help contribute something to such a revival.

---

5. The New Deal's efforts in the minimum wage are covered in George Paulsen, *A Living Wage for the Forgotten Man: The Quest for Fair Labor Standards, 1933-41* (Selingsgrove, PA: Susquehanna University Press, 1996).

6. The Australian law was discussed by an early American visitor Matthew B. Hammond, "The Minimum Wage in Great Britain and Australia," *Annals of the American Academy of Political and Social Science* 48 (1913), 22-36. The British experience is covered in G. D. H. Cole, *A History of the Labour Party from 1914* (New York: Augustus Kelley, 1949), chapters 1 and 2.

A NOTE ON TERMINOLOGY

There is often some confusion about the differences among a *minimum* wage, a *fair* wage, a *just* wage, and a *living* wage. People tend to use the terms interchangeably and without clear definition. A minimum wage is any legally mandated wage, no matter what its level or how calculated. A fair wage usually refers to a wage that provides the worker with a portion of the sales price of the product he or she makes. Its measure is the contribution to production. A just wage refers to the principle of the medieval church fathers that justice had a role to play in wage determination. They never chose exact criteria for its calculation. It is more uncertain, therefore, than other terms. A living wage, finally, looks to the needs of the employee.

Therefore, a minimum wage may be a living wage, or it may not be. And, an employer could voluntarily pay a living wage absent any government-set minimum wage. Thus, these two may overlap, but they are not coterminous. Similarly, a minimum wage could be a fair wage or a just wage, or neither. Again, a living wage might also be a fair wage, and would probably be a just wage by any measure.

My argument throughout this book is that the national minimum wage ought to be a living wage.

2. CIVIC REPUBLICANISM, POVERTY, AND INEQUALITY

The Anglo-American political tradition is composed of two distinct strains, liberal individualism and civic republicanism. For several reasons, liberal individualism largely came to occupy the field in both academic and popular political discourse in the thirty odd years following the end of World War II. Within the last decade or so, however, academics have been busy resurrecting and rehabilitating civic republicanism.[7] Yet, in the public domain liberal individualism still retains a relatively strong grip, shaping many contemporary political attitudes on both the right and the left.

Liberal individualism begins with the sanctity of the individual, who is thereby endowed with a fundamental right to personal liberty.[8] All individuals, it follows, should be free to lead their lives according to their own preferences. No one, consequently, can define the good life for another. The state emerges from a "social contract" to which individuals consent for the better protection of their rights. Majoritarian democracy is grafted onto this system as the legitimate way to conduct political business. The task of political institutions is to aggregate as accurately as possible the political preferences of the voters. If the procedures are fair and open, then what results must be just for it reflects the

---

7. See, for two major examples, Michael Sandel, *Democracy's Discontent: America in Search of a Public Philosophy* (Cambridge: Harvard University Press, 1996) and Robert Bellah, et al., *Habits of the Heart: Individualism and Commitment in American Life* (Berkeley: University of California Press, 1985).

8. Although it addresses a rather specific question, an excellent and recent spirited defense of liberal individualism is Brian Barry, *Culture and Equality: An Egalitarian Critique of Multiculturalism* (Cambridge: Harvard University Press, 2001).

preferences of those who cast ballots. However, the problem arises when the outcome of this procedure violates the rights of the individuals who compose the society. This the state should not do, since the people never gave it that power in the first place. Therefore, some checking mechanism must be at the ready. Liberal individualist politics thus exhibits two basic features. First, there is the contest between political forces, usually organized into political parties, for votes, which they carry out by seeking to convince the voters that their respective positions are more in accord with the voters' self-interest than their opponents'. Second, when the political coalition representing the majority enacts its policies, there is a contest testing whether these measures violate the rights of at least some of the citizenry, rights which are inviolate. There is, therefore, plenty of room for controversy here, especially given the tension between majoritarian democracy and individual rights. But it is controversy framed within an accepted corpus of rules and values. Party A and Party B differ over whether your self-interest is this or that. You choose, with no referent but your own system of values. (Perhaps even your altruistic sense may be addressed as self-interest, in that it makes you feel good or worthy. Or, your "enlightened self-interest," requiring a longer view, may be enlisted. It is still your choice, though.) One party wins and enacts its program. A march to the courts by the losers follows, claiming this or that "right" has been violated.

The triumph of this model over civic republicanism has been unfortunate for several reasons, but our chief concern here is how it has impoverished our economic debate. In this area, it has allowed the right to marry liberal individualism's concern with rights to an exaggerated form of protection for property rights. Claiming that property rights are equal to, and at the same time supportive of, other legal and political rights, the right has argued that the state is morally prohibited from interfering with how people exercise their property rights.[9] Even modest regulations which indirectly decrease the value of one's property — such as environmental regulations in wetlands that keep me from building a tract of vacation homes — are held to violate the property holder's "rights."[10] The "free market's" transaction value must be considered hallow, and off limits to state interference. It is, in this view, a matter of individual liberty, pure and simple.

---

9. The most powerful statement remains Milton Friedman, *Capitalism and Freedom* (Chicago: University of Chicago Press, 1962). A more directly political work is Robert Nozick, *Anarchy, State, and Utopia* (New York: Basic Books, 1974).

10. A forceful statement of this position can be found in Richard Epstein, *Takings: Private Property and the Power of Eminent Domain* (Cambridge: Harvard University Press, 1985).

On the left, the triumph of liberal individualism has produced two tendencies regarding economic policy: an attempt to uncouple property rights from other rights and a brief for the recognition of certain "social rights." The first is a defensive posture designed to convince courts not to hold economically redistributive policies invalid, one that began in the New Deal era, and until the 1980s was largely successful.[11] The second followed the British sociologist T.H. Marshall, who erected a developmental scheme of legal, political, and social "rights," each building on and in turn expanding the others.[12] Social rights, he held, consist of a series of rights to the benefices of the modern welfare state. If claims on society's product can be made a right, then the whole corpus of political debate, as well as the legal issues actionable in the courts, would change. In the end, redistributive policies enacted by the processes of majoritarian democracy are protected (and how difficult should it be to convince the lower 51% of income recipients that they can benefit from redistribution?) while new social rights are judicially actionable by plaintiffs, typically poor plaintiffs, seeking to secure state benefits.

What both the right and the left have shared is a view of the citizenry as an atomized collection of rights bearing individuals bound together purely by self-interest. Both have overlooked the moral character of citizenship and the importance of community life. In short, they have neglected the civic republican tradition, a tradition which, as Adrian Oldfield has stressed, "is at least as resilient a strain in western thinking as liberal individualism."[13]

THE CIVIC REPUBLICAN POLITY

Civic republicanism's origins lie in the ancient world, in the political theory undergirding several notable Greek city-states and the Roman republic.[14] Thereafter, it lay dormant until resurrected in the Italian city-states of the Renaissance, and then by the "Commonwealth men" of seventeenth-century

11. An excellent recent history, which takes issue with some of the previous historical consensus on the New Deal's constitutional implications, is G. Edward White, *The Constitution and the New Deal* (Cambridge: Harvard University Press, 2000).

12. T. H. Marshall, *Citizenship and Social Class* (Cambridge, UK: Cambridge University Press, 1950).

13. Adrian Oldfield, *Citizenship and Community: Civic Republicanism and the Modern World* (London: Routledge, 1990), 3.

14. The best and most thorough analysis of republican political theory is Phillip Petit, *Republicanism: A Theory of Freedom and Government* (Oxford: Oxford University Press, 1997).

England. From the latter, it was transported to the American colonies and flowered during the Revolutionary era and immediately afterward. While republican thinkers from these various periods parted company on several matters, their unifying focus was that the polity is a self-governing community of citizens.

The aim of the civic republican polity is maintaining the liberty of its citizens. Since liberty cannot be achieved outside a community — a wild animal can be "free" but it cannot be said to have "liberty" — the individual citizen must be intimately connected to the community. He must believe that his interests are inseparable from those of the community, and that the role of citizen is a natural part of life. The state can rely on its citizens, who after all are the state, to exercise civic virtue and to consider the needs of the community along with their own. The citizenry governs itself by the process of deliberation, a deliberation devoted to finding and pursuing the public interest. To this end, political institutions in a republic should evidence a certain balance and be rather slow acting, at least under ordinary circumstances. Representative democracy, which allows republics to be larger than city-states, is a method for the further protection of liberty. It is not, pointedly, an end in itself.

Unlike liberal individualism, which posits no overriding end for the polity, civic republicanism stands emphatically on liberty as its central value. Liberty is taken to mean being free from domination. More formally, according to Richard Petit, a leading contemporary republican theorist, "One agent dominates another if and only if they have a certain power over that other, in particular a power of interference on an arbitrary basis."[15] Domination can therefore take either of two forms. In the first, one private individual holds power over another (*dominium*); in the second, it is the state which exercises the domination (*imperium*). Both are equally odious to republicanism. If I am dominated, I am not free, no matter what the source of the domination. To be a citizen is to be at all times and all places free of domination, since citizenship is synonymous with the enjoyment of liberty.

Prohibiting *dominium* presupposes that no citizen can be the servant of another, for servanthood brings domination with it by its very nature. If you are my servant and I order you around, you are quite clearly being dominated. Nevertheless, it is important to note that you are dominated even if I choose not to order you around (for whatever reason). You still cannot look me in the eye as an equal, for we both know that "The Remains of the Day" is more realistic than

---

15. Petit, *Republicanism*, 52.

Wooster and Jeeves. Not only may I alter my reserved role at any time without consulting you, but you will also be ever mindful of my ability to do so, and that cannot help but affect how you think, feel, and act. You and I are both aware that there may come a time when you will have to tread gingerly. Citizens of a republic simply cannot have such a relationship. As Petit said of civic republicans:

> The heights that they identified held out the prospect of a way of life within which none of them had to bow and scrape to others; they would each be capable of standing on their own two feet; they would each be able to look others squarely in the eye.[16]

Or, as Walt Whitman succinctly described a citizen, "Neither a servant nor a master am I."[17]

Governmental power can of course be a source of domination also, for the enormous power of the state is ever pregnant with the potential for domination. There is, however, a critical difference here. Whereas interference, real or potential, by one individual over another's choices is by its nature domination, governmental interference in one's affairs may or may not be. This is because liberty can only be made meaningful in a community, and the needs of the community will necessarily at times come into conflict with one or more individuals' autonomy, or at least with individuals' autonomy as they would define it. It is the community that makes liberty possible, and a citizen's freedom is inseparable from the interests and health of the community. As Blackstone noted, "Laws, when prudently framed, are by no means subversive but rather introductive of liberty."[18]

What is required for governmental interference to be legitimate and not *imperium* is that it be adopted by proper procedures, that it be non-arbitrary, and that there remain a "contestability" to the policy, an opportunity for citizens to overturn it if they deem a different direction to be in the public interest. If these criteria are met, then you cannot assert that you have some kind of *a priori* right not to be interfered with. Your freedom consists in your not being dominated; it is not the right to be shielded from the operation of just laws.

This is where civic republicanism and political theories based in neoclassical economics (as well as those based on extreme versions of a right to

---

16. Petit, *Republicanism*, 133.

17. Quoted in Lawrence Glickman, *A Living Wage: American Workers and the Making of a Consumer Society* (Ithaca, NY: Cornell University Press, 1997), 61.

18. Quoted in Petit, *Republicanism*, 41.

privacy, it should be added to be fair) clash. Take Milton Friedman's argument that the right to buy and sell property at market prices is a fundamental liberty that should be guaranteed in the Constitution.[19] The civic republican would reply that, first, while a citizen certainly has property rights (and indeed that they are important rights), he/she also has property in rights. James Madison endorsed this sentiment in 1792 when he wrote that "as a man is said to have a right to his property, he may be equally said to have a property in his rights." Government, he went on, should "impartially secure to every man whatever is his own."[20] What he meant is that the liberty of the person, considered as a citizen, is the central concern. The right of property refers not merely, and certainly not exclusively, to the right to possess and accumulate physical goods; a person's property includes the possession and exercise of civil and political liberties.

Moreover, our civic republican would continue, economic life is not separable from political life. It is the pursuit of the collective interest of the citizenry in preserving their liberty that is paramount. Thus, I cannot claim that the state can brook no interference in my right to sell my apples at price X or construct a high-rise office building on my real estate. Of course it may interfere with my doing these, and a host of other activities for that matter. Its only constraints are utilizing proper procedures in adopting the policy, non-arbitrariness in carrying it out, and the maintenance of contestability. My rights are as a citizen, not as the owner of a lemonade stand. Thomas Jefferson argued in a letter to a friend in 1816 that governments do not exist to protect property. They exist, rather, to promote access to property, which, he said, is why he changed John Locke's trilogy of "life, liberty, and property" to "life, liberty, and the pursuit of happiness."[21]

Critics sometimes contend that civic republicanism, by granting the state such extensive powers, can suffocate the individual. Of course, it is theoretically possible that it could, but that is a faint threat in a viable republic. Republican politics endeavors to construct a society in which individuals are free to make the choices that they wish, to be truly free from domination today and the threat of domination tomorrow. If the citizenry, though, becomes selfish and

19. Milton and Rose Friedman, *Free to Choose: A Personal Statement* (New York: Harcourt Brace, 1980).

20. Quoted in Lance Banning, *The Sacred Fire of Liberty: James Madison and the Founding of the Federal Republic* (Ithaca, NY: Cornell University Press), 357.

21. Joyce Appleby, *Liberalism and Republicanism in the Historical Imagination* (Cambridge: Harvard University Press, 1992), 304.

irresponsible, then, yes, republican governments could become arbitrary and destructive of liberty. It is often, though, a rampant individualism that undermines individual freedom. In part, this is because it turns a blind eye to the domination that can be inherent in individuals' relations with each other. But it is also because that by asserting that there is no higher good than self-interest it destroys the whole. Tocqueville, it is worth recalling, was strongly in favor of "individuality," attainable only when people are free from domination, but deeply skeptical of "individualism," where people acknowledge no higher good than the pursuit of their own self-interest. In fact, one of the major concerns voiced throughout his writing was whether republican liberty could be maintained as democracy spread, or whether the offspring would swallow the parent.[22]

Consequently, "rights," whether the economic rights favored by Friedmanites or the privacy rights cherished by the left, cannot stand as impenetrable barriers to policies designed to achieve the public good.[23] To do so is to champion an individualism that is the path to isolation and ultimately to anarchy. Rights are a means to the accomplishing of liberty, not zones that by absolutely restricting state action are subversive of it.

POVERTY

Republics are composed of and governed by their citizens. Seeking to secure and protect the liberty of the citizenry, republics depend on both widespread civic virtue and active participation in public affairs. The role of citizen is not merely a legal status conferred by the state; it is rather a central component of the individual's life.

To be free in the republican sense, free from domination, requires that each citizen be autonomous. Without autonomy, the citizen cannot make the choices that are the benefits of liberty. Further, without autonomy the citizen is liable to be unduly swayed by others, and unable to reach her own conclusions about the needs of the community. Richard Dagger has defined autonomy as "the right to the protection and promotion of the ability to lead a self-governed life."[24]

---

22. Tocqueville's views on civic republicanism are discussed in Oldfield, *Citizenship and Community*, chap. 6.

23. Mary Ann Glendon has put this argument well in her *Rights Talk: The Impoverishment of Political Discourse* (New York: Free Press, 1991).

Autonomy is not a dichotomous variable, however, something either present or absent. "Autonomy, like other abilities," Dagger explains, "is not something we either do nor do not have; it is something we may possess to a greater or lesser extent, just as the ability to speak English or play chess varies considerably among English speakers and chess players."[25] It is a continuum, therefore, and it is not necessary that every citizen have an identical amount; what is required instead is merely that no citizen should be below a certain *threshold* of autonomy. Above that, "increasing someone's autonomy by widening the range of choices available . . . becomes less and less valuable. Rather than maximize autonomy, either in a select few individuals or in some abstract sense, as if we could pile up units of autonomy, we ought to be concerned with bringing as many people as possible up to that threshold. The idea is to promote autonomy by recognizing the right of autonomy, not to produce more and more autonomy for its own sake."[26]

What must we as citizens have, then, to reach this threshold of autonomy? First, of course, we must possess certain basic civil liberties, such as those found in the Bill of Rights. We must be free from unjust criminal prosecutions; we must be free to speak our minds and write what we wish; we must be free to exercise freedom of conscience; our private effects must be shielded from arbitrary intrusions; and our property must not be taken without just compensation. Additionally, we must have a guarantee of political participation, participation in which each counts as one and only one. In a representative democracy, this means voting, running for office if we choose, petitioning government, and organizing with others to promote our views.

But it also requires something more, namely the ability to live without depending on others. James Harrington, the foremost of English republican writers of the seventeenth century, included these among his aphorisms regarding politics:

> The man that cannot live upon his own must be a servant; but he that can live upon his own may be a freeman.
>
> Where a people cannot live upon their own, the government is either a monarchy or aristocracy; where a people can live upon their own, the government may be a democracy.[27]

---

24. Richard Dagger, *Civic Virtues: Rights, Citizenship and Republican Liberalism* (Oxford: Oxford University Press, 1997), 32. "Self-governing," it should be pointed out, stops considerably short of the concept of "self-actualization" used by psychologists such as Abraham Maslow.

25. Dagger, *Civic Virtues*, 30.

26. Dagger, *Civic Virtues*, 194.

Or, as Richard Petit put it in more modern language, "To be independent in the intended sense is to have the wherewithal to operate normally and properly in your society without having to beg or borrow from others, and without having to depend on their beneficence."[28]

If you do not live upon your own, therefore, your citizenship is wanting. Not only are you not free of the domination your purse-string holders have over you; your capacity for developing the independence of mind needed for the expeditious and just conduct of public business is also called into serious question. You must have the capacities to make choices both in your private sphere and when you participate in public affairs.

Without question, the economist and philosopher Amartya Sen has done the best thinking in this area.[29] He begins by laying out two concepts, "functionings" and "capabilities." Goods, he maintains, have four discrete aspects. There is first the notion of the good, say bread. We have a referent for "bread," defining it as a mixture of so much dough, so much water, and so forth. Second, there are the characteristics of goods, in this instance its color or nutritional value. Third, there is the function of the good, preventing hunger and providing nourishment in bread's case. Fourth, there is the utility of the good, that is, how much pleasure one derives from consuming it.

It is the "functionings" of the goods that are germane here. What we want people to possess is adequate health and vigor. It follows that to achieve an acceptable level of these "functionings," people must have the "capabilities" to secure certain goods. They need what Sen refers to as an adequate "capability set." In a modern society, part of the "capability set" will consist of non-material matters, such as the ability to read, to have access to knowledge, and the like.[30] Part of it, however, will be purely economic, the enjoyment of a certain standard of living. "In this approach what is valued is the *capability* to live well, and, in the specific economic context of standard of living, it values the capabilities associated with economic matters." Being free, therefore, he argues, requires a "basic capability set" composed of both economic and non-economic elements. Without this, one cannot be a citizen as republicans envisage citizenship.

---

27. Quoted in Charles Blitzer, ed., *The Political Writings of James Harrington* (New York: Liberal Arts Press, 1955), 4.

28. Petit, *Republicanism*, 158.

29. See "The Living Standard," *Oxford Economic Papers*, 36 (November 1984), Supplement, 74-90; *Commodities and Capabilities* (Amsterdam: North Holland, 1985); and "Capability and Well-Being," in Martha Nusbaum and Amartya Sen, eds., *The Quality of Life* (Oxford: Oxford University Press, 1993).

30. Sen, "Living Standard," 78.

Moreover, the capability set and the functionings it produces vary significantly from one society to another. Merely to have a roof over one's head, one set of clothes, and three bowls of gruel a day cannot fulfill the functioning requirement in a modern, prosperous society. Adam Smith himself addressed this point in 1776 in *The Wealth of Nations*:

> By necessaries I understand, not only the commodities necessary for the support of life, but whatever the custom of the country renders it indecent for creditable people, even of the lowest order, to be without. A linen shirt, for example, is, strictly speaking, not a necessary of life. The Greeks and Romans lived, I suppose, very comfortably, though they had no linen. But in the present times, through the greater part of Europe, a creditable day-labourer would be ashamed to appear in public without a linen shirt, the want of which would be supposed to denote that disgraceful state of poverty, which, it is presumed, no body can well fall into without extreme bad conduct. Custom, in the same manner, has rendered leather shoes a necessary of life in England. The poorest creditable person of either sex would be ashamed to appear in public without them . . . Under necessaries, therefore, I comprehend, not only those things which nature, but those things which the established rules of decency, have rendered necessary to the lowest rank of people.[31]

Sen made the same point two hundred years later regarding peoples' basic standard of living in modern, rich countries.

> Can they take part in the life of the community? Can they appear in public without shame and without feeling disgraced? Can they find worth-while jobs? Can they use their school education? Can they visit friends and relations if they choose? It is a question of what the persons can do or can be, and not just a question of their earnings and opulence, nor of their being contented. Freedom is the issue; not commodities, nor utility as such.[32]

Thomas Jefferson saw as clearly as Amartya Sen the link between republican citizenship and a base line of economic independence, and was more than willing to use public policies to bring people up to that level. Daniel Boorstin has argued that Jefferson was deeply concerned throughout his public career with how best to use government to provide the conditions for people to reach their potential.[33] Joyce Appleby adds that, as early as 1784, he wished "to use constitutional and statutory measures to make the poor independent."[34] He

---

31. Adam Smith, *The Wealth of Nations* (London: Methuen, 1911). Edited by Edwin Cannan. Vol. II, 354-55. (Originally published 1776)

32. Sen, "Living Standard," 86.

33. Daniel J. Boorstin, *The Lost World of Thomas Jefferson* (Boston: Beacon Press, 1960).

34. Appleby, *Liberalism and Republicanism*, 301.

proposed, for example, adopting a 50-acre property qualification for the right to vote in Virginia — and giving every landless adult white male 50 acres.

Jefferson's praise of the role of independent small farmers is often painted as a nostalgia trip, a utopian fantasy that, if it were ever feasible in the past, certainly was not in the emerging commercial republic of his middle age. A laudable ideal, perhaps, but hopelessly naive as a social blueprint in the early nineteenth century. But that is simply inaccurate. Jefferson in fact looked forward to and actively supported the commercialization of agriculture. "Working with a completely commercial mode of agriculture, Jefferson projected for America a dynamic food-producing and food-selling economy which promised the best of both worlds: economic independence for the bulk of the population and a rising standard of living."[35] It was the expansion of the stock of available arable land that was the key to securing the republican ideal of small farmers into the foreseeable future. If the land could be provided, Jefferson was optimistic about the American future of commercialized agriculture. In 1817 he wrote to a French correspondent that his optimism was "built much on the enlargement of the resources of life going hand in hand with the enlargement of territory, and the belief that men are disposed to live honestly, if the means of doing so are open to them."[36]

In sum, to be a citizen one must have a certain basic level of economic well-being, and that level must be judged by the standards of each society. Without it, no person can be free, and when people are not free the republican polity disintegrates. Adrian Oldfield has summed it up this way:

> For activity of any kind, including that involved in the practice of citizenship, people need certain resources. Some of these have to do with . . . civil, political, and legal rights. Others have to do with economic and social resources. Without health, education, and a reasonable living income, for instance, individuals do not have the capacity to be effective agents in the world, and the possibilities of a practice of citizenship are thus foreclosed in advance. Such rights and resources have to be secured for citizens, for citizenship is an egalitarian practice."[37]

Richard Petit put the same point more briefly. "If a republican state is committed to advancing the cause of freedom as non-domination among its

---

35. Appleby, *Liberalism and Republicanism*, 270.
36. Letter to Barre de Marbois, June 14, 1817, quoted in Appleby, *Liberalism and Republicanism*, 319.
37. Adrian Oldfield, *Citizenship and Community: Civic Republicanism and the Modern World* (London: Routledge, 1990), 27-28.

citizens, then it must embrace a policy of promoting socioeconomic independence."[38]

Poverty, therefore, has decided political consequences. By stunting the mind and warping the spirit, it makes people unfit for republican citizenship. Since the freedom of all citizens is dependent on the health of the political system, which in turn is dependent on the continuing practice of citizenship, the viability of a republican polity is threatened, and ultimately destroyed, by the threat of poverty.

To be sure, even at its most generous, the reach of who could be considered a citizen in the historical republics was quite restricted — to a small coterie of property-owning males who stood ready for military service. However, republican theory loses none of its cogency when the definition of citizen is expanded to include all adults. Rather than limit citizenship to those who already have the educational attainments and a degree of personal prosperity, the question for modern societies is how to make all adults fit for citizenship. The framework for political organization civic republicanism embodies can be as relevant to the politics of today as at those historical moments when it was dominant, if steps are taken to make citizenship a condition of every adult.

We must be at pains to point out that securing an acceptable level of material well-being for all is not a sufficient condition for keeping a republic, merely a necessary one. Republican citizenship requires that citizens utilize their well-being responsibly and for wise ends. They are free to be foolish and intemperate, but a republic cannot endure if they are. Rereading Harrington's aphorisms, the use of the word "may" in both of them is striking, and far more than merely suggestive. Here, of course, is where the role of education in the promotion of virtue becomes critical, but that is another avenue entirely. For the moment, we must address ourselves solely to the best mechanism for securing a basic level of material well-being to every citizen. First, however, we need to take up the issue of equality and inequality.

INEQUALITY

Republics, we have established, must address the problem of poverty. Further, the attack on poverty must be mounted by the state, for to leave it to private efforts is to leave its eradication uncertain. Citizenship must be

---

38. Petit, *Republicanism*, 159.

preserved by removing citizens from poverty, opening up the vistas of choice that are the essence of freedom. But what about equality of choice? Citizenship is by its nature egalitarian, as each person has to count and measure as one and only one. Does it follow that republican governments must secure material equality among their citizens? In a word, no.

A viable republic will, instead, have to adhere to three conditions. First, it must free all its citizens of the stain of poverty. Second, it must establish and maintain what Richard Petit calls "structural equality" among the citizenry. Third, it must soften the extremes of material inequality.

The issue of poverty has already been addressed. Passing on, we need only pause momentarily to dispense with the structural issue. What is required to meet this criterion is complete legal and political equality. When people appear before the courts and other institutions of government, they must be treated as equals. No citizen may stand outside the law, or have special rules apply to him. The principles and practices of the law must be shaped and applied in a completely non-arbitrary fashion. Turning to political equality, it is essential that political participation be conducted on the basis of one person one vote. No citizen may be denied the right to participation (in all its guises) and none can have more voice than another.

Let us turn now to the matter of material equality. As with poverty, a moral case can be made for material equality, but that is irrelevant here. In political terms, furthermore, an arguable case can be made that a republic would function better if there were material equality among its citizens. None would surely then have to bow and scrape. They could all eat at the same restaurants, afford similar clothes, and ride in the same section of the train or plane; and the similarity of their economic condition would bind their interests tightly together. If a society existed, then, with absolute, or even rough, pre-existing material equality, a republic would be an ideal and natural choice for the political system. However, republican political theory is not designed merely to provide a guide to what would be desirable in a social utopia; it is designed to be a program for the real world.

Therefore, two factors must be kept in mind. First, a market economy is the natural outgrowth of republican political structure. If people have even qualified property rights, then they must have the right to dispose of their property as they see fit. Transactions among private parties will thereby automatically characterize much of the economic activity in a republic. Because people have different endowments and different luck, inequalities in the possession of property will be an inevitability. Such inequalities are simply a natural byproduct of a market economy, and it cannot be otherwise. Since there is no way to maintain republican freedom without an accompanying market economy, we must accept that some economic inequality is going to be a fact of life in a republic.

Second, any attempt to legislate material equality would vest far too much power in the state to suit republican tastes. It would lead, that is, to *imperium*, which would demolish what you were trying to save. This is because the magnitude of the undertaking would create a state the scale of which would make it extremely difficult, if not impossible, to tether it to republican political institutions. Besides, how could it be done? If some people have a certain skill (say, hitting a little white ball with a stick) which others do not, and if people are willing to pay to watch those with the skill demonstrate it, how would you achieve material equality? You could not physically endow everyone with the skill. So, you would have to lower the skill level of those with it to make abilities equal. At my physical peak, for example, for Barry Bonds and me to be equal at the plate, he would have to have 25-pound weights attached to each wrist and wear a blindfold (at least). While the republic might not collapse if everyone was made equal in sports, if you did this to artists, musicians, dancers, and various other talented individuals, it would be a drab and oppressive world. Or, you could make the recipients of the largesse fork all of it over to a common pool, to be distributed to everyone. But would not at least some of the incentive go away? And what about the rules, regulations, and bureaucracy that would be required? At the same time, there are entrepreneurs who do serve the greater good while pursuing riches for themselves. New products and better ways of doing things spring from people whose creative abilities lie in these areas. To deprive them of the reasonable fruits of their labors hardly seems fair, and would surely lessen their propensity to tinker in the garage. No, a republican state that tried to utilize governmental power to enforce anything approaching material equality would likely not survive.

Nevertheless, too much inequality in material possessions is an equally serious problem. Again, both the moral case and the economic efficiency case against too much inequality, powerful though they may be, must yield to the political case. Severe inequalities in material conditions, to put it straightforwardly, can destroy the very bases on which legal and political equality are built. This is true for three reasons.

First, when citizens enjoy vastly different incomes, they begin to lose the sense of seeing each other as equals. When housing, clothes, vacations, food, and so forth differ enormously, people invariably become detached from those who are on the other side of the chasm. Their experiences cannot help but disconnect them, and they begin to see fellow citizens as somehow the "other," different from themselves, unapproachable and perhaps vexing. Everyone need not be able to afford an identical house, but the square footage and the acreage on which it sits should not be too far apart. If it is a matter of choice, of course — citizen A spends his discretionary income on a large house while citizen B enjoys expensive wines in a smaller house — that is altogether different. That very act of choice makes them similar.

Second, too much economic inequality can lead to skewed political participation. Any form of clientelism is obviously incompatible with republicanism. However, even far short of that, marked economic inequalities open up the possibility that some can, if not the guarantee that they will, buy ever larger megaphones to amplify their voices. In a healthy republic, every citizen's views need to be heard and considered, much as in a Quaker meeting. If one group of citizens can drown out others' voices, then a republic cannot be maintained. It is inevitable that economic power is going to lead to political power. And with the disparities that accompany a market economy, it is also inevitable that in a republic some are going to have more wherewithal to invest in the political debate than others. But that gap should be narrow rather than large. If we cannot eliminate megaphones, we can at least restrict their size.

Third, vast economic inequalities impair the public institutions that are a vital component of republican life. Republics require more domains than the courtroom and the polling station where citizens meet as equals, unaffected by wealth and income. Public parks, for example, are much more than attractive and pleasant locales. They are places where citizens can see each other and interact as equals. When those with superior wealth erect their private enclaves to enjoy tennis, picnics, and the outdoors, a link in the citizenship chain is broken. The same is true for public transport and public schools. When people do not see their personal fate linked to public institutions, they lose interest in them. Why should I, the wealthy begin to think, pay for these facilities which I do not use? When that happens a vital thread of a common citizenship is cut. Of even more central concern is the military. Citizen service in the military is the hallmark of a republic. When the army becomes largely a semi-mercenary force of those for whom it presents an attractive economic alternative, one of the central vestiges of citizenship is removed.

Republican theorists down through the ages have, consequently, been concerned with the political implications of economic inequality. James Harrington, for example, proposed an "agrarian law" that would limit the amount of land someone could own, a law "designed to control the distribution of land in such a way that there should always be enough free proprietors to constitute a many."[39] Throughout his writings, he speaks of the need for "balance," and part of that balance was in the distribution of material resources. Charles Blitzer explained that "Harrington is disturbed by the existence of extremes of wealth and poverty and prefers a more equal distribution of small holdings. But his justification was not a moral one; rather he argues that it will be economically efficient and productive as well as politically desirable."[40]

In the United States, James Madison, according to the respected historian Lance Banning, seconded Harrington believing "that power follows property [and] that great extremes of poverty and wealth are incompatible with freedom."[41] During the Revolution, Jefferson wrote to Madison that "Legislators cannot invent too many devices for subdividing property."[42] In 1792 the Republican party-oriented *National Gazette* published an article critical of policies that would serve to "increase inequalities of wealth, and to undermine the character of the people."[43] Banning sums up the ideology of the early Republican Party leaders as follows:

> America had come to be defined, in part, in terms of its relatively equal, agrarian balance of property. Republicans held it as a first principle that private morality and public virtue depended on the maintenance of this dis-tribution of wealth, a distribution profoundly threatened in their minds by the rise of the monied favorites of a Federalist administration.[44]

At the end of the day, then, inequalities of wealth corrode republican politics. They separate citizens one from another, lead to disparities in political participation, and weaken public institutions. While an attempt to effect absolute, or even near, economic equality among citizens would indeed pose a serious danger, failing to adopt public policies to soften the gargantuan inequalities that invariably result from the normal operation of a market economy is equally dangerous. While the state must tread cautiously in this area,

39. J. G. A. Pocock, *The Political Writings of James Harrington* (Cambridge, UK: Cambridge Univer-sity Press, 1977), 47.

40. Charles Blitzer, *An Immortal Commonwealth: The Political Thought of James Harrington* (New Haven: Yale University Press, 1960), 233.

41. Banning, *Sacred Fire of Liberty*, 40.

42. Quoted in Appleby, *Liberalism and Republicanism*, 300.

43. Lance Banning, *The Jeffersonian Persuasion: Evolution of a Party Ideology* (Ithaca, NY: Cornell University Press, 1978).

44. Banning, *Jeffersonian Persuasion*, 204.

therefore, it must not hesitate to tread. Adam Smith can be adduced again in support of this point.

> Is this improvement in the circumstances of the lower ranks of the people to be regarded as an advantage or as an inconveniency to the society? . . . [W]hat improves the circumstances of the greater part can never be regarded as an inconveniency to the whole. No society can surely be flourishing and happy, of which the far greater part of the members are poor and miserable.[45]

CONCLUSION

The noted journalist E.J. Dionne has written that "Talk of citizenship and civic virtue sounds utopian. In fact, it is the essence of practical politics. Only by restoring our sense of common citizenship can we hope to deal with the most profound — and practical — issues before us."[46] When we take the civic republican perspective on political economy, three conclusions press themselves on us. First, the state is not hobbled in economic matters by an undue attachment to property rights. Property rights are to be respected but not transformed into an untouchable icon. Second, poverty is incompatible with citizenship. Seeking to keep its own base solid, therefore, a republic must strive to make certain that none of its people live in poverty. Third, a republican state must guard against the growth of unhealthy material inequalities. While a measure of inequality will spring from the normal operation of an economy based in private property, the state must retain a watchful eye on income gaps lest they erode republican values and practices.

Civic republicanism does not, it must be stressed, point directly to the details of public policies in any of these areas. Specific policies emerge from intensive public discussion weighing the strengths and weaknesses of alternatives and through the operation of the balanced political institutions that are the hallmark of a republic. Republicanism, to quote Petit again, "presents us with a programme for developing policy, not with a policy blueprint."[47]

After we examine the religious foundations for a living wage and survey the extent of poverty and inequality in the United States and the United Kingdom, I will try to show that the living wage is the best available alternative for addressing poverty and inequality.

---

45. Smith, *Wealth of Nations*, 1, 80.
46. E. J. Dionne, *Why Americans Hate Politics* (New York: Simon and Schuster, 1991), 333.
47. Petit, *Republicanism*, 147.

3. Religious Foundations of a Living Wage

Religiously grounded arguments about public policy make many people nervous, often with good reason. History's annals are filled with examples of religious fanatics seeking to impose their views of the world on believers and non-believers alike, unhesitatingly, even eagerly, employing governmental coercion as a ready-made tool. In either a secular political order or a religiously plural society, allowing religious values to shape public policy, therefore, poses uncommon dangers.

Does it necessarily follow, though, that citizens who hold religious values must always refrain from arguing that the state should adopt policies they favor for religious reasons? Must we all come, as the saying goes, "naked to the public square"? John Rawls, representing a widely held view, certainly thought so, arguing that in the public realm citizens of a liberal polity must address each other only through the prism of "public reason." Public reason is defined as being composed of only those "presently accepted general beliefs and forms of reasoning found in common sense, and the methods and conclusions of science when these are not controversial."[48] We must not submit therefore political positions resting on appeals "to comprehensive religious or philosophical doctrines — to which we as individuals or members of associations see as the whole truth."[49] In a liberal society, if that position holds, arguments for a living

---

48. John Rawls, *Political Liberalism* (New York: Columbia University Press, 1993), 224.
49. Rawls, *Political Liberalism*, 224.

wage that are grounded in religious understandings would have to be kept off the table.

Rawls' position, however, is far too confining. Aside from the obvious problem that neither the American nor the British — indeed the entire Western — version of "public reason" is intelligible without knowing its religious origins, there is the matter of evolution and change. By Rawls' criteria, William Wilberforce's advocacy of ending the slave trade, William Lloyd Garrison's attack on slavery, and Martin Luther King's pleas for civil rights would all be illegitimate. In an attempt to correct this problem, Rawls later granted a rightful place to religious advocacy that *improves* public reason. However, this presents a fresh problem: Is contemporary American or British public reason capable of any further improvement? If so, we may well need some religiously motivated reformers. If not, isn't it rather arrogant to believe that we have reached some kind of end state regarding our public reason? In any event, is it really appropriate that citizens with religious convictions, or any strong viewpoints, be saddled with special handicaps in public discussions? Why should one group of people suffer special disabilities in explaining why they think government should do this or that?

Ronald Thiemann has offered a much sounder approach for measuring the appropriateness of religious arguments in the political arena.[50] Aware of both the dangers to a secular political order and the problems posed by religious pluralism, he sets out three guidelines religious arguments have to meet before they can be welcomed at the public square.

The first is "public accessibility." The premises of the argument, that is, must be open for public inspection. The theological framework supporting the argument must be spelled out and the way it supports the policy at issue must be specified with reasonable precision. Such openness cannot be demanded; but if it is not granted, then citizens should ignore the argument.

Second, there is the matter of "mutual respect." This condition means that those making religiously based arguments must travel beyond mere tolerance of other viewpoints. Religious advocates, while able to believe ardently that their position is correct, must absolutely refrain from questioning the motives or the integrity of their opponents. It is a political foul, leading to ejection from the public arena, to portray citizens with opposing views as anything other than honorable.

---

50. Ronald F. Thiemann, *Religion in Public Life: A Dilemma for Democracy* (Georgetown: Georgetown University Press, 1996).

Finally, religious arguments must possess "moral integrity." Borrowing from two other political philosophers, Amy Guttman and Dennis Thompson, Thiemann lays out three facets of this type of moral integrity. To achieve it, an argument must demonstrate 1) consistency of speech: the position taken must be truly moral, and not one that is merely self-serving; 2) consistency between speech and action: what is advocated must be accompanied by appropriate action; more colloquially, practice what you preach; and 3) integrity of principle: the implications of the argument must be taken seriously and followed to their logical conclusions.

If these three conditions are met, then policy arguments flowing from religious convictions should be welcomed into public discussions. Furthermore, once there, they should be addressed seriously by those holding opposing views, not shunned simply because people disagree with the rationale for the argument.

Three different religious arguments can be used to support a living wage: the just wage tradition, the command to care for the poor, and the problem that Christianity has with human inequality. All three of them meet the conditions elaborated by Thiemann.

THE JUST WAGE TRADITION

Christianity has always had an ambivalent relationship with market economics. On the one hand, the motor of market exchange, the desire to accumulate material possessions, at best sits uncomfortably with the way the ideal Christian is supposed to order his or her life, seeking first the Kingdom of God. At worst, the pursuit of worldly goods can easily slip over into greed, one of the deadly sins. On the other hand, merchants and wage earners were common enough throughout the biblical era, and the Scripture is replete with references to trade in wares as well as the earning of wages. Numerous parables from the Gospels, in fact, employ the language of mercantile exchange and the payment of wages.

Measuring the value of something by its "price" nonetheless cannot, in the final analysis, be squared with most Christian theology. This is especially true when the labor of a human being, a child of God, is involved. It is an unease that is reflected in the long history of the theory of the just price and, most importantly for our purposes, the just wage. This teaching has been primarily, although by no means exclusively, a product of Catholic social thought.

31

Its roots lie with the scholastics of the late medieval period. New Testament verses such as Matthew 10:10 ("for the worker is worth his keep"), Luke 10:7 ("for the laborer is worthy of his hire"), and I Timothy 5:8 ("the worker deserves his wages") were combined with concepts drawn from the patristic tradition and Roman and canon law to develop a complex and sophisticated theory of the just wage. Odd Langholm has written that:

> [W]henever economic exchange was being discussed, one of the funda-mental principles of scholastic ethics in the medieval period was that hon-est labor deserves its material reward. The adage repeatedly stated in the Bible, that "the laborer is worthy of his hire," and other scriptural texts to this effect, interpreted in material terms, was commonplace.[51]

Immediately prior to this period, Church teaching disdained the life of this world. Virtue, it taught, was to be found by withdrawing from the inevitable sinfulness of the world. Spurning its temptations and embracing the monastic life was the ideal. By the late medieval period, though, a more accommodating view of the world had taken root. Theologians, consequently, felt a need to apply Christian ethics to the whole range of human activities, including economics. For if the Godly life can be led in the world, then a theology of ethics must reach there also.

The principle of the just wage derived initially from the concept of the just price.[52] According to St. Thomas Aquinas and the other major scholastics, especially the Italians Sant'Antiono and San Bernardino, the just price of a product was its "normal and customary" price set in ordinary market transactions. From one perspective, then, it would appear that any price agreed on by a buyer and a seller is inherently just because it is simply a product of the law of supply and demand. However, that is not quite what the scholastics envisaged. They meant the "normal and customary" price determined by transactions in general, not that agreed on by any given buyer and seller.

This approach has echoed down through the centuries. The *New Catholic Encyclopedia* has this to say under the "Just Price" entry:

> The price of a thing is its value in terms of money. Value, in this context, is the capacity of goods to satisfy human wants . . .

---

51. Odd Langholm, *The Legacy of Scholasticism in Economic Thought: Antecedents of Choice and Power* (New York: Cambridge University Press, 1998), 119.
52. A general discussion of the just price and the just wage can be found in Diana Wood, *Medi-eval Economic thought* (New York: Cambridge University Press, 2002), chap. 6.

How can the equal capacity of commodities for satisfying human wants be calculated? Extreme answers [fixed values and pure market prices] must be rejected...

In opposition to such views, the traditional natural law theory maintains that the just price should be determined not by the usefulness of a commodity to this or that individual but to men generally.

For any given transaction to reflect a just price, several conditions must be met, conditions designed to ensure both that the bargaining between the parties was fair and that the result has truly been agreed to voluntarily by both. To begin, any type of violence or coercion makes the transaction completely unjust. Further, there must be no fraud or even deception. Pope Innocent IV (d. 1254), for instance, gave I Thessalonians 4:6 (which, referring to sexual conduct, commands that "no one shall wrong his brother or take advantage of him") a commercial meaning.[53] Thus, it was a combination of fair bargaining and informed consent that yielded a just price. Similarly, a just wage occurred only when both employer and employee knowingly and voluntarily agreed to the wage.

In addition to violence, fraud, and coercion, the scholastics also recognized the problem of unequal bargaining position. If one of the parties is desperate to make the bargain and the other not, then there is in effect compulsion. John Duns Scotus stressed that no one could take advantage of another in driving a bargain, and several writers condemned those who took advantage of shortages to drive up prices.[54]

Unequal bargaining power was seen as a special problem where wages were involved, for often the employee is more in need of obtaining the wage than the employer is of the service. Low income and dependency can easily lead to a bargain that has an odor of compulsion. Antonio stated explicitly that it was "unfair and sinful to pay less than the just wage because a worker had mouths to feed."[55] Free markets for workers' labor, in this view, could contribute to social good *if* they reduced the opportunities for employer compulsion by providing the worker with options. Conversely, a market was not just if, for whatever reason, alternatives were restricted. Moreover, the existence of a market certainly did not relieve the employer of the moral responsibility to pay a just wage.

---

53. Steven A. Epstein, "The Theory and Practice of the Just Wage," *Journal of Medieval History* 17 (1991), 66.

54. Epstein, "Theory and Practice of the Just Wage," 56.

55. Quoted in Edd Noell, "In Pursuit of the Just Wage: A Comparison of Reformation and Counter-Reformation Economic Thought," *Journal of the History of Economic Thought* 23 (2001), 473.

It is interesting to note that the modern tax law recognizes the same basic features of the just price as the scholastics did. The U.S Internal Revenue Code defines "fair market value" as "the amount at which the property would change hands between a willing buyer and a willing seller when the former is not under any compulsion to buy and the latter is not under any compulsion to sell, both parties having reasonable knowledge of the relevant facts."[56] Appropriately modified, that would suffice as a good definition of the just wage.

Edd Noell sums up the scholastics' position on the just wage as follows:

> By the time of the Protestant reformation in the sixteenth century, there was general agreement among scholastics on several facets of the just wage. Justice in the labor market was to be pursued through fair bargaining, and wages should be set according to the markets' common estimate in the absence of fraud or violence. Beyond physical violence, economic compulsion was possible due to disadvantages in bargaining power held by either the employee or employer; competition in the labor market could check such compulsion.[57]

By the time of the Counter-reformation, many noted Catholic theologians became more approving of markets.[58] Individual transactions were given more standing as reflective of justice in setting prices and wages. Even so, these theorists never completely removed ethics from the economic world. People were not relieved of their moral responsibility, especially when it came to wages, merely because the market allowed a certain price to be paid. Business people were still, as all people, accountable for the morality of their actions.

Subsequently, while the just price was never erased entirely from Catholic social teaching, it did become dormant until the late nineteenth century. Pope Leo XIII then gave it a new and vibrant life with the papal encyclical *Rerum Novarum* (On the Condition of the Working Classes) in 1891. The first part of this famous encyclical sanctifies the private possession of property and dwells on the evils of socialism. Workers were admonished to perform their tasks conscientiously, to avoid ideas of class conflict, and to be skeptical of unions. As for employers, though, the payment of a just wage was held to be a fundamental requirement.

---

56. Internal Revenue Service, *Revenue Ruling 59-60*, 1959.

57. Noell, 474-75.

58. The most notable were associated with the Salamancan School headquartered in Spain. Noell, "Pursuit of the Just Wage" contains a brief discussion. A fuller treatment is Marjorie Grice-Hutchinson, *Early Economic Thought in Spain, 1177-1740* (London: Allen and Unwin, 1978).

Workers are not to be treated as slaves; justice demands that the dignity of human personality be respected in them, ennobled as it has been through what we call the Christian character. If we hearken to natural reason and to Christian philosophy, gainful occupations are not a mark of shame to man, but rather of respect, as they provide him with an honorable means of supporting life. It is shameful and inhuman, however, to use men as things for gain and to put no more value on them than what they are worth in muscle and energy. . .

Among the most important duties of employers, the principal one is to give every worker what is justly due him. Assuredly, to establish a rule of pay in accord with justice, many factors must be taken into account. But, in general, the rich and employers must remember that no laws, either human or divine, permit them for their own profit to oppress the needy and the wretched or to seek gain from another's want. To defraud anyone of the wage due him is a great crime that calls down avenging wrath from Heaven, "Behold, the wages of the laborers . . . which have been kept back by you unjustly, cry out: and their cry has entered into the ears of the Lord of Hosts". . .

We are told that free consent fixes the amount of a wage . . . Let it be granted then that worker and employer may enter freely into agreements and, in particular, concerning the amount of the wage; yet there is always underlying such agreements an element of natural justice, and one greater and more ancient than the free consent of the contracting parties, namely that the wage shall not be less than enough to support a worker who is thrifty and upright. If, compelled by necessity or moved by fear of a worse evil, a worker accepts a harder condition, which although against his will he must accept because an employer or contractor imposes it, he certainly submits to force, against which justice cries out in protest.

Contemporary Catholic social teaching continues to echo these themes. Pope Paul VI reiterated a commitment to the just wage in *Guadium Spes* (The Church in the Modern World), issued in 1965 in wake of the Second Vatican Council. After contending that labor "is superior to the other elements of economic life," the encyclical turns to compensation.

Finally, remuneration for labor is to be such that people may be furnished the means to cultivate worthily their own material, social, cultural, and spiritual life and that of their dependents, in view of the function and productiveness of each one, the conditions of the factory or workshop, and the common good.

On the one hundredth anniversary of *Rerum Novarum*, John Paul II celebrated its publication with another encyclical, *Centesimus Annus*, pointing once again to the need for a just wage. Finally, the *Catechism of the Catholic Church* (#2434) contains this provision:

A just wage is the legitimate fruit of work. To refuse or withhold it can be a grave injustice. In determining fair pay, both the needs and the contributions of each person must be taken into account. Remuneration for work should guarantee humans the opportunity to provide a dignified livelihood for themselves and their family on the material, social, cultural and spiritual level, taking into account the role and the productivity of each, the state of the business, and the common good. Agreement between the parties is not sufficient to justify the amount to be received in wages.

That such statements are more than window dressing can be seen in the way Catholic institutions struggle with issues of compensation. Take American Catholic hospitals, for instance. The group Senior Human Resources Executives of Large Catholic Health Systems drew up a statement of seven "Principles Concerning the Just Wage" in 2001.[59] The first principle says clearly that "Catholic health care organizations should establish plans to move them toward a just wage." The fourth maintains that "Competitive pay rates and market position can significantly challenge a Catholic organization's ability to pay just wages. At least in the case of lower-paid workers, however, such organizations should pay wages at or above the prevailing market rates and provide benefits that support family needs and the development of the worker." A number of Catholic health care systems have adopted and tried to implement the principles.

One issue that bedeviled the scholastics, and is evident still in contemporary statements such as that from the Catholic hospital executives and the Catechism, is how a just wage is to be calculated. Aquinas thought more in terms of what was called commutative justice, as opposed to distributive justice. He would try to measure the "worth" of the work, which is its contribution to the price of the product. This is not surprising, given that in his day craftsmen produced goods individually and the selling price was thought to include a return to his labor. If the craftsman employed someone, it followed that the employee should receive a fair amount for his contribution also. Other scholastics spoke more about distributive justice, the needs of the worker. In either case, though, it is important to stress that the market price, standing alone, is not the measure of justice.

Protestants, for their part, have not entirely ignored the just wage. Luther, for example, harbored a strong suspicion of commercial life in general. He did, however, talk of the Christian calling to serve God in all that one does,

---

59. These can be found, along with an enlightening discussion, in Jeffrey W. Hamlin, "A 'Just Wage': More than Dollars," *Health Progress*, March-April 2002.

presumably in commercial occupations as much as in others. Furthermore, he sometimes mentioned that prices should be tied to costs, not to what could be had in the market. In a 1524 essay entitled "Trade and Usury," he wrote

> Now it is fair and right that a merchant take as much profit on his wares as will reimburse him for their cost and compensate him for his trouble, his labor, and his risk. Even a farmhand must have food and pay for his labor. Who can serve or labor for nothing? The gospel says, "The laborer deserves his wages."

Otherwise, Luther concentrated far more of his energies on other topics.

John Calvin is often credited with giving theological sanctification to, if not spawning, the commercial revolution of his day.[60] Even more than Luther, he stressed the concept of a "calling." Each person's occupation was a calling and an opportunity to serve God. Making a success of that calling was therefore satisfying to God. Some of his supporters, the most prominent of whom were the Puritans of seventeenth century England and America, moved a little further, holding that the acquisition of worldly goods signified divine approval of one's work. Prosperity was a measure of the degree to which one was succeeding in pleasing God in the pursuit of his call. This "more is better" philosophy, equating the accumulation of worldly goods with Godly favor, can quickly put an unregulated market on theological footing. Calvin himself, though, did not believe that excessive profits should be taken through exploiting the vulnerability of workers. In a sermon from 1555 he warned that God wished "to correct the cruelty of the rich who employ poor people in their service and yet do not sufficiently compensate them for their labor."[61]

Some modern day Protestants have joined Catholics in calling for a just wage. For example, the Evangelical Lutheran Church in America's 1999 statement *Sufficient Sustainable Livelihood for All* does so explicitly. After pointing out that seeking the Kingdom of God is the first priority of human life but that committed Christians cannot neglect economic affairs, the statement addresses a number of areas of concern. At one point it declares that "Employers have a responsibility to treat employees with dignity and respect. This should be reflected in employees' remuneration, benefits, work conditions, job security, and ongoing job training." The church promises to "compensate all people we

---

60. This is the famous Weber thesis. Max Weber, *The Protestant Ethic and the Sprit of Capitalism* (New York: Scribners, 1958), translated by Talcott Parsons. Originally published in 1905. See also Roger Tawney, *Religion and the Rise of Capitalism* (Gloucester, MA: Peter Smith, 1962). Originally published in 1926.

61. Quoted in Noell, "In Pursuit of the Just Wage," 479.

call or employ at an amount sufficient for them to live in dignity." All other employers are then urged to do the same.

To implement the just wage, the scholastics restricted themselves to moral exhortation. But this approach inevitably falls apart on the shoals of economic reality. What if some employers are convinced by the churchmen's teachings and adopt a just wage policy but others do not? The first group is immediately placed at a competitive disadvantage. The experience reported by Christopher Ringwald, a Catholic layman and owner of a construction company is a good example.[62] He tried paying just wages but came to the conclusion that government mandated minimums are the only rational and fair option. A level playing field for fair-minded employers simply cannot be accomplished without a public policy.

In sum, the just wage has an ancient lineage and a contemporary relevance. Human life is not about, in the first instance, getting and spending, but rather the pursuit of a satisfactory relationship with God. Nevertheless, no domain of human activity is immune from the strictures of Christian theology. As church tradition has not hesitated to develop, for instance, a doctrine of just war, so too has it embraced the concept of a just wage. An impersonal market does not justify anyone jettisoning the ethical teachings of the church. Practicality dictates that government action is the correct way to procure the just wage.

RELIGIOUS TEACHINGS ON POVERTY

Some readings of the Old and New Testament have encouraged a fatalism about poverty. It was, is, and always will be present. A sympathetic Stoicism is the best that can be hoped for, it seems, regarding this world. Another perspective glorifies poverty, seeing in wealth a flirtation with — if not an outright capture by — evil. The more ascetic perspective urges the virtuous person to turn himself or herself completely toward higher matters. The cynical version preaches to the poor that they should be glad they are poor and to wait patiently for the rewards of the next world. (This is the rendering Marx, rightly, called an "opiate.")

Most Western religious traditions, however, bear a different witness. The presence of the poor and destitute is a blight on God's world, and the faithful are called on to take positive steps to help alleviate their condition. Since each is

---

62. Christopher Ringwald, "Make Minimum Wage a Just Wage," *Salt of the Earth*, May 1999.

built on a slightly different theological tradition, it will be helpful to briefly survey the attitudes of (in no order of preference) mainstream Protestantism, Judaism, evangelical Protestantism, and Catholicism.

Mainstream Protestantism and Poverty[63]

Although to some degree Anglo-American mainstream Protestantism's concern with poverty can be traced to John Wesley, who preached to the poor in outdoor worship services in defiance of the Anglican authorities and who took their condition to heart, it was the development of the social gospel movement of the late nineteenth and early twentieth centuries that forms the direct root. The most widely used definition is still the one offered by the contemporary Shailer Matthews, "the application of the teaching of Jesus and the total message of the Christian salvation to society, the economic life, and social institutions . . . as well as to individuals."[64]

Historically, the British theologian F.D. Maurice was the first key figure in this movement. In 1838, he penned *The Kingdom of Christ*, in which he argued that it was the task of the modern church to build a society based on Christian compassion. Removed from his professorship at King's College, London, in 1853 for his unorthodox views, he and his followers continued to urge "Christ in every man." Maurice was joined by the Congregationalist R.J. Campbell and the Anglican Frederick W. Robertson. Both "preached that one must appreciate the human nature of Christ before proceeding to a proper understanding of his divine nature."[65]

It was the doctrine of Divine Immanence, therefore, that was at the base of the movement. This doctrine stresses the presence of God in all creation, in all of nature and all of humanity, including social organizations and institutions. The Kingdom of God, therefore, encompasses all that is and all that we touch in our lives. Creating the Kingdom of God then means making it real in the here and now. "The metaphor of the Kingdom," the historian Paul Philips has stressed, "repeatedly surfaced in the writings of the Social Christians long after Maurice's

63. In the interest of full disclosure: I am an active member of a mainstream Protestant denomination.

64. Quoted in Christopher Evans, "Historical Integrity and Theological Recovery: A Reintroduction to the Social Gospel," in Christopher Evans, ed., *The Social Gospel Today* (Louisville, KY: Westminster John Knox Press, 2001), 2.

65. Paul Phillips, *A Kingdom on Earth: Anglo-American Social Christianity, 1880-1940* (University Park: Pennsylvania State University Press, 1996), 5.

death in 1872. . . The Kingdom was the community of righteousness about to be established on earth."[66]

American theologians, some of whom had studied in England, were equally involved in the social gospel movement.[67] Walter Rauschenbush was undoubtedly the most accomplished theologian of the cause, and the doctrine of the Divine Immanence runs throughout his writing. In his most widely read book, *Christianity and the Social Crisis*, he took the position that

> Whoever uncouples the religious and the social life has not understood Jesus. Whoever sets any bounds for the reconstructive power of the religious life over the social relations and institutions of men, to that extent, denies the faith of the Master.[68]

In one sense, the social gospel can be seen as a reaction to nineteenth century intellectual trends. Theologians felt they had to take account of high biblical criticism, the search for the historical Jesus, and the findings of the natural sciences. However, it would be a mistake to view it merely as a reactive movement. Its leaders were reared in the evangelical tradition, with its emphasis on preaching salvation. They simply broadened the meaning of salvation to include "social salvation." In line with most nineteenth-century thinkers, they believed that progress was possible, and with the appropriate energy emanating from the churches it could be channeled toward realizing the Kingdom of God on this earth. Personal faith could not be, they felt, separated from the command to act to make the world a more just place. The result was the advocacy of any number of social and economic reforms designed to address the deplorable conditions created by industrialization.[69]

To be sure, in both Britain and the United States, social gospel adherents were rocked by World War I and the 1920s.[70] Further, some of them easily slipped into theological sloppiness and shallowness, making of the gospels little

---

66. Phillips, *Kingdom on Earth*, 1.

67. A good survey is Gary Dorrien, *The Making of American Liberal Theology: Idealism, Realism, and Modernity* (Louisville, KY: Westminster John Knox Press, 2003). John Atherton, *Christian Social Ethics: A Reader* (Cleveland: Pilgrim Press, 1994) should also be consulted.

68. Walter Rauschenbush, *Christianity and the Social Crisis* (New York: Macmillan, 1907), 48-49.

69. Of late it has been fashionable to criticize adherents of the social gospel for not being sensitive to the problems of African-Americans, women, and Native Americans. However, that is surely reading history backwards, judging them by the standards of another time. See, for example, Susan Curtis, *A Consuming Faith: The Social Gospel and Modern American Culture* (Baltimore: Johns Hopkins University Press, 1991), which also lays the growth of a consumer culture at the feet of the social gospel.

70. See Gary Dorrien, "Social Salvation: The Social Gospel as Theology and Economics," in Evans, ed., *The Social Gospel Today*, chap. 7.

more than a social reform tract. However, the social gospel's core commitments to a vital faith made evident by a concern for the downtrodden of the earth remained an important strain of mainstream Protestantism.

Any number of modern examples could be cited from the myriad position papers issued by Protestant church bodies in both Britain and the United States through the years.[71] A recent one from the American United Methodists can be taken as indicative, though. It is *One Shared Dream: The Beloved Community*, issued by the denomination's Council of Bishops in 2003. It takes its vision from Isaiah 65:17-18a: "For I am about to create new heavens and a new earth; the former things shall not be remembered or come to mind. But be glad and rejoice forever in what I am creating." God is always actively creating, therefore, and calls the faithful to participate in what they call the Beloved Community. In outline,

> In the Beloved Community [all people] know themselves to be formed and empowered to love others by the grace of God in Jesus Christ. Their thoughts and actions are one in knowing self-interest is satisfied only when all people are valued and all have enough to live. . . The Beloved Community is to be a visible sign of the body of Christ in the world.

The problem of poverty occupies a special place in the Bishops' concern. "The Beloved Community represents the possibility of a truly inclusive human family that embraces everyone but holds in especially high regard the lives and gifts of the most vulnerable: children and the poor." Justice cannot be done, the Beloved Community cannot come into existence, until "the least of these" are brought fully into the human family, spiritually and materially.

Judaism and poverty

Jewish traditions place a strong emphasis on caring for the vulnerable and the dispossessed: the sick, the elderly, the orphan, the disinherited, even the stranger at the gate. The Old Testament and the compilations of Jewish law speak clearly and directly to this issue. From them, we can discern three general principles.

There is first the concept of community. Being less otherworldly than many religions, Judaism has stressed the ties of humans to each other. Within the Jewish community, there is a responsibility to care for all its members, especially those who have various calamities fall upon them. However, Jewish ethical

---

71. A good discussion of the Church of England's pronouncements during the eighties is Henry Clark, *The Church Under Thatcher* (London: Society for Promoting Christian Knowledge, 1993).

teaching has also emphasized that there is a wider community. The care the Jewish community provides to its own must also be extended to all.

Second, Judaism puts even more emphasis on God's ties to the human community in this life and his role as an active agent in that community than does Christianity. The covenant relation puts God at the center of all human activity. Moreover, it creates a special place for the oppressed within the community. Based on God's deliverance of the people of Israel from bondage in Egypt, "Judaism proclaimed a message of potentially universal significance: the power that created the universe *is the same power* that champions the powerless and creates the demand for a moral universe infused with justice and compassion."[72]

Third, poverty is seen as a curse. It is a curse not only in that it deprives people of material goods, but also because it undermines their dignity. One's place in the community is a vital element of dignity, and this is put in jeopardy when he or she falls into poverty. Thus, avoiding poverty is an important goal for the individual, but seeing that no one is in poverty is also a responsibility of the community.

A variety of specific teachings follow from these general principles. For example, according to the Mishnah, the early statement of the law, the land belonged to God. Thus, those who held it did so in partnership with God, a fact that carried important consequences.

> Since the Mishnah's framers regard the land as God's property, when Israelite farmers claim it as their own, and grow food on it, they must pay for using God's earth. The householder therefore must leave a portion of the field unharvested as *peah* and give this food over to God's chosen representatives, the poor.[73]

The gleanings then that are gathered by the poor are not left simply at the discretion of the landholder; they constitute instead as much an obligation as any other required payment.

Furthermore, there is the command of Deuteronomy 15:1-4 that debts are to be forgiven every seven years. The rationale for this, according to the well-known contemporary scholar Jacob Neusner, is to keep the poor from becoming mired in accumulated debt.[74]

---

72. Michael Lerner, "Jewish Liberation Theology and Emancipatory Politics," in Michael Zweig, ed., *Religion and Economic Justice* (Philadelphia: Temple University Press, 1991), 131.

73. Jacob Neuser, *The Economics of the Mishnah* (Chicago: University of Chicago Press) 1990), 121.

74. Neusner, *Economics of the Mishnah*, 130.

Maimonides, the noted medieval Jewish legal theorist, listed eight categories of charity, prime among which was ensuring against poverty. "[P]reventing a faltering individual from falling into the throes of poverty is given first ranking by Maimonides in his eight categories of charity. The position of someone in that predicament must be stabilized."[75]

However, more than the mere transfer of money is called for. Charity is sometimes distinguished from benevolence, the latter requiring "the commitment of one's person as well as one's purse."[76] The most important stipulation is that the recipient must have his or her dignity preserved.

> [O]ne can give money and yet forfeit the reward of the *mitzvah* because of the manner in which one gives. The Talmud teaches us that to humiliate the recipients is a cardinal sin. In fact, the highest form of giving, as Maimonides pointed out, is to help the recipient be independent of charity — to enable the needy to be self-sufficient."[77]

Or, as Morris Adler has put it:

> But helping a man was not exhausted by providing him recurringly with the elementary necessities. The responsibility of the community was to raise him out of the condition of dependence to the status of a self-supporting individual.[78]

Taken together with the traditional Jewish emphasis on the importance of work, this injunction to make the poor independent supports the need for a living wage. Even menial work was always held as superior to begging. And, as Barend de Vries has pointed out,

> In facing issues in welfare assistance, the Jewish tradition demonstrates compassion, but also affirms the crucial importance of work as central to the dignity of the human being. Biblical, rabbinic, and contemporary Jewish tradition are replete with admonitions exalting the virtues of work as a way to honor God and man.[79]

In fact, Aaron Levine has said that "the stated goal of minimum wage legislation, ensuring the working poor a 'living wage,' is an objective Halakah

---

75. Aaron Levine, *Economic Public Policy and Jewish Law* (New York: Yeshiva University Press, 1993), 23.

76. Emanuel Rackman, *Modern Halakhah for Our Times* (Hoboken, NJ: KTAV Publishing House, 1995), 57.

77. Rackman, *Modern Halakhah*, 57-58.

78. Morris Adler, ""Torah and Society," in Abraham Ezra Millgram, ed., *Great Jewish Ideas* (Clinton, MA: Colonial Press, 1964), 116.

79. Barend de Vries, *Champions of the Poor: The Economic Consequences of Judeo-Christian Values* (Washington: Georgetown University Press, 1998), 184-85.

[Jewish law] would fully embrace."[80] He goes on to argue, it is true, that the minimum wage is counterproductive because it leads to unemployment. However, if this proposition could be refuted, as I hope to do in Chapter 7, then the Jewish law, and even Levine, would stand clearly behind a living wage. As for the living wage being mandated by government, Levine has no problem with this. For as he says, "Government involvement in the charity obligation is . . . an integral part of the social welfare program of the Torah society."[81] Indeed, Frank Loewenberg traces this back to the early days of Hebrew history.

> Jewish kings were commanded to practice [justice and charity]. Classi-
> cal as well as modern commentators agree that the command does not refer
> to 'courtroom justice and charity' but to *social justice*. The major wrongdoing
> to which the prophets objected was not the perversion of the judicial pro-
> cess, but the oppression and exploitation of the poor by the political elite
> and the wealthy classes.[82]

Evangelical Christians and poverty

"Evangelical" is an uncertain descriptive adjective.[83] Technically, all Christians are "evangelical," in the sense that they take the Great Commission seriously. After the Resurrection, Jesus appeared to the disciples and said,

> All authority in heaven and on earth has been given to me. Therefore, go
> and make disciples of all nations, baptizing them in the name of the Father
> and of the Son and of the Holy Spirit, and teaching them to obey everything
> I have commanded you. And surely I am with you always, to the very end of
> the age. (Matthew 28: 18-20)

The distinguishing mark of evangelicals is that they take these verses as the centerpiece of the Christian commitment. Moreover, they have usually viewed it in individual terms. That is, they have focused their efforts on convincing people to accept the Christian notion of the Trinity ("converting" them), securing thereby their personal salvation in the life of the world to come. Generally, too, evangelicals seek authority directly from the Bible and are, to varying degrees, prone to take it in a more literalistic fashion than other Christians.

By concentrating their energies on their own personal salvation and sharing the blessings of that salvation with others, historically evangelicals were

---

80. Levine, *Economic Public Policy*, 23.

81. Levine, *Economic Public Policy*, 23-24.

82. Frank M. Loewenberg, *From Charity to Social Justice: The Emergence of Communal Institutions for the Support of the Poor in Ancient Judaism* (New Brunswick, NJ: Transaction Publishers, 2001), 159.

83. Furthermore, it is often confused with fundamentalism, the absolute literal reading of the Bible. Though often linked, the two are conceptually distinct and are not always found together.

disinclined to enter the political arena. To them, Christianity was a personal religion, from which social concerns were largely removed. Therefore, the movements for economic justice and civil rights found them primarily on the sidelines.[84]

When evangelicals did enter politics in the United States in the 1970s, it was mostly to push for family issues.[85] Abortion more than anything else is what galvanized the evangelical churches into politics, but they have spoken out on a number of other matters: defense of the traditional family, homosexuality, prayer in the public schools, the structure of the school curriculum, and so forth.

In economics and economic policy, many evangelicals have lined up with their neoconservative allies and defended the free market. Ronald Nash, for instance, has argued that while concern for the poor is admirable, and there is a clear Christian imperative for private charity, only the market can secure social justice in the long run.[86]

However, we should not forget that there are other dimensions to evangelical Christianity, historically and in its contemporary guise. For example, William Jennings Bryan was solidly in the evangelical tradition. Most of Bryan's career was spent promoting economically progressive causes, as a Senator and presidential candidate. Few serious politicians of his day (or ours) were more radical than he. His most famous utterance, it should be recalled, accused the rich of crucifying mankind on a "Cross of Gold." There was no inconsistency between this economic populism and his later defense of Tennessee's banning of the teaching of evolution. Both involved using government to secure what Bryan, and other evangelicals, believed to be a righteous society.

Today, there is a vibrant cohort of evangelicals who, contrary to many of their brethren, find in their theology, with its deep emphasis on fidelity to the Bible, a commitment to take up the cause of the poor.[87] John F. Alexander is one example. He has stressed how much the Bible has to say on poverty.

---

84. There were always, of course, many notable exceptions.

85. Evangelical Christianity has only a minute presence in Britain. Thus, I am largely ignoring it here.

86. Ronald H. Nash, *Poverty and Wealth: The Christian Debate over Capitalism* (Westchester, IL: Crossway Books, 1986).

87. A balanced summary and analysis of the debate within the evangelical camp can be found in Craig Gay, *With Liberty and Justice for Whom? The Recent Evangelical Debate over Capitalism* (Grand Rapids, MI: Eerdmans, 1991).

Throughout Scripture, you find a special concern for the poor. It varies in its intensity and in whether it includes a special suspicion of the rich and powerful, but that special concern is always there. At times this concern points toward the poor and weak as an ideal, and weakness begins to be portrayed as the force to stop evil. This concern for the poor suggests a class consciousness, and at times it develops into that. [88]

The widely respected Jim Wallis is another. "Issues of wealth, poverty, and economic justice," he argues, "are central in the Bible. The sheer bulk of the biblical teaching about the rich and the poor is overwhelming." The thrust of the teaching of the New Testament is clear: "Jesus warns those who would call his name that they will be judged by how they respond to the hungry, the poor, the naked, the imprisoned, the sick, and the stranger."[89]

The group Evangelicals for Social Action (ESA), founded by Ronald Sider, is the largest and most active of several evangelical organizations inhabiting the political left.[90] Its statement of beliefs both places it squarely in the evangelical tradition and argues for a commitment to the world's poor. To quote but a few lines:

We, members of the Church of Jesus Christ, praise God for his great salvation and rejoice in the fellowship he has given us . . . We believe the gospel is God's good news for the whole world, and we are determined by his grace to obey Christ's commission to proclaim it to all humankind and to make disciples of every nation.

We affirm the divine inspiration, truthfulness and authority of both the Old and New Testament Scriptures in their entirety as the only written word of God, without error in all that it affirms, and the only infallible rule of faith and practice.

We affirm that God is both the creator and the Judge of all people. We therefore should share his concern for justice and reconciliation throughout human society and for the liberation of people from every kind of oppression. Because humankind is made in the image of God, every person . . . has an intrinsic dignity because of which each person should be

---

88. John F. Alexander, *Your Money or Your Life: A New Look at Jesus' View of Wealth and Power* (San Francisco: Harper and Row, 1986), 232.

89. Jim Wallis, *Agenda for Biblical People* (San Francisco: Harper and Row, 1984), 63.

90. See Sider's books *Rich Christians in an Age of Hunger: A Biblical Study* (Downers Grove, IL: Inter-Varsity Press, 1984) and *Just Generosity: A New Vision for Overcoming Poverty in America* (Grand Rapids, MI: Baker Books, 1999). The movement is analyzed in Timothy Tseng and Janet Furness, "The Reawakening of the Evangelical Social Consciousness," in Evans, ed. *The Social Gospel Today*, chap. 8.

respected and served, not exploited. . . The message of salvation implies . . . a message of judgment upon every form of alienation, oppression and discrimination, and we should not be afraid to denounce evil and injustice wherever they exist. . . Faith without works is dead.

Even a brief glance through ESA's magazine *Sojourners* will show how deep this commitment runs.

If we accept the evangelical position on the need to address poverty, there are still two steps to the living wage. First, we must accept public policy alongside private charity as a legitimate tool for the Christian to realize his/her obligations. Second, we must show that, among the policy alternatives available, the living wage is the most preferred. The next chapter is devoted to the latter task, but a word regarding the former is appropriate here.

No religious person in Great Britain or the United States, of any tradition, denies that charitable efforts toward the poor are an obligation of faith. In both countries, churches and synagogues operate an enormous variety of social welfare institutions, and in general they are highly effective at what they do. However, should they be the exclusive mechanism for helping the poor?

First, the scale of the undertaking is more than religious groups ought to be asked to do alone. Given the numbers of people in poverty in the United States and Britain and the magnitude of the pathologies that surround them — unemployment, poor housing, deteriorating schools, unsafe streets, inadequate health care, lack of day care facilities, etc. — it is simply unreasonable and unrealistic to expect churches and synagogues to meet all the need. Can they accomplish much? Yes. Can their service delivery systems serve as models for public agencies? Certainly. Can they manage it alone? Hardly.

Second, private provision of social services is unsystematic. In the nineteenth century, for example, any number of British observers noted with dismay the overlapping and uncoordinated nature of the work charities were doing. There is simply no way to effectively match private efforts with needs. Furthermore, even when there is a good match between needs and efforts, the contingent nature of private funding means that programs may lack consistency. If people lower their giving to churches and synagogues, programs may have to be cut; and in practice they may be cut when they are needed most, say in an economic downturn.

Therefore, the charitable work of religious (and secular) social welfare agencies is admirable and necessary. However, public policy has a legitimate role to play also if we want to embark on a serious effort to attack poverty.

Two arguments frequently mounted by some evangelicals (but others also) against public provision of social welfare services can actually be used to support the living wage. First, E. Calvin Beisner takes the position that even if it were desirable for government to secure social justice through erecting a welfare state, the dangers attending the size of the resulting state outweigh the potential gains.[91] An inflated state inevitably becomes overweening, a "nanny state," as is often said. There is admittedly something to this argument. The inherent tendency of bureaucratic growth can seldom be legislated away. However, a living wage avoids this problem. It is the most slimmed down social welfare policy there is. Its enforcement requires only a very small and tightly focused bureaucracy. Second, some people have asked whether or not a governmentally operated welfare state might not lead committed religious people to lower their giving. Might not an "I gave at the office" and a "the government will take care of that" mentality seep into the pews?[92] While this position is problematical, a living wage, again, would hardly be conducive to the growth of this attitude. It would not require the expenditure of the taxpayer's money (except for the miniscule amount for enforcement) and no one believes a living wage would cure all social problems. Therefore, there would still be plenty of need for the social agencies of the churches and synagogues.

In conclusion, there is a lively evangelical tradition that focuses on the needs of the poor. Private charity is praiseworthy, and can even be accompanied by other private activities such as boycotts. (For example, Brian Bolton has asked "Where would Jesus Shop? Not Wal-Mart," because of its treatment of workers.) [93] However, such private initiatives must be supplemented by public action, and many evangelicals have not hesitated to say so.

> Real progress in reducing social ills cannot be made by only volunteering and making donations. Charity is needed, but true justice requires a different kind of commitment — a commitment to change... Will we tap into the power of our identity and witness, incorporating Christ's example to change the face of poverty in this country? Will we continue to toss crumbs from the table to poor people, instead of giving them a seat at the table?[94]

---

91. E. Calvin Beisner, "Justice and Poverty: Two Views Contrasted," in Herbert Schlossberg, Vinay Samuel, and Ronald Sider, eds., *Christianity and Economics in the Post-Cold War Era: The Oxford Declaration and Beyond* (Grand Rapids, MI: Eerdmans, 1994), 57-80.

92. This idea stems from applying rational choice theory to religion and religious institutions. See Lawrence A. Young, ed., *Rational Choice Theory and Religion: Summary and Assessment* (New York: Routledge, 1997).

93. Brian Bolton, "Where Would Jesus Shop? Not Wal-Mart," *Sojourners*, February 2004.

94. Yonce Shelton, "What's Charity Without Justice?" *Sojourners*, January 2004.

Roman Catholicism and poverty

The Catholic Church has a long and honorable history in taking up the cause of the poor, although at times that concern has admittedly been more pronounced than at others. Since the nineteenth century, however, the problem of poverty has been a major preoccupation of both Catholic theologians and the hierarchy. The Catechism (#2444) provides "'The Church's love for the poor . . . is part of her constant tradition.' This love is inspired by the Gospel of the Beatitudes, of the poverty of Jesus, and of his concern for the poor."

Contemporary Catholic thinking has been heavily influenced by the writings of Gustavo Gutierrez.[95] While not generally endorsing his rather extreme "liberation theology," there has been a widespread acceptance of his idea of a "preferential option" for the poor. Catholic social teaching, for example, contends that "In teaching us charity, the Gospel instructs us in the preferential respect due to the poor and the special situation they have in society." Again, as the American bishops put it in their famous 1986 pastoral letter *Economic Justice for All*, "As followers of Christ, we are challenged to make a fundamental 'option for the poor.'"

However, what the poor are due is not merely charity. Rather, their needs should be met because of the justice of doing so. The well-off cannot claim any absolute sense of ownership of their riches, which is what the giving of alms implies. In contrast, the Catechism (#2446) says

> St. John Chrysostom vigorously recalls this: "Not to enable the poor to share in our goods is to steal from them and to deprive them of life. The goods we possess are not ours but theirs." "The demands of justice must be satisfied first of all; that which is already due in justice is not to be offered as a gift of charity."

Catholic social teaching reiterates this position by quoting St. Ambrose: "You are not making a gift of your possessions to the poor person. You are handing over to him what is his." Some form of sharing of the output of the economy through redistribution is therefore an ethical command, and the mechanism for such redistribution cannot be mere voluntary donations.

In company with Jewish teachings, Catholic moral philosophy exalts the role of work. The Catechism (#2427) is quite explicit.

---

95. See especially his *The Power of the Poor in History* (Maryknoll, NY: Orbis Books, 1983).

Human work proceeds directly from persons created in the image of God and called to prolong the work of creation by subduing the earth, both with and for one another. Hence, work is a duty: "if any one will not work, let him not eat." Work honors the Creator's gifts and the talents received from him.

In *Laborem Exercens* (On Human Work, 1981), Pope John Paul II added dignity to the virtues called forth by work. "Work remains a good thing, not only because it is enjoyable, but also because it expresses and increases the worker's dignity. Through work we not only transform the world, we are transformed ourselves, becoming 'more a human being.'" *Economic Justice for All* also underscored the importance of work: "Labor has a great dignity, so great that all who are able to work are obligated to so."

Work is therefore not only a duty but an activity that makes us more human. Since the Church has never believed that unregulated markets should set the compensation a worker receives, it is not surprising that the Catechism (#2428) adds "Everyone should be able to draw from work the means of providing for his life and his family, and of serving the human community."

Even Catholic leaders who put a great deal of faith in the institutional welfare state have stressed the importance of work. The English bishops, for example, noted in *Taxation for the Common Good*, a document mostly defending expenditures on traditional welfare state measures, "[W]e bear in mind that [Church teaching] includes a warning about becoming too dependent on welfare and it is the responsibility of the state to ensure that this does not happen by assisting those on welfare benefits who could be usefully employed to seek work."[96]

Catholicism has, historically, not harbored the animosity to the state that sometimes animates certain branches of Protestantism. While a cynic might say that this is traceable to the Church's established position throughout much of European history, it is also deeply imbedded in its political philosophy. Given the universalistic claims of the Church and its natural law heritage, it is not surprising that it is more comfortable with political power than others. The American bishops have said that "Society as a whole, acting through public and private institutions has the moral responsibility to enhance human dignity and protect human rights."[97] (Note that "public" precedes "private.") Therefore, Catholics have generally not been reluctant to utilize the power of the state to

---

96. The document was composed by Caritas, an agency of the Catholic bishops. It is available on the organization's website.

97. *Economic Justice for All*, 1986 pastoral letter.

fight poverty. As the English bishops have formulated it, government "has an obligation to watch over the interests of the poor and most disadvantaged because power is not distributed evenly in society."[98]

Catholic teaching puts a special premium on caring for the poor through justice rather than charity. A just portion of the fruits of our collective labor must be made available for the poor. Work is a central component of human life, more forcefully stated by the general teachings of the Church than by the English bishops to be sure, but still important even to them. All who work should be able to earn adequate means to support themselves and their families. Couple these propositions with a legitimate role for the state and you have the recipe for a living wage.

CHRISTIANITY AND INEQUALITY[99]

Some Christian traditions, especially modern Catholicism, worry over inequality for the same reason civic republicans do, that massive economic inequalities undermine if not destroy the sense of community necessary for a healthy society.[100] For other Christians, though, there is a rather different concern. Human equality before God is a fundamental tenet of Christian theology. To what extent, then, should human institutions seek to reflect that fact? Tocqueville noted the way Christian thinking manifested itself in the law. "Christianity, which has declared all men equal in the sight of God, cannot hesitate to acknowledge all citizens equal before the law."[101] Is it only in the procedures of the law, one might ask, that Christianity points toward the eradication of inequality? Or, should it be extended to other spheres of life as well?

---

98. The bishops must be referring to economic power, for if they were speaking of political power, then you would most certainly *not* want government paying special attention to the poor because it would likely adopt policies inimical rather than helpful to them. The way out of this dilemma would be for government, if it is political power that is the referent, to listen carefully to the guidance being offered by the church. However, that would be a curious position for Catholics in Britain.

99. Much of this section is based on Douglas Hicks' excellent book *Inequality and Christian Ethics* (New York: Cambridge University Press, 2000).

100. Although, of course, Catholics would define a "healthy society" rather differently than civic republicans.

101. Alexis de Tocqueville, *Democracy in America* (New York: Harper, 1969), 16. Originally published in 1840.

The most serious Christian thinker to grapple with this issue was the American H. Richard Niebuhr.[102] Niebuhr begins with the assertion that all people receive both their being and their value from God. We are first, then, equal in our creation. But we are also equally valued, a fact which overwhelms and trivializes the rankings humans place on each other.

Two avenues of thought germane to inequality flow from this framework. One is more theological in nature and bears only indirectly on how inequality is to be dealt with by humans. The other goes more directly to issues of social and political organization.

Taking the theological thrust first, three important implications can be drawn from Niebuhr's position. First, the equality instilled by God is universal. No one and no group can legitimately be excluded when we speak of our relations to others. Human institutions, of whatever sort, that grant equality to some but not others therefore cannot be justified. Second, life should be lived as a grateful response to him who created us. A central measure of being grateful for our life is how we treat our fellow human beings. Third, there is what Douglas Hicks and others have called "relationality." People, Niebuhr said with Aristotle, must live in community. This fact makes it impossible to develop any sense of self apart from our communal lives. Therefore, when we fail to place a high value on the needs of the community we detract from the dignity of others (as well as ourselves).

As stimulating and intriguing as the propositions are, they do not directly address specific social and political issues. For that, we need to turn to Niebuhr's position on sin.

Inasmuch as we are all equal because we have all been created by God, we are also equal in being touched by sin. Niebuhr does not subscribe to the inherent evil of man thesis, though, nor does he contend that all individuals sin in equal amounts. Rather, what he means is that sin is universal. It touches every person *and* every realm of life. "While neither of these aspects — the *universality* of persons or the *whole* person — destroys the prior sacredness and goodness of each human being, this understanding of 'total depravity' does call for vigilant attention to the actions of individuals and groups."[103]

Niebuhr absolutely rejects the conservative position some holders of this same view of sin take, that the presence of sin in all people and all arenas of life

---

102. Hicks, *Inequality*, chap. 6 contains a discussion of Niebuhr's thought. Niebuhr's most germane works are *Radical Monotheism and Western Culture* (New York: Harper and Row, 1970) and *The Responsible Self: An Essay in Christian Moral Philosophy* (San Francisco: Harper and Row, 1963).

103. Hicks, *Inequality*, 122.

means that people must be controlled by government in order to minimize how much damage they can do. He argues that the correct lesson is that we must be suspicious of any system that allows for undue concentration of power. Power can, of course, be used for good, but because of sin it can also be used for evil purposes. Therefore, there is a strong need for balance in human institutions. While he spoke more often of the dangers of concentrating political power, an analogous argument could be made about concentrations of economic power. When some people have vastly more economic power than others, the sinfulness that can result should lead us to seek a better balance.

Niebuhr's teachings on suffering are also relevant. Suffering, such as that resulting from war, is tied to human sinfulness. However, such suffering is never spread evenly; it falls disproportionately on the poor and the weak. The suffering that accompanies the comings and goings of economic allocation shares this characteristic. It is not the wealthy who worry about what their children will wear, whether the car will break down, or most distressingly where they will live next month — or eat tomorrow.

For Niebuhr, the touching of humanity by God through Jesus Christ offers the redemption needed to overcome sin and all its ramifications. Christ points humans toward God's will, which is for us to be reconciled to him. Christians should strive, therefore, to transform their lives individually and collectively to make the world more in line with that reconciliation.

We should add that Niebuhr was no utopian, and believed that sometimes doing nothing was the best available option. Because of sin's ubiquity, our actions, even our good actions, will have unintended consequences. It is incumbent on committed Christians to study carefully what they advocate, and not merely assume that the purity of their motives will sanctify their concrete proposals.

What Christianity has to offer here is the unqualified stance that all people stand equal before God, in both creation and value. What we can draw from Niebuhr is that, at the least, we must think creatively about how far that equality should be something we strive for in every corner of human life. Economic inequality is, therefore, at least worrisome on this score.

Some of the religious arguments we have surveyed — the just wage tradition and the Jewish and Catholic positions on poverty — point directly to a living wage. The general concern about poverty manifested by mainline and evangelical Protestants and the disquiet over inequality Christianity engenders call for a serious weighing of the various alternatives for alleviating poverty and inequality. It is to that task we now turn.

4. POVERTY AND INEQUALITY IN THE UNITED STATES AND GREAT BRITAIN

Drive through the south side of Chicago or the Mississippi Delta, and then through some of the posh suburbs of Dallas or Boston. Walk through parts of Greenwich or East London, then catch the subway to Belgravia or the train to Finchley. You simply cannot conclude anything but that there is a substantial amount of poverty and a very significant degree of inequality in the United States and Great Britain. Intelligent and well-meaning people, or even those with only one of those traits, will come away from such tours with different views regarding the causes of these conditions, and the appropriate remedies, but the facts will be undeniable

The extent of poverty and inequality, however, is more complex than such a snapshot would convey. It will be helpful, therefore, to survey the terrain systematically. Impressions aside, how much poverty and inequality is there really? Two notes before we begin. First, data tend to hide the human dimension. We need to remember that these statistics represent real people, not faceless numbers. Second, as with all data, those on poverty and inequality can be tweaked, or cited selectively, to support a particular conclusion. People with a defined agenda, especially but not only on the left, often do so.[104] A common tactic is to list a number of "myths" about poverty, and then debunk each. This is an area, though, where candor and balance are essential to coming up with realistic and workable policy prescriptions.

MEASURING POVERTY IN THE U.S.

Any statistical measure of the number or percentage of people in poverty requires, first, drawing some sort of line. Doing so, however, presents several problems. First, we must decide what the line is to measure. There are three possibilities: the resources people have (wealth), the funds they receive in a given time period (income), or what they spend (consumption). Wealth measures something very important, but let us put it aside for the moment. While some analysts believe consumption is a better measure, we ordinarily use yearly income.

If we settle on income, we must next decide what counts as income. Clearly, wages, salaries, pensions, and cash payments from government, such as veterans' benefits, should count as income. But what about non-cash items such as food stamps, free (or reduced price) school lunches, Medicaid, and subsidized housing? Should pre-tax or after-tax income be used? A heated debate has ensued through the years over these issues because the number of people officially in poverty will rise or fall depending on the choices made here.[105] Similar decisions would have to be made if either wealth or consumption were chosen (although there are fewer decisions with consumption).

Then, how are we to determine what income people actually receive? Official government reports, such as income tax returns, are one source. However, they often do not measure income the same way as our poverty definition. For example, housing subsidies are not taxed. Furthermore, they have inaccuracies of their own. No one believes, for instance, that all income gets reported to the Internal Revenue Service. Applications for certain types of benefits (such as food stamps) are also available, but you cannot be sure that all those who are eligible have applied. The other tack is to take surveys. These too, though, are subject to errors. Accurate sampling among the poor is very difficult. And, of course, there is no guarantee that people are telling the truth. (They are unlikely to mention income from illegal activities, for example.)

104. A particularly egregious example, among many, is Anne Marie Cammisa, *From Rhetoric to Reform: Welfare Policy in American Politics* (Boulder, CO: Westview, 1998), pp. 7-17. Her myths are Welfare Causes Poverty; Once a Family Went on AFDC, They Usually Stayed on It for Many Years; Welfare is the Cause of the Federal Deficit; Most of the Money Spent on Welfare is for Adults; Most Welfare Families Are Black; Prior to the New Deal, the Government Did Not Spend Money on Welfare, Leaving It to Private Charities; and Most Welfare Families Have Lots of Children. All of these are straw men of one sort or another, and have little or nothing to do with the defects of the old Aid to Families with Dependent Children program.

105. Many of these issues are discussed in Contance Citro and Robert Michael, eds., *Measuring Poverty: A New Approach* (Washington: National Academy Press, 1995).

All these problems pale, however, compared to the difficulties inherent in determining where the line should fall. It is always a judgment call (and even when set there are always those immediately above and immediately below it). In the United States, our official poverty line dates from the efforts of a civil servant named Mollie Orshansky of the Social Security Administration, who was asked in 1963 to devise a poverty threshold.[106] She obtained a Department of Agriculture calculation on the cost of a rudimentary food plan. Then, using a 1955 government study that concluded that the average American family of three (all families, not just poor ones) spent one-third of its *after-tax* income on food, she multiplied the cost of the basic food plan by three. Until 1969, the amount was adjusted according to price changes in the basic food budget. After that, the Consumer Price Index has been used to provide updated figures annually.

After the line has been set, some account has to be taken of the varying size of households. It would be easy to simply multiply the poverty line for one person by the number of people in a household. However, this would not factor in economies of scale. It costs less per person, for instance, to house four people than one. This means that some type of equivalence scale must be developed. There is, to put it mildly, no acceptable method for doing this, and small variations can produce significant differences. Then, finally, there is the problem of regional variations, chiefly related to housing costs.

Returning to the line itself for a moment, everyone surely agrees that it is wildly inadequate. Looking at Table 4-1, does anyone think that someone could live on $9,359 a year? For starters, remember that the original metric was erected on *after-tax* income, but the official poverty line is drawn with *pre-tax* income. While it is true that few people in these low income brackets pay federal or state income taxes, they do pay social security payroll taxes if they work. Furthermore, many people have argued that the percentage an *average* family spends on food is not a good basis for a formula measuring the number of our fellow citizens who are poor. Even Ms. Orshansky herself said later that the multiplier should be four rather than three.[107]

Consequently, the "official poverty line" is more like a compilation of tea-leaf readings than a scientific measure.[108] It has become part of the policy tool kit

---

106. The intriguing story of this episode is told in Gordon Fisher, "The Development and History of the Poverty Thresholds," *Social Security Bulletin*, 55 (1992), 3-14.

107. See Gordon Fisher, "The Development and History of the U.S. Poverty Thresholds: A Brief Overview," *Newsletter* of the Government Statistics Section and the Social Statistics Section of the American Statistical Association, Winter 1997.

108. See Patricia Ruggles, *Drawing the Line: Alternative Poverty Measures and Their Implications for Public Policy* (Washington: Urban Institute Press, 1990).

Table 4-1

Size of faimily unit	Related children under 18 years								
	None	One	Two	Three	Four	Five	Six	Seven	Eight or more
One person (unrelated individual):									
Under 65 years	9,359								
65 years and over	8,628								
Two people:									
Householder under 65 years	12,047	12,400							
Householder 65 years and over .	10,874	12,353							
Three people	14,072	14,480	14,494						
Four people	18,556	18,859	18,244	18,307					
Five people	22,377	22,703	22,007	21,469	21,141				
Six people	25,738	25,840	25,307	24,797	24,038	23,588			
Seven people	29,615	29,799	29,162	28,718	27,890	26,924	25,865		
Eight people	33,121	33,414	32,812	32,285	31,538	30,589	29,601	29,350	
Nine people or more	39,843	40,036	39,504	39,057	38,323	37,313	36,399	36,173	34,780

Poverty Threshholds in 2002 by Size of Family and Number of Related Children Under 18 Years
(Dollars)

Source: U.S. Census Bureau, *Poverty in the United States*, 2002, p. 4.

of social scientists, however, and is used continually in public debate. It cannot be stressed too strongly, in addition, that the line was initially developed to try to ascertain how many people were truly destitute; it was not designed, and should not be used, to measure policy success if X per cent of people merely climb above it.[109] Being above it hardly means you are out of poverty.

A far more realistic approach has been taken by the Economic Policy Institute. Three careful researchers sorted through the myriad of studies on family budgets in order to build a basic family budget for Baltimore.[110] Included were amounts for food, housing, transportation, health care, child care, taxes, and "other necessities" (telephone service, clothing, personal care and household items, bank fees, union dues, reading materials, school supplies, and television). Excluded entirely were any expenditures for restaurant meals (not even fast food), movies, vacations, appliance purchases or repairs, and savings for any kind for emergencies, education, or retirement. For a family of two adults and a seven year old and a three year old, the annual amount came to $34,732.28 (for 1998). Parallel studies for several other cities and states have produced similar results.[111] The official poverty line for a family of four in 1998, by way of comparison, was $16,600.

When asked, the American public agrees that amounts far above the poverty level are needed just to live. For example, a 2000 survey of Maryland residents found that 77% of the respondents felt that a family of four would need

---

109. Gordon Fisher, "Income (In-) Adequacy? The Official Poverty Line, Possible Changes and Some Historical Lessons," *Community Action Digest* 1 (1999).

110. Jared Bernstein, Chauna Brocht, and Maggie Spade-Aguilar, *How Much is Enough? Basic Budgets for Working Families* (Washington: Economic Policy Institute, 2000).

111. A list of these studies is contained in the appendix to Bernstein, Brocht, and Spade-Aguilar, *How Much is Enough?*

Table 4-2
Economic Policy Institute Family Budegt
for Baltimore, 1998
Two Parents, Two Children (Seven and Three)

Item	Monthly amount
Food	$500.20
Transportation	222.22
Health care	266.65
Housing	628.00
Child care	626.08
Other necessities	338.46
Taxes	312.74
Total	$2,894.36
Annual	$34,732.28

Source: Economic Policy Institute

$35,000 to make ends meet, while nearly half, 44%, thought they would need $45,000.[112]

Despite the shortcomings of the official federal definition of poverty and the inherent limitations of survey research, the Census Bureau's Current Population Survey studies nonetheless provide a helpful glimpse of the extent and profile of poverty in the United States. The latest compilation, issued in September 2003 using 2002 data, makes grim reading, indeed.

First, for the genuinely shocking numbers: In 2002, 34.6 million people — 12.1% of the entire population — roughly one in every *eight* people — lived in a household with income below the official poverty level. Another 12.5 million (4.4% of the population) were below 125% of the poverty line. Altogether, that is about the population of California, Washington state, and Missouri combined. Most disturbing of all, 14.1 million — about as many people as inhabit Minnesota and Georgia combined — or 4.9% were under 50% of the poverty level. These numbers, granted, are above those of the late 1990s because of the recession, but only slightly. For instance, we have never had fewer than 15.6% of our population below 125% of the official poverty level. The bald truth is that there is a lot of poverty in this country.

---

112. "A Statewide Survey of Maryland Residents About Low-Wage Workers and Maryland's Economy," Conducted by Lake Snell Perry and Associates, November 2000.

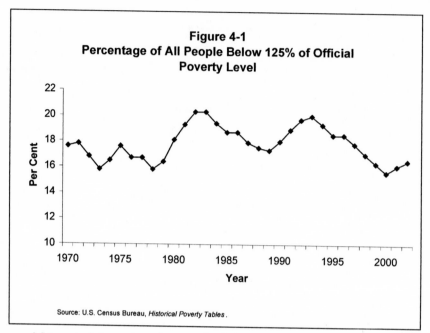

Figure 4-1
Percentage of All People Below 125% of Official Poverty Level

Source: U.S. Census Bureau, *Historical Poverty Tables*.

Moreover, it is not true that people glide in and out of poverty because they experience temporary spells of unemployment, move from one locale to another, return to school, etc. Of course, there is a good bit of movement in and out of poverty, but consider: In the six years ending in 2000, according to the Organization for Economic Co-operation and Development (OECD), the average number of Americans having "low income" at any given time was 14.2%.[113] At the same time, 4.6% had continuously low incomes, while 26% of the population had experienced low income at some time in their lives. That 4.6% figure translates into 12.9 million people.

The demographic breakdown of poverty is largely what anyone would expect. Geographically, the lowest levels are found in the Midwest, 10.3%, and the Northeast, 10.9%, the highest levels in the South, 13.8%, with the West in between at 12.4%. Central cities have higher rates than either the suburbs or small towns and rural areas, 16.7% compared to 8.9% and 14.2% respectively.

Both the types of families and the number of children in poverty are justifiably sensitive issues for people in every ideological camp. The stark fact is that a married couple is very unlikely to have an income so low as to fall under the poverty line. Only 5.3% of these intact families fail to rise above the government's poverty threshold. Among male-headed families with no wife

---

113. The OECD defines "low income" as two-thirds of median earnings.

present, the rate more than doubles, to 12.1%. For female-headed families with no husband present, it doubles again, to 26.5%. In short, families headed by women are five times more likely to be in poverty than married couples. From another angle, one in every four female-headed households is in poverty, even as measured by the paltry federal standard. It is easy to see, from these statistics, why some people feel encouraging people to get and stay married would decrease poverty. Marriage without good wages, though, will not solve the problem.

Over 12 million children, 16.7% — one in six — of all children are in poverty. The statistical reason that the rate exceeds the 12.1% of the total population is that poor families tend to have more children than more affluent ones. Therefore, while only 9.6% of all families are in poverty, many more children are.

Though the Census Bureau's categories can be a bit confusing, the general picture of racial and ethnic differences is evident. Non-Hispanic whites have only an 8.0% poverty rate, while 24.1% of blacks and 21.8% of Hispanics are in poverty. Nonetheless, it is important to remember that because there are many more whites than either blacks or Hispanics in the population, the number of whites in poverty exceeds minorities. Of all Americans in poverty, 45.0% are white, 24.9% black, 24.7% Hispanic, and 5.4% other groups.

It is often alleged that poverty and joblessness go hand in hand, and there is a strong element of truth in that. Table 4-3 shows that one in five adults who did not work were in poverty, whereas less than three per cent of those who worked full time, year round were. Working full-time, year-round, then, will almost always get you out of poverty. But what if you get laid off? Or, what if you have insurmountable transportation or child care problems? Many entry-level jobs are now in the suburbs, in places such as shopping malls, and difficult for inner city residents to reach. Child care is a perpetual problem for that most vulnerable of poverty categories, the female-headed household. (More on this when we discuss welfare reform.) And, remember, this is only getting you out of poverty as officially defined; it says nothing about getting to the EPI's basic budget, much less being able to aspire to what most Americans consider a decent life. Working full-time, year-round is a likely ticket out of abject poverty (except for 2.6 million people, we must continue to bear in mind), but what we need to insure is that it is a punched ticket to a decent life.

If we take the people below the officially defined poverty line as our base rather than the general population, we see something more disconcerting. While 62.1% of all those of working age did not work, 11.2% held full-time year-round

Table 4-3 Work Experience for Those 16 and over, 2002 (Numbers in Millions)			
Characteristic	Total	Number in Poverty	Percent in Poverty
All workers	151.5	9.0	5.9
Worked full time year round	100.7	2.6	2.6
Not full time year round	50.9	6.3	12.4
Did not work at least one week	69.6	14.6	21.0

Source: U.S. Census Bureau, *Poverty in the United States*, 2002, p. 7.

jobs and still could not lift themselves out of poverty. Any full-time year-round job should surely do better than that.

POVERTY IN THE UNITED KINGDOM

Although, as seen in Figure 4-2, the percentage of people in Britain (here measured by children) who are below the American poverty line is lower than in the United States, it is still relatively high by international standards. Officially, Britain measures poverty differently from the U.S., using 60% of median income (in line with European practice).[114] By whatever definition, though, there is still plenty of it. Refreshingly, the Blair government has pledged to attempt the eradication of child poverty within a generation. Accordingly, some serious steps have been taken, mostly to get at the root causes of deprivation. However, the sheer magnitude of the problem is daunting.

One important calibration in official British data is the weight given to housing costs. Calculations are made on both a before housing cost (BHC) and after housing cost (AHC) basis. The reasons are 1) housing costs vary enormously by household type (e.g., a pensioner with a paid up house versus a young couple having to rent); 2) housing is a critical and necessary item in every household budget but one people often have little control over; and 3) it introduces some type of control for regional variations.

According to the most recent AHC data, 12.5 million British citizens, 22.2% of the population, reside in low-income households. If BHC data are used, 17% are in poverty, with 9.6% receiving below half the median income and 4.8%

---

114. Incidentally, the Economic Policy Institute's budget discussed earlier is roughly 60% of American median earnings for a family of four.

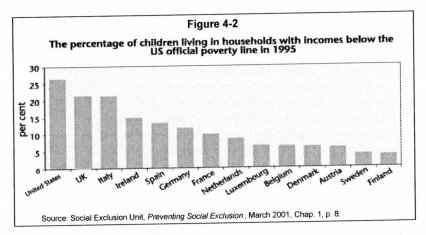

Source: Social Exclusion Unit, *Preventing Social Exclusion*, March 2001, Chap. 1, p. 8.

below 40% of the median.[115] Compared to other European Union nations, Britain's poverty rate is exceeded only by Greece and Portugal.[116]

The geographical differences in poverty rates in the United Kingdom are as pronounced as in the United States.[117] Using AHC data, 28% are in poverty in the depressed Northeast, followed by the West Midlands at 26%. The Southeast and Eastern regions contain the lowest rates, 16% and 17% respectively. London is in the midrange at 23%.

The breakdown of family types in poverty mirrors that in the United States, although the data are put together in slightly different form. Couples without children have a 12.2% poverty rate (AHC); couples with children come in at a 20.9% rate of poverty. Being single without children gives you a 21.7% chance of being in poverty. If you are single with children, though, your rate climbs to 53.8%, nearly four and a half times the couple without children rate.[118]

As for child poverty, it too is higher in the U.K. Nearly a third, 30.3%, of Britain's children are in poverty under the AHC standard, compared to 21.3% of all households. As in the United States, ethnic minorities suffer more poverty than the general population.

As is true in the U.S., Table 4-4 confirms the role of work in removing people from poverty in the U.K.. When the adults in a household, whether there is one or two of them, work full time, the odds of being in poverty are negligible.

115. Office of National Statistics, *Social Trends 33*, Figure 5.14.

116. Guy Palmer, Jenny North, Jane Carr, and Peter Kenway, *Monitoring Poverty and Social Exclusion 2003* (London: Joseph Rowntree Foundation, 2003), 32.

117. Unless otherwise noted, all data are from Office of National Statistics, *Social Trends 33.*

118. Stephen Nickell, "Poverty and Worklessness in Britain," Royal Economic Society Presidential Address, 2003, Table 1.

At the opposite extreme, when no adults work, the rate of poverty is huge, approaching nearly two out of three. From another angle, 20.7% of all British children live in families characterized by worklessness in 2000-01. Among these children, 77.4% were in poverty. Still, it is worth stressing, four per cent of all people working full time cannot manage to lift themselves and their families up to the 60% of median level. Furthermore, many people are surely just slightly above the threshold.

Table 4-4

Individual Poverty in Households with Different Employment Characteristics, 2000-01 (UK)

Characteristic	Percent of people in each type	Percent of people in each type in poverty
Workless	17.0	64.4
One or more part-time	10.0	29.4
Head self-employed	10.9	24.6
Couple, one full time	14.5	19.7
Couple, one full time, one part time	17.5	5.1
Single or couple, all in full time work	30.1	4.0

Source: Stephen Nickell, "Poverty and Worklessness in Britain", Royal Economic Society Presidential Address, 2003, Table 2.

British researchers have lately taken an interestingly different approach to measuring poverty, focusing on "social exclusion."[119] They asked a national sample of people to identify the necessities of life (from a checklist). The lineage of this approach stretches back to Adam Smith, recalling his comments on leather shoes cited in Chapter 2. All the responses that received more than 50% are listed in Table 4-5. It is clear that not only the physical needs of life are considered necessary, but also many items that touch on social customs and obligations. Visits to friends and family, the ability to celebrate Christmas, attendance at weddings and funerals, and the need for a hobby are all widely recognized as important components of life in contemporary society. The ability

---

119. Palmer, *et al., Monitoring Poverty and Social Exclusion 2003.*

to do these things says something about belonging, both to those who can and those who cannot afford them.

Then, through similar surveys, the research team set out to find out how many people cannot afford these items.

Overall, 58% of the population lacks none of them. However, many lack one or more. Quoting the report:

• Roughly 17% of households cannot afford adequate housing conditions as perceived by the majority of the population. That is they cannot afford to keep their home adequately heated, free from damp or in a decent state of decoration.

• About 13% cannot afford two or more essential household goods, like a refrigerator, a telephone or carpets for living areas, or to repair electrical goods or furniture when they break or wear out.

• Almost 14% are too poor to be able to engage in two or more common social activities considered necessary, visiting friends and family, attending weddings and funerals or having celebrations on special occasions.

• About 33% of British children go without at least one of the things they need, like three means a day, toys, out of school activities or adequate clothing. Eighteen per cent of children go without two or more items or activities defined as necessities by the majority of the population.

• About 11% of adults go without essential clothing, such as a "warm waterproof coat," because of lack of money.

• Around 7% of the population are not properly fed by today's standards. They do not have enough money to afford fresh fruit and vegetables, or two meals a day, for example.

• Over 28% of people in households suffer from some financial insecurity. They cannot afford to save, or insure their house contents or spend money on themselves.[120]

THE BLAIR INITIATIVE

The renewed emphasis on social exclusion has reached the higher rungs of government. In 1997, the freshly elected Tony Blair established a Social Exclusion Unit to attack social exclusion by focusing on welfare to work policies and improving schools. Composed of a combination of civil servants and people borrowed from various private organizations, it has since been moved to the Deputy Prime Minister's office to increase its visibility. While some of its work has been publishing the usual reports that provide grist for the academic

---

120. Palmer, *et al., Monitoring Poverty and Social Exclusion,* 4-5.

Table 4-5
Percentage of British Public Who Believe Various Items Are "necessary, which all adults should be able to afford and which they should not have to to without."

Item	Per cent identifying it as necessary
Beds and bedding for everyone	95
Heating to warm living areas of the home	94
Damp-free home	93
Visiting friends or family in hospital	92
Two meals a day	91
Medicines prescribed by doctor	90
Refrigerator	89
Fresh fruit and vegetables daily	86
Warm, waterproof coat	85
Replace or repair broken electrical goods	85
Visits to friends or family	84
Celebrations on special occasions such as Christmas	83
Money to keep home in a decent state of decoration	82
Visits to school, e.g. sports day	81
Attending weddings, funerals	80
Meat, fish or vegetarian equivalent every other day	79
Insurance of contents of dwelling	79
Hobby or leisure activity	78
Washing machine	76
Collect children from school	75
Telephone	71
Appropriate clothes for job interviews	69
Deep freezer/fridge freezer	68
Carpets in living rooms and bedrooms	67
Regular savings (of £10 per month) for rainy days or retirement	66
Two pairs of all-weather shoes	64
Friends or family round for a meal	64
A small amount of money to spend on self weekly not on family	59
Television	56
Roast joint/vegetarian equivalent once a week	56
Presents for friends/family once a year	56
A holiday away from home once a year not with relatives	55
Replace worn-out furniture	54
Dictionary	53
An outfit for social occasions	51

Source: Joseph Rowntree Foundation, *Poverty and Social Exclusion in Britain*, September 2000, Table 1.

mills (including mine), but that are soon shelved and forgotten after the initial press release, some important actions have resulted also. For instance, £900 million has gone into a thoughtful program to revitalize many of the country's poorest areas. A "Connexions Service" has put 17,180 young, unemployed school absentees either to work, in training, or back in school.[121] While the self-congratulatory claims of far-reaching results noted by the Unit cannot be taken at face value, the project does seem to be more than window-dressing.

Nonetheless, the most important commitment Blair made came in 1999. Giving the Beveridge lecture for that year, he proclaimed that "Our historic aim will be for ours to be the first generation to end child poverty." Given 20 years as the usual measure of a generation and providing a year to get started, that means 2020. Chiefly, and importantly, this is to be done by tackling the roots of poverty and social exclusion rather than focusing on more cash transfers. As Robert Walker and Michael Wiseman say,

> Labour's commitment to tackle social exclusion reflects European influences on British policy learning. However, Labour has used the phrase as shorthand for multiple deprivations but with an emphasis on the processes that generate deprivations rather than, as is common elsewhere in Europe, on the immediate circumstances of individuals and families. In so doing, Labour has sought to shift action and expenditure away from dealing with immediate problems and more to preventing problems in the future.[122]

Whether or not Blair's Labourites meet their ambitious goal, they are at least making an effort. I will try to show later that converting the new (1999) National Minimum Wage into a living wage would go far toward realizing this dream.

Analyzing Inequality

If we turn from poverty to inequality, the situation in both Britain and the United States is equally bleak. Even if poverty were eradicated, there would still be inequalities in both societies of such a magnitude as to pose a looming danger of severing the bonds of a common citizenship. Of course, a certain amount of

---

121. Social Exclusion Unit, *Preventing Social Exclusion*, March 2001.
122. Robert Walker and Michael Wiseman, "Sharing Ideas on Welfare," in Robert Walker and Michael Wiseman, eds., *The Welfare We Want: The British Challenge for American Reform* (Bristol: Policy Press, 2003), 18.

economic inequality, as stressed in the discussion of civic republicanism, is inevitable, and it might be conceded, further, that some inequality of economic outcomes might foster other desirable goals, such as economic growth (a position noted again later). However, the political health of a society must be weighed into any discussion of a nation's economic life. Vitamin A contributes to health, too, but too much of it can be ruinous. Even if it transpired that the mean or median income or wealth in a society were a little lower but the gap between the top and the bottom — or the top or the bottom and the middle also — were a little less, that would surely be better than a high average accompanied by crushing inequalities. What is economic growth for anyway? As an end in itself, it is both vacuous and morally bankrupt. Its only justification is as a means to make life better. In the end, if we were to obtain a surfeit of it, but in the process erode the very bonds that form an orderly society, what would be won? It is the aggregate version of the admonition "What good is it for a man to gain the whole world, yet forfeit his soul?"[123]

Inequalities within a society can be measured, as with poverty, using consumption, income, or wealth. Whatever the base, two traditional measures of inequality are the most often used.[124] One involves simply comparing how much of the base various percentages of the population possess. For example, we can compare, say, the income claimed by the top 10% or 20% with that passing through the hands of the bottom 10% or 20%. Or, a comparison could be drawn other ways, laying the top 10% figure alongside the 50th percentile, for instance. To gain a better perspective, it is always instructive to examine how these figures stack up against other nations', and to look at how they have changed over time.

The second measure, the Gini coefficient, is a bit more complex. The fundamental idea is based on a Lorenz curve, as depicted in Figure 4-3. The horizontal and vertical axes are stated in percentages, although note that the vertical axis is a cumulative percentage. Consider the 45° line, which would represent perfect equality. If it were a measure of income, then each person would receive the same income. A Lorenz curve is the curved line in the diagram. In this case, the people in the lower levels are receiving less income than their percentage of the population. Put another way, their place on the vertical axis is lower than on the horizontal axis.

---

123. Mark 8:36 (NIV).

124. There are some other technical ways to measure inequality, but they need not detain us here. See Alissa Goodman, Paul Johnson, and Steven Webb, *Inequality in the UK* (New York: Oxford University Press, 1997), 50-52 for a discussion.

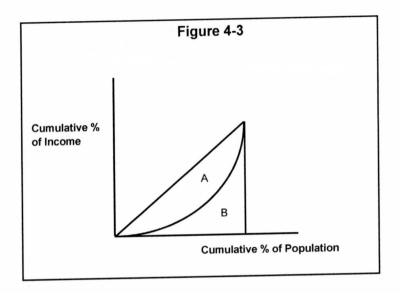

A Gini coefficient states the ratio of area A in the figure to area B. If there were perfect equality, if the 45° line were the curve, then the Gini coefficient would be zero. The higher the Gini coefficient, the greater the area, that is, covered by A, the higher the degree of inequality there is.

By any measure, the United States and Britain are both sharply inegalitarian societies. Table 4-6 presents the income shares claimed by the income quintiles in the mid 1990s compared to several other industrial nations. Table 4-7 gives a comparative glimpse at the income Gini coefficients from the same period.

INEQUALITY IN THE UNITED STATES

According to the latest figures from the U.S. Census Bureau, the lowest 20% of American households receive 3.5% of total income while the top 20% claim 49.7%, a per person average of over 14 times as much.[125] The top 5% take in 21.7%, over six times the *total* amount received by the bottom 20%. If we look at dollars rather than percentages, the figures are revealing in a different way.

---

125. U.S. Census Bureau, *Income in the United States: 2002*, September 2003. As noted in the text, there are several definitions of income, and each produces a slightly different number. The figures cited here are money income. The technical differences among five possible definitions are discussed by the Census Bureau on page 2 of the study cited.

Table 4-6 Comparative Income Percentages			
Percentage of Income Going To (mid 1990s)			
Bottom 10%	Bottom 20%	Top 20%	Top 10%
U.S. 1.8	5.2	46.4	30.5
U.K. 2.6	6.6	43.0	27.3
Australia 2.0	5.9	41.3	25.4
Switzerland 2.6	6.9	40.3	25.2
France 2.8	7.2	40.2	25.1
Canada 2.8	7.5	39.3	23.8
Germany 3.3	8.2	38.5	23.7
Denmark 3.6	9.6	34.5	20.5
Sweden 3.7	9.6	34.5	20.1

Source: World Bank, *World Development Report 2000-01*, Table 5.

Median household income — counting down to the household where half of all households lie either above or below it — was $42,409.

Table 4-7 Comparative Income Gini Coefficents	
	Income Gini Coefficients (mid 1990s)
U.S.	34.4
U.K.	32.4
Australia	30.5
Canada	28.5
Germany	28.2
France	27.8
Switzerland	26.9
Sweden	23.0
Denmark	21.7

Source: OECD

Meanwhile, mean income — totaling all households' incomes and dividing by the number of households — stood at $57,852. The only way this is statistically possible is if a few large incomes pull up the mean. Consider lining up, say, 30 college students from a typical class by height and calculating the median and mean height. Then, remove the five tallest students and replace them with the college basketball team and recalculate the median and mean height.

Part of this inequality can be explained by the natural life cycle. People just starting out on their careers earn less; their incomes rise as they advance to

Table 4-8
Shares of Aggregate Income by Quintiles 2002 (U.S.)

Lowest 20%	Second 20%	Middle 20%	Fourth 20%	Top 20%
3.5%	8.8%	14.8%	23.3%	49.7%

Source: U.S. Census Bureau

middle age, then decline as they retire. Confirming this pattern, those 25-24 years old have a median income of $27,828, while those who are 45-54 enjoy a median of $59,021. For the over-65 cohort, the median drops to $23,152. However, there are vast family and racial/ethnic differences that have nothing whatever to do with age. Married couples have a median income of $61,254. Male-headed households with no wife slide to $41,711, but female-headed households with no husband present fall dramatically, to $29,001. If the household is non-Hispanic white alone (that is, not a mixed household), the median is $46,900. Hispanic households have a median of $33,103 while black households come in at only $29,026. Regional differences, and of course differences in work experience and educational and skill level, also exist. As for the composition of income, for the average household, earnings from wages and salaries make up about three-quarters of the total.

In analyzing inequality, wealth is as important as income. As Lisa Keister explains:

> In addition to telling a different story about advantage and disadvantage, wealth comes closer both theoretically and empirically to our general understanding of well-being. When we talk about economic well-being, we are referring to how prosperous people are, to how financially secure they are. Income is an indicator of short-term security, a type of security that may be lost if markets change abruptly, if the income earner becomes ill or dies, or if one relocates with a spouse. Wealth implies a more permanent notion of security and an ability to secure advantages in both the short and long terms. It is this latter concept that likely fits our shared conception of well-being. This is also perhaps why most people, including social scientists, use the terms *income* and *wealth* interchangeably. It is the latter concept, however, that we should probably understand if we are to understand how well people are doing and what it really means to be disadvantaged.[126]

126. Lisa A. Keister, *Wealth in America: Trends in Wealth Inequality* (New York: Cambridge University Press, 2000), 11.

If we follow Keister and turn to wealth, the picture of relative advantage and disadvantage is even more disturbing. In 2001 (the latest year for which full figures are available), the bottom 25% of families had a median net worth (assets minus debts) of a little over a thousand dollars.[127] The top 10%, in contrast, had a median net worth of $1,301,900. As for the means, they paint an even more compelling portrait. For the bottom quarter, the mean is not even enough register if measure in thousands of dollars. (The fact of a large number with no or even negative net worth could work the same effect on a mean as a few high figures, but in the opposite direction.) For the top 10%, the mean was $2,754,900. The Gini coefficient for the distribution of American wealth is .822.

If we look at the percentage of wealth owned by various groups of the population, perhaps an even better measure, we see the same yawning gaps.[128] The bottom 40% of our citizens control one fifth of one per cent (0.2%) of all the nation's wealth. The next 40% own 16.4%, which leaves 83.4% in the hands of the top 20%. In fact, if we break it down into smaller cohorts of the top 20%, it gets worse. The top 10% own 70.9%, the top 5% 59.4%, and the top 1% a whopping 38.1%. This, incidentally, is the highest percentage of wealth in the hands of this few people since 1929. In short, over 83 cents of every dollar's worth of wealth in this country is controlled by 20% of the population and nearly half of that by only 1%. It is not an overstatement to characterize it as the title of a recent book put it, *Economic Apartheid in America.*[129]

One final note regarding wealth. We often hear that half the American public now owns stocks. If you count mutual funds and retirement accounts, that is true. However, the implication, often merely suggested or sometimes drawn overtly, that there has been a great democratization of the stock market is blatantly false. Ten per cent of Americans own 78.7% of all equities, and 10% of those fortunate people, 1% of the public, own 42.1%. (If, in fact, we count only stocks and mutual funds owned directly, then the figures are 85.1% and 49.4% respectively.)

Moreover, and even more distressingly, these skews in both income and wealth are getting worse. Some historical perspective is helpful. Between 1947

127. Contemporary wealth data can be found in Ana Aizcorbe, Arthur Kennickell, and Kevin Moore, "Recent Changes in U. S. Family Finances: Evidence from the 1998 and 2001 Survey of Consumer Finances," *Federal Reserve Bulletin* 89 (2003), 1-32. Table 3 contains a summary.

128. These figures are from Edward Wolff, *Recent Trends in Wealth Ownership, 1983-1998,* Jerome Levy Institute Working Paper, 2000.

129. Chuck Collins and Felice Yeskel, *Economic Apartheid in America* (New York: New Press, 2000).

and 1979, all income quintiles gained, with the bottom even gaining slightly more than the others. (Figure 4-4) Keep in mind, though, that these are percentages of growth; the 99% growth at the top 20% level represented far more dollars than the 116% growth enjoyed by the bottom. These varying income growth percentages, nonetheless, did result in a slight, ever so slight in fact, shift in income percentages claimed by the different quintiles.

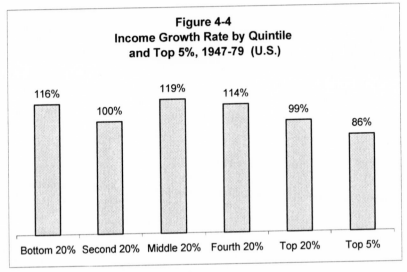

Figure 4-4
Income Growth Rate by Quintile
and Top 5%, 1947-79 (U.S.)

Source: Inequality.com (Compiled by Chris Hartman)

Since 1979, however, the income growth pattern has shifted dramatically. Between then and 2001, the lowest quintile grew at a paltry 3%, while the top quintile enjoyed a 53% boost — over 17 times the *percentage* gain of the worst off — and the really fortunate, the top 5%, found a bonanza, with their incomes growing at an astounding 81%. (It bears noting that this is *before* either of the Bush tax cuts, both of which were heavily weighted toward the well-off, took effect.) The trend line of the Gini coefficient reflects the result.

The Congressional Budget Office has translated these percentages (through 2000) into after-tax dollars. On this score, the bottom fifth, on average, had a $1,100 gain in income since 1979 (in 2000 dollars). In the meantime, the top 1% garnered an average of $576,400 in disposable cash.[130] Put another way by Robert Greenstein and Isaac Shapiro of the Center on Budget and Policy Priorities, who analyzed the CBO data:

---

130. Congressional Budget Office, *Effective Federal Tax Rates, 1997-2000*, August 2003.

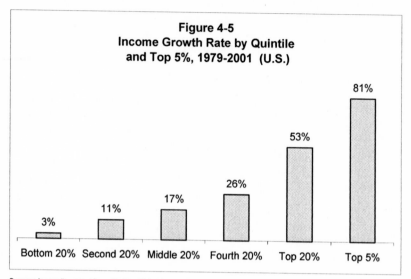

Source: Inequality.com (Compiled by Chris Hartman)

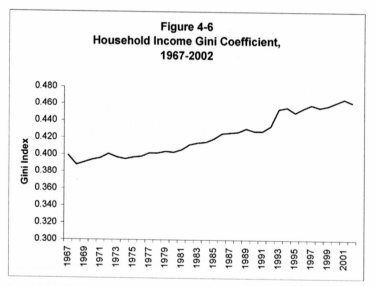

Source: Census Bureau
Note: In 1993 the method of calculating the Gini was modified somewhat.
Thus, those after that date, while valid as a comparison with each other, are
not strictly comparable to the earlier figures.

In 1979, the share of the nation's after-tax income flowing to the top one percent of the population was less than half the share received by the bottom 40 percent of the population. But in 2000, the share of income received by the top one percent exceeded that of the bottom 40 percent. As a result, the 2.8 million people who made up the top one percent of the population received more after-tax income in 2000 than did the 110 million Americans in the bottom 40 percent of the population.[131]

The year 2000 is a revealing time to view the data, since the 1990s were always talked of as an economic boom time for all. While there were some gains at the bottom, the authors of *The State of Working America, 2002-03* summed it up this way:

> Along with the slower growth rates discussed thus far, the other trend in the analysis of American family incomes has been increased income inequality. Even the strong, full-employment economy of the late 1990s, which generated large wage gains for workers at the bottom, was unable to reverse the trend.[132]

Changes in wealth mirror the changes in income, not surprisingly since wealth usually reflects savings from one's previous income.[133] Tables 4-9 and 4-10 say it all. As a percentage of total wealth, the bottom 40% fell the furthest, from holding a bare 0.9% to holding a miniscule 0.2% of national wealth. The next 20% fell also, as did even the fourth 20%, albeit only slightly. The top 20%, though, surged forward. Putting absolute numbers to the mean wealth of the quintiles is perhaps more revealing. Over the 15 years in question, the citizenry's mean net worth increased by over $57,000 (measured in constant dollars), or 27.1%. However, the mean net worth of people in the bottom 40% actually declined from $4,700 to $1,100, a loss of 76.3%. The middle 20% became a little better off, gaining about $5,500 on average, or 10%. The top two groups' asset holdings, though, really climbed. In other words, there was both a percentage and an absolute redistribution of wealth, from the bottom to the top.

---

131. Robert Greenstein and Isaac Shapiro, *The New, Definitive CBO Data on Income and Tax Trends* (Washington: Center on Budget and Policy Priorities, 2003), 2.

132. Lawrence Mishel, Jared Bernstein, and Heather Boushey, *The State of Working America, 2002-03* (Ithaca, NY: Cornell University Press, 2003), 51.

133. In fact, it has to represent savings from someone's income, yours, an ancestor's, or society's generally.

Table 4-9
Percentage of Net Worth Owned by Various Segments
of the American Population, 1983 and 1998

	Bottom 40%	Middle 20%	Fourth 20%	Top 20%	Top 1%
1983	0.09	5.2	12.6	81.3	33.8
1998	0.02	4.5	11.9	83.4	38.1

Source: Edward N. Wolff, *Recent Trend in Wealth Ownership, 1983-1998*, Income Levy Institute, 2000, Table 2.

Table 4-10
Mean Net Worth of People in Various Segments of the
American Population, 1983 and 1998
(in 1998 dollars)

	Bottom 40%	Middle 20%	Fourth 20%	Top 20%	Top 1%
1983	4,700	55,500	133,600	864,500	7,175,000
1998	1,100	61,000	161,300	1,126,700	10,204,000

INEQUALITY IN THE UNITED KINGDOM

The latest British figures show an income distribution that is not as unequal as that in the United States, but is still remarkably unequal. Table 4-11 (utilizing BHC measures) show that the top 10% are ten times as well off as the bottom 10% and that the top 30% have 54% of the nation's income coming to them while the bottom 30% receive only 13%. AHC data, incidentally, would accentuate these inequalities. For example, the 90/10 ratio (the ratio of the person standing at the 90th percentile to the person standing at the 10th percentile) is 4.1 when BHC income is used and 4.9 when AHC income is used.

As in the United States, age plays a role. A pensioner couple has an average BHC income of £301 per week while nonpensioner couples without children enjoy an average of £449 per week.[134] The comparable figures for single pensioners and singles without children are £274 and £383. It bears noting,

---

134. Alissa Goodman and Andrew Shephard, *Inequality and Living Standards in Great Britain: Some Facts*, Institute of Fiscal Studies Briefing Note No. 19, December 2002.

Table 4-11									
Share of Aggregate Income by Deciles, 2000-2001 (UK)									
Bottom 10%	Second 10%	Third 10%	Fourth 10%	Fifth 10%	Sixth 10%	Seventh 10%	Eighth 10%	Ninth 10%	Top 10%
2.8%	4.7%	5.6%	6.5%	7.6%	8.7%	10.1%	11.9%	14.5%	27.7%

Source: Institute of Fiscal Studies

though, that the spread of incomes within the couples without children group (Gini= .335) is greater than among pensioner couples (Gini=.300), as it is in the single without children segment (Gini=.354) compared to single pensioners (Gini=.272). Nevertheless, the work status of adults in the household explains much of the variation. When all adults in a household work full time, the average income is £480 per week; if one works full time and one part time the average is £387; if one is employed and one not working, average income falls to £359; if all are part time then the figure is £307; for the unemployed, meanwhile, the figure is only £173. It is easy to see that work, therefore, especially full-time work, is the path to higher income. Incidentally, the within group inequality is highest among those families in which one works full time and one does not (Gini=.339).

If we turn to wealth, although the figures are compiled somewhat differently from those in the United States, again, we see yawning inequalities. Table 4-12 provides the net worth of people standing at various points in the percentile distribution in 1995 US dollars. The 50th percentile (the median) finds a person having a net worth of $49,700. By the time we get to the 90th percentile that has more than quadrupled to $232,100. At the 98th percentile it is far over 10 times the median. Table 4-13 is perhaps more revealing, breaking down median and mean net worth by income deciles and age (again in 1995 US dollars). First, look at how far apart the medians are in each age group; then glance at how much higher the mean is in every grouping than the median. In fact, in the lowest age group, when people have had the least amount of time to accumulate assets, the ratio of the overall mean to the median is highest, two and a half times. A lot of people are obviously starting life with a significant head start.

Although there has been a slight leveling under the Blair government in income growth rates (both the richest and poorest quintile have grown at a little under 3%), the unmistakable trend since 1971 has been widening inequality.[135]

---

135. For recent growth rates, see Andrew Shephard, *Inequality Under the Labour Government*, Institute of Fiscal Studies Briefing Note No. 33, March 2003.

 KALAMAZOO VALLEY COMMUNITY COLLEGE LIBRARY

Table 4-12
Percentile of Net Worth (UK)
(in 1995 US dollars)

50th percentile	$ 49,700
70th percentile	100,100
90th percentile	232,100
95th percentile	372,600
98th percentile	551,000

Source: James Barks, Richard Blurdell, and James Smith, *Wealth Inequality in the United States and Britain.* London: Institute for Fiscal Studies, 2000, Table 6.

Figure 4-7 compares the growth of BHC incomes of the 90th and 10th percentiles. To round out the picture, Figure 4-8 provides the AHC Gini from 1961 to 2000.

Table 4-13
Median and Mean Net Worth by Income
Decile and Age Cohort, UK
(in 1995 US dollars)

Income Decile	Age < 40		Age 40-59		Age 60+	
	Median	Mean	Median	Mean	Median	Mean
1	200	18,600	900	38,500	1,600	44,500
2	900	23,700	34,500	67,500	11,600	42,700
3	2,100	16,300	49,400	70,000	6,200	48,000
4	9,400	35,500	61,600	88,900	6,300	40,200
5	17,100	35,300	65,200	115,400	65,200	75,600
6	27,500	47,400	91,600	109,500	85,000	96,600
7	45,400	68,300	98,700	136,100	93,900	132,900
8	39,400	62,200	115,300	166,300	118,200	137,500
9	49,700	89,100	130,600	164,800	151,400	201,100
10	74,900	126,000	210,000	308,700	284,100	345,700

Source: Barks, et.al., *Wealth Inequality*, Table 12.

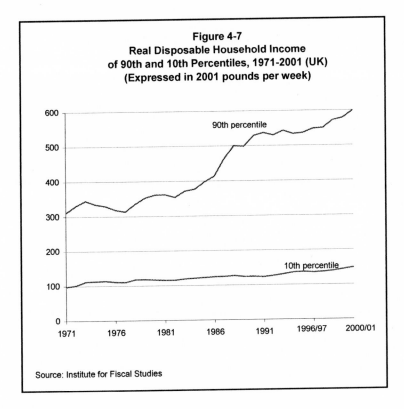

Figure 4-7
Real Disposable Household Income
of 90th and 10th Percentiles, 1971-2001 (UK)
(Expressed in 2001 pounds per week)

Source: Institute for Fiscal Studies

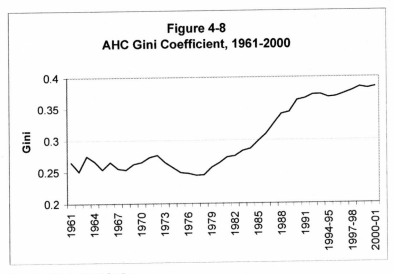

Figure 4-8
AHC Gini Coefficient, 1961-2000

Source: Institute for Fiscal Studies

Statistics on the changes in wealth are not readily available for Britain. However, given the close link between income and wealth, there is no reason to believe that there has not been a parallel concentration of wealth in the top brackets.

THE ROOTS OF INEQUALITY

We need first of all to dispatch to the trash bin some of the specious contentions that inequality can either be explained away or does not matter. The first argument is that income inequality is not a good measure of true inequality, and that consumption would be far better. In Britain, at least, there is some evidence that expenditure inequality has not grown as fast as income inequality.[136] However, using expenditure as our measure would merely temper the trend, not counter it. And, Lawrence Mishel and his colleagues have shown that in the United States consumption inequality has grown in almost perfect tandem with income inequality.[137] Wal-Mart and Nieman Marcus, that is, have replaced J.C. Penney and Sears. The next item in the critical refrain is that demographics, especially the growth of single parent families, are at the root of the reported inequality. However, while this fact may contribute marginally, it cannot account for the bulk of the trend. The heaviest growth in inequality is *within* family types. Then, other critics argue that there is substantial mobility in the United States and Britain. Therefore, while there may be more dispersion among income quintiles or deciles than in the 1970s, snapshots at different points in time pick up different groups of people. The problem is that there is not any evidence whatever of increased social mobility in either society.[138]

As a momentary aside, some people have acknowledged that economic inequality has grown but cheered the fact, maintaining that economic growth and inequality are tied together. One version has it that inequality is a necessary condition for economic growth because it provides incentives for hard work and judicious investment strategies. Others say that economic inequality is the inevitable byproduct of economic growth (however it is generated) because some will either be lucky or astute (by working or investing in the right industries, such as computers in the 1980s) while others will fall behind since

---

136. Goodman, Johnson, and Webb, *Inequality in the UK*, chap. 2.

137. Mishell, *et al.*, *State of Working America, 2002-2003*, 74.

138. See, for example, Lorraine Dearden, Stephen Machin, and Howard Reed, "Intergenerational Mobility in Britain," *Economic Journal* 107 (1997), 47-66.

they work or hold investments in declining industries.[139] These ideas have generated a host of studies, and their evidence for the early stages of economic growth in particular is contradictory. However, Lane Kenworthy has performed the most complete study of the issue for advanced industrial countries.[140] He found that in 15 affluent countries in the 1980s and 1990s there was no correlation in either direction between more equality and economic growth. He then looked at the historical trends in the United States since World War II and conducted an analysis of the American states. In both cases, the data supported his initial finding. In advanced industrial societies, then, it seems, at least to the degree it has been softened so far, inequality is not connected to economic growth, either as cause or effect.

Returning, though, to the causes of our growing inequality, the real explanations come down to two, and one is far more important than the other. The first is increased workforce participation by women. The reason this has added to household income inequality is that wives' educational and skill level closely correlates with that of their husbands. In 2001, for example, the average hourly wage for a woman with less than a high school education was $8.21 while for a woman with an advanced degree it was $24.35.[141] Consequently, if two women, one from the former group and one from the latter, enter the full-time work force, and if their husbands are already significantly apart, the gap will simply rise even further.

However, the gravamen of income inequality is the growing wage inequality, since wages and salaries account for about three-fourths of the average American family's income. Begin with the scandal of CEO pay.[142] In 1982, the typical corporate chieftain earned 42 times as much as the average worker in his or her company. By 2002, that ratio had skyrocketed to 282 times, an almost sevenfold gain.

But CEO pay is only the most obvious indicator of the disparity of what people earn. Table 4-14 shows the change in real wages for both males and females by wage percentile (not total income percentiles) between 1979 and

---

139. There is another side to this. We know that increased welfare expenditures are tied to more economic equality (why is another matter). But nations with higher public budgets generally tend to have more welfare expenditures. Therefore, some critics allege, cutting welfare expenditures reduces the size of the state in the economy, freeing up resources for more growth producing activities in the private sector. Thus, growth and inequality go together.

140. Lane Kenworthy, *An Equality-Growth Tradeoff*, Luxembourg Income Studies Working Paper No. 362, November 2003.

141. Mishell, *et al.*, *State of Working America, 2002-2003*, 161.

142. United for a Fair Economy publishes an annual report on CEO compensation. The latest one, available at UFE's website is from August 2003.

2001. Taking males first, while the middle decile roughly broke even, although even they lost slightly, the bottom groups really lost ground. The bottom 40% all earned less per hour in 2001 than they did in 1979, while those in the deciles above 50 gained. And within the top 40%, the higher the decile the greater the gain. As a result, if we look at the ratio between the bottom and top deciles, we find that in 1979 it was 3.7. By 2001 it had climbed to 4.5.

Table 4-14
Real Hourly Wage by Percentile, 1979-2001 (US)
(in 2001 dollars)

Wage levels by percentile

Males	10	20	30	40	50	60	70	80	90
1979	7.35	9.95	11.26	12.91	14.63	16.59	18.25	21.01	26.76
1989	6.57	8.23	10.10	11.95	13.91	16.38	18.94	22.19	27.80
2001	7.15	8.90	10.41	12.38	14.60	17.06	19.97	24.20	32.19
% change	-2.6	-4.7	-7.3	-5.3	-2.4	0.4	4.8	9.3	19.4
Females									
1979	6.37	6.90	7.49	8.36	9.38	10.66	11.87	13.81	17.19
1989	5.34	6.58	7.61	8.75	10.17	11.62	13.68	16.40	20.58
2001	6.23	7.49	8.71	9.97	11.40	13.20	15.56	18.89	24.82
% change	-2.2	8.5	16.3	19.4	21.6	23.9	31.0	36.8	44.4

Source: Lawrence Mishel, Jared Bernstein, and Heather Boushey, *The States of Working America, 2002-2003* (Ithaca, NY: Corenll University Press, 2003), 130 and 132.

Female wages show a somewhat different pattern. The lowest group, in company with their male counterparts, actually lost ground, but others in the bottom half made gains. However, the gains were not equally spread across the wage spectrum. The percentage gains and losses for the deciles: -0.14, 0.58, 1.22, 1.62, 2.02, 2.54, 3.68, 5.08, and 7.63 — form an almost exact linear progression. The 1979 90/10 ratio was 2.7, the 2001 ratio 4.0. Therefore, the wage dispersion for females, while it started at a lower level, has actually grown more than the male dispersion as a percentage. The male 90/10 ratio increased by 21.6% but the corresponding female ratio grew by 48.1%. Nevertheless, given the differences in male and female participation in the workforce, the difference in full versus part time work by the two groups, and the larger dependence (in families with a male adult present) on male wages, the dramatic climb in male wage disparity has contributed mightily to the gaps in family living standards we now see around us. Add to that the rise in the number of female-headed households, and the picture is rounded out.

Combined then, the growth in wage dispersion for both males and females is the major culprit of rising income inequality.

In Britain, too, "earnings are still by a large distance the biggest single source of income, and make by far the biggest contribution to overall inequality."[143] Gender wage patterns over time in Britain show a similar pattern to that in the U.S.[144] The gap between the 90th and 10th percentiles for male wages has grown significantly since the 1960s. Wage growth for both genders has been slightly compressed in the early years of this century, but only to the point that most segments of the labor market are growing at similar rates. Thus, the gap is not narrowing.

In short, the startling inequality in earnings is what is primarily driving the inequality in incomes. And inequality in incomes is making, in turn, for ever widening gaps in the distribution of wealth. Any serious attempt to address either type of inequality, therefore, requires addressing what people earn.

CONCLUSION

Poverty is certainly not rare in either the United States or Britain. Despite sustained economic growth and a variety of government policies, it remains stubbornly high and shows no signs of diminishing. At the same time, inequality has come to a gallop, and literally threatens to overwhelm us. There are truly two Americas and two Britains. One lives in an opulence unmatched in human history, enjoying a cornucopia of quality goods, lifestyle choices, enjoyable vacations, and access to clean, healthy neighborhoods and services of all kinds. The other lives in a situation of near despair, in decaying, crime-filled neighborhoods, making do with second hand goods and shoddy services.

To some degree, of course, culture drives economics, and those in poverty often engage in activities that make their situations worse. However, economics also drives culture. When you live in hopelessness, when the future appears no brighter than today, when you have dilapidated, or non-existent, public services, when your neighborhood is plagued by crime, you begin to lose your self-respect and your sense of connection to the community. When also your job is low paid in addition to being dirty, demeaning, and perhaps dangerous to boot, you have little if any core of decency to hold onto.

It seems clear that work is the way out of poverty, but it must be work that pays well. At the same time, closing the income and wealth gap is hardly feasible without closing the wage gap. A living wage, better than any alternative, can do both of these simultaneously.

---

143. Goodman, Johnson, and Webb, *Inequality in the UK*, 153.
144. See the graphs in Goodman, Johnson, and Webb, *Inequality in the UK*, 163.

5. THE SUPERIORITY OF THE LIVING WAGE

If we accept the proposition that both poverty and severe economic inequalities are unacceptable, and the complementary proposition that both should be addressed by public policy, the next question is the best policy or mix of policies to achieve these ends. No policy, of course, is going to be a panacea, as there will always be downsides and tradeoffs. The questions to be asked are these: Does the policy stand a reasonable chance of ameliorating the undesirable conditions, in this case poverty and gaping inequalities? Is the design of the policy, including its administrative and institutional aspects, practical? Can the policy attract enough political support to be considered a serious proposal? Naturally, each of these assessments must be made in light of the possible alternatives.

I will argue in this chapter that the living wage is the most appropriate antidote to the twin problems of poverty and inequality. It is certainly not perfect, let me hasten to add. However, it would reduce poverty almost to the vanishing point and take a large step toward making citizens somewhat more equal. It has a relatively simple design, and, as social policies go, uncomplicated enforcement mechanisms. Furthermore, it enjoys enormous political support. Finally, and of utmost importance, it is not only congruent with but also supportive of the values of civic republicanism. None of the known alternatives, tried and untried alike, offers as many positives with as few drawbacks.

These alternatives include economic growth, means-tested transfer payments, worker training, a basic income guarantee, a participation income, the

85

Earned Income Tax Credit, and subsidized private sector jobs. I will first lay out the virtues of the living wage, and then compare it to each of these other options.

A Living Wage

A living wage can be defined as *a wage that would provide someone who works full-time year-round with a decent standard of living as measured by the criteria of the society in which he/she lives.* Although I will take up the structural details in the following chapter, it is worth noting at this point, first, that the law would apply to anyone, regardless of age, type of employer, or size of employer, and, second, that the wage would have to be continually adjusted, usually upward (but conceivably downward), to reflect changes in living standards stemming from economic growth (or decline).

The Importance of Work

The first, and quite considerable, positive attribute of the living wage is that is based on work. For many years, economists taught that work was purely a negative. That is, you worked merely to produce the income that enabled you to buy those items which gave you satisfaction. Logically, therefore, the less you could work for a given level of income, the better. However, that viewpoint wholly overlooks the personal and social dimensions of work. Here, as elsewhere, too much emphasis on the economics of an activity obscured more than it enlightened. Fortunately, we are now coming to appreciate how important the non-economic aspects of work are.[145]

In the first place, work provides a structure to life. The tendency to entropy pervades human activity as much as it does the physical world. Only a precious few of us can keep our lives on course without structure and routine. Stories from the Great Depression are poignant reminders of this. People were lost without routines, and an aimlessness soon infected every corner of life. Orderly life began to crumble, for individuals, for their families, and for their communities. Similarly, today's retirement counselors advise people to retire only if they have something they want to do. As William Julius Wilson put it, regular employment "determines where you are going and when you are going to

---

145. A good summary of the social ramifications of work is Alan Wolfe's review essay, "The Moral Meanings of Work," *American Prospect*, October 1997.

be there. In the absence of regular employment, life, including family, becomes less coherent."[146]

Second, work gives most people a sense of accomplishment, which invariably makes them feel better about themselves. Well-educated people may find it hard to believe that jobs they view as repetitive and stultifying actually challenge people, and that they find them rewarding, but interviewers continue to find this to be the case.[147] People repeatedly report enjoying their jobs and feeling a deep sense of satisfaction in knowing that they do them well. Of course, some jobs are deadening and demeaning, but we should not overlook the overwhelmingly positive aspects most jobs provide merely because of that. Furthermore, I would argue that even a dull job can be given more meaning if it carries a living wage.

Third, and closely related to the second, work provides a sense of identity. We all know what the question "What do you do?" means. "I play softball and collect toy soldiers" is not the type of answer most people expect. Think of how we develop euphemisms ("between jobs") or give a qualification ("I am retired") to avoid saying "I do not work." Of course, this can be overdone, in that some people take their work role too seriously; but the healthy side of the feeling that "I am this" should not be ignored either.

Fourth, work forces us to confront the social world. We learn how to interact with others and how to perform in groups, formal and informal. We learn what society's expectations of us are, as at the same time we develop expectations of certain behavior from others. This clearly leads to greater mental health and better social adjustment.

Fifth, work contributes to the development and maintenance of a healthy civic life. For example, one Australian study found that people with regular jobs had a higher level of trust, especially institutional trust, than those not working, holding all other factors constant.[148] Robert Putnam pointed out that individuals who work are more apt to join groups and participate in civic life

---

146. William Julius Wilson, *When Work Disappears* (New York: Knopf, 1997), 179.

147. See, for example, Robert Wuthnow, *Poor Richard's Principle: Rediscovering the American Dream Through the Moral Dimensions of Work, Business, and Money* (Princeton, NJ: Princeton University Press, 1996).

148. David Hogan and David Owen, "Social Capital, Active Citizenship and Political Equality in Australia," in Ian Winter, ed., *Social Capital and Public Policy in Australia* (Melbourne: Institute for Family Studies, 2000).

than others.[149] Thus, the personal advantages of work spill over easily and naturally into the public realm.

All these aspects of work are cogently summed up by the conclusions of an intensive study of the unemployed in three Dutch cities. They exhibited, the researchers found,

> a loss of time structure, purposelessness, self-blame, strain on mental and physical health, a decline of interest in hobbies and in regular social contacts, loss of identity, a gradual loss of employability, and a distinct decline in involvement in political affairs and civic activities.[150]

To be sure, work can be onerous, unpleasant, degrading, and productive of stress. But then, anything that is good can have a down side. Furthermore, we need to distinguish between the sometimes negative side of work for individuals and the requirements of good social policy. Any social policy that contains unemployment incentives can only be suspect, for the importance of work both for the dignity it gives to people's lives and the position it allows them to assume in the wider society is too basic to be ignored.

Some critics point out that not all paid work is socially useful (making cigarettes, for example) and that much socially useful work (caring for children, engaging in voluntary activities, etc.) occurs outside the market. Both these allegations are true; however, the implications these critics draw for social policy are misguided. The solution to the first is to regulate markets in more desirable ways. Turning to the second, what the critics usually really stress, it does not follow that because someone cares for an elderly parent or leads a Girl Scout troop that they should receive a public subsidy. All kinds of activities that do not show up in the GDP are socially useful, and indeed we ought to work on better methods for measuring production that include these in our reckonings of national well-being.[151] Nevertheless, there is a sharp and useful distinction between paid work in the regular economy and all other activities. By focusing on wages in regular work, the living wage works with a clear and identifiable aspect of the economy.

---

149. Robert Putnam, "Bowling Alone: America's Declining Social Capital," *Journal of Democracy* 6 (1995), 65-78.

150. Quoted in Anton Hemerijck, "Prospects for Basic Income in an Age of Inactivity?" in Robert van der Veen and Loek Groot, eds., *Basic Income on the Agenda: Policy Objectives and Political Choices* (Amsterdam: Amsterdam University Press, 2000), 143.

151. Several attempts have been made at this. See Richard England, "Economic Development and Social Wellbeing: Alternatives to Gross Domestic Product," Unpublished paper, Whittemore School of Business and Economics, University of New Hampshire, 1996.

But the living wage does not stop with the value of work alone. It seeks to underscore the value and dignity of work, all work, by supplying an ample reward for performing it. If we hold that work is so central to psychological well-being and that people's identity is closely tied to their work, then the remuneration they receive for that work cannot help but affect how they view themselves. I and my work are worth "this." Therefore, paying everyone who works a living wage will make him or her have more self-confidence and feel better about the world around them. From that can only flow better citizens. On one of my visits to the local employment office to interview people regarding their feelings about the minimum wage, one young man told me, "When you are paid more, you are motivated. You are motivated to work and you feel better about yourself. When you get $5.15 an hour [the minimum wage], you just don't feel worth very much." Adam Smith expressed the same sentiments two centuries earlier.

> The liberal reward of labour . . . increases the industry of the common people. The wages of labour are the encouragement of industry, which, like every other human quality, improves in proportion to the encouragement it receives. . . Where wages are high, accordingly, we shall always find the workmen more active, diligent, and expeditious, than where they are low.[152]

Thus, the living wage takes both sides of the work equation equally seriously. It rests on the fact that work is an essential ingredient of a normal life *and* on the recognition that both the individual worker and the society at large measure the value of someone's work to a considerable degree by what it pays.

No Connection to the Government's Budget

The second point in the living wage's favor is that it is not embroiled in the government's budget. A living wage would, of course, require a statute setting the wage, and seen from one angle, this would constitute an indirect "tax" on employers. That is, if I operate a shoe store and can get employees willing to work for me for 80% of the living wage, the extra amount I must pay them is an expenditure mandated by government, hence a "tax." Economists would then want to study shifting and incidence in an effort to ascertain who actually "paid" the "tax." Whatever economists might tell us, though, the politics of a living

---

152. Adam Smith, *The Wealth of Nations* (London: Methuen, 1911). Edited by Edwin Cannan. Vol. I, 83. (Originally published 1776.)

wage policy would be decidedly different from the politics of any policy that required the direct expenditure of public funds.

Budgetary politics have their own unique rhythm. It involves both fixing a total for expenditures and allocating that total among various programs. While there is always some rational and dispassionate analysis (and even more talk about it) on display, in the end political considerations rule the day. Members of Congress are besieged by claimants for a place at the public trough, and these must somehow be sorted. Economic and moral logic inevitably mix with old-fashioned, sordid political calculation and give-and-take.

In this messy and high-stakes political struggle, groups with large numbers (retirees), an intense following (farmers), high legitimacy (veterans), or pockets loaded with actual or potential campaign contributions (realtors, doctors, any business trade organization) are going to fare best most of the time. Given that the poor register and vote in smaller numbers than other citizens, and given that they sponsor no political action committees, programs aimed at the poor are always going to be politically vulnerable at budget time. Of course, the poor don't lose out entirely. Members of Congress have consciences and, contrary to popular opinion, are not immune to public interest arguments.[153] In addition, there are several groups that lobby for increased funding for poverty-fighting programs.[154] Occasionally, too, an activist president, such as Lyndon Johnson, will mobilize political capital for expanded social expenditures. Nevertheless, as is often said, the race may not always be to the swift, but that is the way to bet. Year in and year out, the practicalities of budgetary politics customarily find the funding of programs to alleviate poverty or soften inequality on or near the chopping block. And it is naive to believe it will ever be otherwise.

Moreover, budgets breed budgetary analysis, one perpetual feature of which is who pays and who receives. Any public program that entails direct cash payments to the poor makes for a study that can be done by any undergraduate. The payers and the payees are, consequently, clear and readily identifiable.

This fact leads us straight to the matter of dependency. No citizen, we argued earlier, can be dependent on another, and that includes political majorities, no matter how benign. To return to republican theorist Richard Petit, he notes that however the state provides for economic independence, it "must not have the aspect of a gift that may be withdrawn at anyone's whim: not at the

---

153. For a number of illuminating examples, see Joseph Bassette, *The Mild Voice of Reason: Deliberative Democracy and American National Government* (Chicago: University of Chicago Press, 1994).

154. Although it must be pointed out that these are mostly composed of activists working on the poor's behalf, not the poor themselves.

whim of a subsidized employer, not at the whim of a street-level bureaucrat, not even at the whim of an electoral or parliamentary majority."[155] Any public program involving cash payments (or vouchers), therefore, is going to breed dependency, with all its damaging effects, both personal and social.

Living wage politics would not entirely escape these maladies, but it would at least be one step removed from them. There is no need being fanciful. Some of the lopsidedness that characterizes the budgetary process would rear its head, as employers have, and for the foreseeable future will have, more clout than workers. However, because the costs of a living wage (assuming there are any, a matter to be discussed later), would be diffuse and because there would be no direct competition with other programs, the effect of this would be muted. There would not be a need to raise taxes or cut other programs in order to raise the living wage periodically. (Or, as I will recommend in the next chapter, there are ways to put it on automatic pilot.)

Furthermore, people working at regular, paid jobs would have a far stronger political legitimacy than most groups who queue up for a share of the public purse. Lower paid workers would still probably lack PACs to spread money around to current and aspiring politicians, but they could never be stigmatized. True, they would be still dependent in a certain sense, in that their wage level was being set by a political majority. But we are talking about a difference in degree separating them from beneficiaries of direct cash payments that is all but a difference in kind.

Energetic economists, as noted above, could employ their statistical talents to calculate who was actually paying the amount of the living wage that exceeded whatever the "market wage" might be. But the payment would not be funneled through the government's budget. Thus, it would be very unlikely that anyone would look at living wage workers and mutter "The government is taking 'my' money and giving it to 'them.'" Any sense of dependency would be severely eroded if not entirely erased.

This sentiment is echoed by the poor themselves. In one survey of a low-income area of Chicago, for example, 81% of poor African-Americans said they would rather work than receive benefits if the amounts were the same.[156] Surely this attitude flows from an understanding that they could look others in the eye if they were being paid for work, as well as deep feelings regarding how it might better structure their lives.

---

155. Phillip Petit, *Republicanism: A Theory of Freedom and Government* (Oxford: Oxford University Press, 1997), 162.
156. Wilson, *When Work Disappears*, Appendix C, Table 4, 251.

Existing Administrative Machinery

Unlike several proposed programs, the administrative machinery to enforce a living wage is already in place. The Department of Labor has been enforcing the minimum wage provisions of the Fair Labor Standards Act for over sixty years now. Undoubtedly, the number of inspectors would have to be increased and the penalties set at appropriate levels. Nonetheless, the entire administrative structure and the various accompanying procedures, including appeals to the judiciary, are up and functioning.

THE ALTERNATIVES

All these advantages of the living wage come into stark relief when we examine the alternatives. Though not without limitations and difficulties of its own, the universal living wage is superior to each of them.

Economic Growth

Conservatives continually bray about the wonders of economic growth as an antidote to poverty. Sustained economic growth will provide the extra moneys that will raise living standards for all. Hence, government policies to spur growth are in everyone's interest. The frequently used metaphor seems to summarize it all, "A rising tide lifts all boats."

Even a luminary such as John Maynard Keynes touted the benefits of economic growth.[157] Writing in the 1920s, he argued for the need to push economic growth for another half century or so. Then, we would have enough material abundance for everyone to have all that they could conceivably need. More recently, Dinesh D'Souza has taken up the theme in his book *The Virtue of Prosperity*. For D'Souza, the important fact is that everyone's income and wealth are rising in absolute terms so that ordinary people "too will find themselves in a position where they can do what they want with the rest of their lives. Thus they will have crossed the point where money produces diminishing gains."[158]

Let us be clear. Economic growth is definitely a positive good. It does produce the extra dividend that raises living standards in the long run, and at the

---

157. John Maynard Keynes, "Economic Possibilities for our Grandchildren," in *The Collected Writings of John Maynard Keynes* (London: Macmillan, 1971), Vol. IX, 321-32. (Originally published in 1928.)
158. Dinesh D'Souza, *The Virtue of Prosperity: Finding Values in an Age of Techno-Affluence* (New York: Free Press, 2000), 109.

same time, provides a peaceful outlet for much human energy and creativity. Consequently, government policies — such as low interest rates, incentives for technological research and development, and guarantees of reasonable rewards for those who invent and invest — that serve to aid economic growth should be pursued with vigor. Conversely, public policies that impede growth are to be shunned.

However, we should be equally clear that economic growth alone does absolutely nothing to reduce poverty or soften inequality. Standing by itself, economic growth produces . . . well, economic growth. The equally important complementary question is who receives the benefits of whatever growth occurs. As public policies can help or hinder economic growth, similarly, they have an enormous influence on who reaps the rewards.

The basis for the idea that economic expansion leads to a reduction in poverty, as well as reduced inequality, is the experience of the mid-1930s, the 1950s, and the 1960s In all three of those periods, economic growth did lead to a precipitate fall in the prevalence of poverty among the American population. However, what happened in the 1980s and early 1990s demonstrates why no generalization can be drawn in this regard, as economic growth produced no reduction in poverty levels. The reason is that in the 1930s, the 1950s, and the 1960s economic growth was accompanied by both a reduction in unemployment and by rising wages. In the 1980s, on the other hand, unemployment fell, but wages, especially for the less skilled, showed no concomitant rise, and according to most accounts have actually fallen. Consequently, absent a government policy to halt the skid in wage levels, the economic growth of 1980s produced no reductions whatever in the percentage of Americans grappling with poverty.[159] Painfully, too, the gap between the rich and the poor stretched ever wider.

In fact, that whole rising tide metaphor is downright silly. In the first place, the decks of the yachts are already far above the seats in the rowboats. At the same time, a rising tide could swamp the rowboats instead of raising them, or it could even smash them against the yachts. If you are having to swim or hold onto the pieces of a wrecked boat for dear life, a rising tide is the last thing you need.

In short, economic growth by itself is hollow. It is an important component of social policy, true enough, but only the beginning point of the search for justice, not its end. Distributive questions are of equal import. Consider, for illustration, two pies, one with 100 pieces, and one 10% smaller with 90 slices of

---

159. The data are laid out in Rebecca Blank, *It Takes a Nation: A New Agenda for Fighting Poverty* (Princeton, NJ: Princeton University Press, 1997), chap. 2.

the same size. Suppose the bottom 20% of one nation's population has five slices of the former pie and the bottom 20% of another's has seven of the latter. Which country is better off?

Means-Tested Cash Transfer Programs

If, as the English political philosopher Harold Laski said, the main difference between the rich and the poor is money, then an easy way to fight poverty and soften inequality is to redistribute some of what the rich have to the poor. That way, the poor can purchase the commodities they wish, and have at least some of the choices the rich have. Vouchers may limit the choices to a given commodity (housing, food, education), but the argument is the same. Furthermore, collecting money and then disbursing it is something governments do on a regular basis.

However, such programs are bound to fail; indeed, it might not be too shrill to call them nefarious. First, who qualifies and for how much must be decided, an endlessly frustrating political exercise under the best of circumstances. Then, the applicants must demonstrate that they qualify, an exercise that invariably robs people of their dignity. You become a supplicant, with all that entails. If the bureaucrats are quizzical, you become defensive and have to shamefully produce evidence that you are indeed poor. If the bureaucrats are "helpful," showing you how to maximize your benefit, you feel like a child. Either way, it is almost the definition of dependency, stigmatizing people in an ineradicable way. A better formula for destroying the autonomy necessary for effective citizenship could hardly be devised.

In addition, means-tested programs carry calamitous political consequences. Those paying the bills will, in time, become chafed, and look on their fellow citizens with jaundiced eyes. Resentment will divide citizens rather than unify them in a sense of common purpose.

One need only look at the history of the AFDC program to get a sense of the results of means-tested programs. Little more needs to be said. In the end, means-tested programs are destructive of the values of civic republicanism. No citizen should ever have to stand before a government official, whether skeptical or sympathetic, and demonstrate that he or she is poor.

Worker Training

Former president Bill Clinton, along with many others, suggested that worker training was a way to raise wages across the board. The logic is rather simple. It is obvious that better trained workers earn more, and equally obvious that a well-trained workforce is more productive. Therefore, the more and better-trained workers we have, the higher wages will be. Some analysts push the argument to another level, contending that the growth of international trade will allow rich countries such as the United States to export the low-wage, and usually unpleasant, jobs elsewhere and keep the high-paying, more gratifying jobs for Americans. Thus, publicly funded training programs benefit everyone.

But there are several defects with worker training as the path to the alleviation of poverty and the reduction of inequality. The first is the limitations inherent in the development and operation of any proposed training programs. For what are the trainees to be trained? Policy makers have no crystal ball allowing them to see into the future of the job market. Establishing, equipping, and staffing a job-training program can be an expensive undertaking, and the whole enterprise can quickly become a white elephant. In addition, how do you encourage (or coerce) people into the program? Those who are eager to learn already have a plethora of programs available to them, in vocational high schools, community colleges, and numerous private vocational schools. And even if you shepherd recalcitrant people into the program through some type of carrot or stick, how much are they really likely to learn? For all these reasons, publicly operated job training programs, while not without some success, have a patchy record indeed in training people and then placing them in permanent jobs. The usual example worker training advocates point to is Germany, which has a combination of vocational programs meshed into a system of apprenticeships. But these go along with a strong vocational tradition and powerful labor unions, neither of which is found in the United States.

A second problem might be called the overproduction malady. Let us say that a highly regarded training program successfully trained thousands of welders. The resulting marked increase in the supply of welders would drive down the wage level. This might push down the cost of construction, but it would actually harm welders, and do little for the newly-minted welders, as yet another fresh batch would be released onto the job market periodically by continued training.

A third problem is more daunting still. Suppose every adult in the United States had a bachelors degree in engineering, and even suppose further we had exported all those nasty low-skilled manufacturing jobs in textiles and so forth to Third World countries. There would still be plenty of menial tasks to be performed here at home. In short, someone would still have to empty the bed pans at the nursing home, mop the floors at the veterinary clinic, and stock the shelves at Wal-Mart. Thus, no matter how much training there is, jobs that are rote and routine will still exist. People, not robots, will have to do them, and they should be paid a living wage.

None of this is to say that training should be abandoned. Modest, well-designed training programs can have an impact, lifting both some individual's wages and overall productivity. But we need to be realistic; it is not a prescription for increasing the wages of everyone.[160]

Basic Income Guarantee

A number of people on the left, both in the United States and Europe, have been taken with the idea of the basic income guarantee, or BI.[161] Although he does not claim to have invented the idea, the founder of the modern BI movement is the Belgian economist Philippe Van Parijs. Van Parijs says that "a basic income is an income unconditionally paid to all on an individual basis, without a means test or work requirement."[162] Tony Fitzpatrick has expanded this a bit: "A BI would be an income paid unconditionally on either a weekly or a monthly basis to every man, woman and child as an individual right of citizenship and so without reference to employment status, employment record, intention to seek employment or marital status."[163] According to Van Parijs and other BI advocates, the plan is designed to enhance liberty, defined as the right to do what you want and possession of the means to do it.

Actually, the plan has a diverse philosophical parentage, some precedents in practice, and a number of advantages to recommend it. Thomas Paine, for example, advocated a program whereby each year all citizens would receive a portion of society's product. Edward Bellamy's society in *Looking Backward*

---

160. Although their conclusions are somewhat tinged by ideology, and therefore debatable, Colin Crouch, David Finegold, and Mari Sako's book *Are Skills the Answer? The Political Economy of Skill Creation in Advanced Industrial Countries* (New York: Oxford University Press, 1999) presents an excellent overview of the issues involved.

161. The best general source on the BI is the November issue of the journal *Boston Review* (also published as a book by Beacon Press in 2000 under the title *What is Wrong With a Free Lunch?*). It contains essays by Van Parijs and several others, both admirers and critics. A more thorough discussion can be found in Philippe Van Parijs, ed., *Arguing for a Basic Income: Ethical Foundations for a Radical Reform* (London: Verso, 1992) and van der Veen and Groot, eds., *Basic Income on the Agenda: Policy Objectives and Political Choices*. There is an excellent website maintained by Karl Widerquist and the U. S. Basic Income Guarantee Network, www. widerquist.com/usbig/index. html, which has numerous useful links.

162. Philippe Van Parijs, "Competing Justifications of Basic Income," in Van Parijs, ed., *Arguing for Basic Income*, 3.

163. Tony Fitzpatrick, *Freedom and Security: An Introduction to the Basic Income Debate* (London: Macmillan, 1999), 3.

contained a basic income scheme. In more modern times, Milton Friedman once laid out a negative income tax plan that would work something like a basic income grant.[164] The state of Alaska makes annual payments to all its citizens out of its permanent fund, each citizen receiving an identical amount.

There are several strong advantages offered by a BI. First, it would provide a minimum income for all, and one obtained without the deservedly hated means test. By making the payments equal for everyone it would underline the equality of shared citizenship. Further, it would eliminate what are called the poverty and unemployment traps so often caused by the current tangle of benefit programs. The former flows from the fact that as earnings go up, benefits (such as medical and child care benefits) are often withdrawn, while the latter occurs when a job produces less income, or not much more at any rate, than the benefit levels. Such an income guarantee would also enhance individual autonomy, especially for those at the bottom of the income ladder. Finally, the program would be simple to understand and relatively cheap to administer, two advantages that are not negligible. One highly desirable impact is that it would surely raise wages in the lower reaches of the economy, as more people would be able to refuse very low-paying jobs. On another front, it would also likely make more women at least partially economically independent, especially low-income women.

Nevertheless, the objections to a BI are overwhelming, and it must be put to one side. The first and most obvious is the absence of any consideration of the value of work. Van Parijs has argued that we need to avoid a "work fetishism," and forcefully put the case for payments based on the joint ownership of the natural resources of the society. In provocative essays, he has shown why two imaginary citizens, Crazy and Lazy, should have equal claims on their society's economic product, and justified paying the "Malibu surfer" a BI.[165] However convincing these arguments are on one level, they completely ignore the personal and social benefits that accrue to households where at least one person works. The uniformity and the lack of a means test inherent in a BI, coupled with its payment as a matter of right, would make it fit the criteria of republican citizenship, true enough; but its failure to recognize the value of work would serve to undermine the very values upon which the republican polity is built.

---

164. Milton Friedman, "The Case for the Negative Income Tax: A View from the Right," in J. H. Bunzel, ed., *Issues of American Public Policy* (Englewood Cliffs, NJ: Prentice-Hall, 1968), 111-20.

165. Philippe Van Parijs, "Why Surfers Should be Fed: The Liberal Case for an Unconditional Basic Income," *Philosophy and Public Affairs* 20 (1991), 101-31 and "Real Freedom versus Reciprocity," *Political Studies* 46 (1998), 140-63.

Furthermore, there is the practical side. Van Parijs has advocated introducing the BI at a low level, then increasing it over time to match the poverty level. But this highlights the dilemma of the BI. Either the amount would be quite small, making it a trivial component of even low-income people's net receipts, or else it would be significant, carrying enormous costs. If you merely take the poverty level for one person and multiply it by the population of any advanced industrial society, you get scary numbers in a hurry. Now, since in most versions of the plan, the BI would replace many current benefits and tax allowances (but not usually contributory programs such as social security), the numbers would not be as huge as a first glance indicates. Nonetheless, they are still beyond the wildest totals imagined by any budget planner anywhere. Just for illustration, the poverty level for one person in 2002 was $8,860 (for the lower 48 states). The 2000 census counted a little over 281 million Americans. This translates to roughly $2.5 trillion in annual payments. The entire federal budget for fiscal year 2003 is $2.1 trillion. A little over $300 billion of this amount is currently allocated for "income security." Let us assume the BI replaced all of that, and further that there is another $300 billion in various benefits scattered throughout the budget, which would fall out with a poverty smashing BI. That would mean "only" $1.9 trillion in new spending would be necessary. Taxes would then have to go up by 91% to cover this amount; or, looked at another way, the new BI would make up 63% of the revised federal budget ($2.5 trillion of $ 4 trillion).

Still on the budgetary theme, the problem of identifying payees and payers would surface immediately. It would be evident to anyone with a calculator who was paying for whom. This could not help but fuel social tensions, build resentments, and undermine the very common citizenship the BI is designed to build. Using the public budget for any type of redistributive purpose invariably invites unhealthy political divisions.

Finally, while a sizeable BI could eliminate poverty, it is possible that it might actually increase inequality. That is because the more affluent could use theirs to invest in stocks and other forms of assets. The returns these would produce over the long run would put them even further ahead of those who had to spend their BI for immediate consumption. The higher the BI the greater this effect would be.

Scan the advantages of the BI again. Would not a living wage achieve each of them also? Furthermore, it would do so by encouraging work, not bursting the public budget, and not making any redistribution accompanying it plainly evident. It would also have a shot at reducing inequality.

Providing Each Citizen A "Stake"

An innovative and stimulating proposal has come from the pens of Bruce Ackerman and Anne Alstott.[166] They propose that each citizen be given a stake in the nation's resources in early adulthood. The amount they select is $80,000, payable to all high school graduates at age 21. The program would be financed initially by a two per cent tax on wealth. At death, each person would return his or her stake to the common pool if they were able to do so.

Each person could do with her stake what she pleased — advanced education, a seaside cabin, a start on a small business, a wild night of revelry. Their belief is that such a scheme would produce a needed shot of responsibility into many of the young. What to do with your stake would be a momentous decision, with life-determining consequences.

The principal rationale for this program is not addressing poverty but securing the blessings of citizenship to everyone. They wish, that is, to use public policy to help realize the republican dream of a propertied citizenry. For this, there are precedents. The Homestead Act, for instance, was one foray in this direction. Margaret Thatcher's 1980s bid to sell public housing units to their occupants is another, as was the Czech Republic's provision of a voucher signifying an ownership share of the public goods of the elapsed communist state. Nonetheless, Ackerman and Alstott are obviously concerned about poverty and inequality, for those themes form an important subtext to their presentation.

This plan, despite what seems like an air of unreality, is actually better on several counts than BI. The first is that while it may share with BI the philosophical notion that a distribution of the nation's wealth rather than income is involved, by making the payment a one time event and providing for financing it by a wealth tax, stakeholding makes the link more straightforward and much less ambiguous. The second is that providing a sizeable stake at one point in time would make people think more carefully about how to spend it. With annual payments, you could easily say, "Well, I will blow this year's, but next year. . ." When there is no more, though, the mind would likely be more sharply focused. Plus, although the public budget is utilized, by setting up a separate fund, it might be possible to make the political case with only a minimal amount of the social division other programs bring. Convincing a majority that everyone would be better off if we went to a stakeholder society would also be a

---

166. Bruce Ackerman and Anne Alstott, *The Stakeholder Society* (New Haven, CT: Yale University Press, 1998).

better bet than convincing a political majority to make sizeable yearly payments to everyone in perpetuity.

I have a few reservations (as I suspect anyone who teaches undergraduates does), but overall the plan has much to recommend it. Nevertheless, there are several problems. What is to be done with those who blow their stake on a BMW or who put their faith in Uncle Marvin's hot tip on flaxseed futures, or even with those who make a reasonable, considered use of their stake (say, purchasing a small farm or opening a small business), but things just turn out badly? We would still have, sadly, the blight of poverty and inequality to deal with. A substantial number of the less well off might indeed use their stake to escape poverty and reach the middle rungs of the economic ladder. But for those who did not, for whatever reason, their citizenship should not be thereby diminished. Furthermore, as with BI, there is a good chance that handing every 21-year-old $80,000 would exacerbate inequality. The affluent would have access to much better investment advice, and the returns they would earn on their stakes would likely dwarf what most less fortunate citizens would be able to garner. Then, if the history of tax legislation is any guide, no matter how air tight the gift and estate tax system (necessary policies if the stakeholding fund is to be self-perpetuating) was, the well-heeled would find ways around it. In time, this would deepen inequality even further. A living wage would have a better chance of handling the first problem and make the second one irrelevant.

Finally, there is the politics. I have trouble seeing, in the foreseeable future anyway, the possibility of selling such a plan politically. In contrast, the living wage already enjoys substantial political backing (as will be discussed in Chapter 6).

In the end, this proposal offers much that is good, and much food for thought. Fortunately, also, it need not be a substitute for the living wage. We could provide each young adult with a stake in our society's resources and enact a living wage at the same time. Given a choice, though, I would argue that the living wage would do a better job of fighting poverty and inequality and put a stronger support under republican citizenship than would going the stakeholder route.

Participation Income

A.B. Atkinson has advocated a somewhat different approach to the BI. While he favors making the payments equal and stripped of a means test, he would restrict the recipients to those who are making a contribution to society.

This contribution could come from paid work, but it could also come from a wide variety of other activities.

> While the qualifying conditions would include people working as an employee or self-employed, absent from work on grounds of sickness or injury, unable to work on grounds of disability and unemployed but available for work, it would also include people engaging in approved forms of education, caring for young, elderly or disabled dependants or undertaking approved forms of voluntary work, etc. The condition involves neither *payment* nor *work*; it is a wider definition of social contribution.[167]

This is certainly an improvement, from a civic republican perspective, on Van Parijs's proposal. Furthermore, as Atkinson says, it is much more likely to gather the needed political support. However attractive in principle, though, it is marred by debilitating political and administrative flaws.

First, the words "approved" and "caring" gloss over hundreds of disputable issues. A statute would have to define "caring" and certify which forms of education and voluntary work counted. If Ms. Smith volunteers full-time at the soup kitchen, I don't suppose anyone would object to her being counted as making a contribution. But what about her neighbor who conducts tours of the local art gallery? What about political activism? What kinds of education would be acceptable? We have seen, for example, what a dead-end nonstop classes in job seeking and self-esteem can become. What would actually constitute "caring"? If you visit Dad in the nursing home and take care of his legal and financial details, does that count? Ad infinitum. Moreover, in order to prevent the rankest kind of abuse, some level of contribution would have to be established. If I go by the homeless shelter once a month and unpack a couple of boxes of supplies, have I contributed enough to get my BI check?

Second, there would have to be some sort of enforcement machinery. Otherwise, the program would have no integrity and breed rampant cynicism. Suppose someone volunteered to work at the Red Cross headquarters two days a week and didn't show up? Or, more seriously, what if someone was supposed to be caring for children but then neglected them? We would, therefore, have to create a National Caregiving and Voluntary Activity Enforcement Board with wide-ranging powers, a substantial staff, and a sizeable budget.

As a start, this body would have to obtain periodic reports from all agencies (including churches, synagogues, and mosques) at which people volunteered. In addition, they would have to have a multitude of enforcement agents to check up

---

167. A. B. Atkinson, "The Case for a Participation Income," *Political Quarterly* 67 (1996), 67-70.

on whether or not those providing the care to the elderly, the young, or the disabled were in fact doing so. Then, there would have to be several layers of administrative machinery to handle the inevitable appeals. ("I could not get to the church because I was sick." "I had to leave my children with a neighbor because my sister in Seattle was having a bout of depression." "I know I shouldn't have spent my check on booze and skipped class, but if you cut me off now I will not be able to buy food. I will do better next time.")

In short, this is an admirable approach, but it is patently unworkable, and it cannot be made to do so.

The Earned Income Tax Credit

The Earned Income Tax Credit (EITC) was adopted in 1975.[168] The U.K. has recently adopted a broadly similar measure, although in the new amendments you do not have to have children to qualify. However, since it is relatively new, I will concentrate on the American version. The EITC provides a "refundable credit" (i.e., a check) to certain people with low wages. The credit schedule is bell shaped, in that it rises with each dollar of earned income up to a point then begins to diminish. In 2001, it phased out completely at $32,121, with the maximum credit being $4,008. Until 1994, you had to be a head of household with dependent children in order to claim the credit. (An increased credit was given for someone with two children, but no more.) A modest credit (a maximum of $364) is now available to those without children. The program has about 20 million household claimants and costs around $32 billion annually. It is also indexed to the inflation rate.

It has long been a favorite of both conservatives and liberals. The former like the work incentives. Unlike many government transfer programs, if you do not work you cannot qualify for the credit. Presumably, by making work pay more, the program pulls more people into the labor market. Liberals like the cash payment aspect, and it does add measurably to the incomes of the poor. According to one study, the EITC lifted 4.8 million people over the poverty line in 1999. It also avoids some of the perpetual problems of means-tested programs by phasing out the benefits gradually. You are always better off to work more.

Despite these advantages, it still comes up short compared to the living wage. First, there is the program's complexity. The IRS booklet (Publication No.

---

168. The best summary and analysis of the EITC is V. Joseph Hotz and John Karl Scholz, "The Earned Income Tax Credit," National Bureau of Economic Research Working Paper #8078, January 2001.

596) explaining it, even though written in very simple language, is 54 pages long. There is disputable evidence regarding the participation rate among those eligible, but it is clearly below 100%. Although there are several plausible reasons for this, the complexity of the rules (particularly regarding what constitutes a "qualifying child") certainly does not help.

The use of households rather than individuals is another problem, and another complexity. For one thing, there are all kinds of variations among American households. For another, it is often not clear how people can end up benefitting most from the Treasury's check. To wit, the structure of the program can have serious marriage penalties or it can have a marriage bonus, depending on the income of various members of a potential household. While the reasons are somewhat complex, the simple fact is that this problem cannot be fixed as long as the income tax is progressive and the taxable unit is the household.

Then, there is the problem of payments to those who are not entitled to them. In a widely noted 1995 study, the IRS admitted that 28.5% of the total expenditures under the program went to ineligible people. Part of this is undoubtedly inadvertent, as people grapple with the complex rules. However, some undetermined, and probably undeterminable, amount is from sheer fraud. A small portion of this occurs by people manipulating their claimed self-employment income, although you have to be pretty knowledgeable to do this. (My accountant friends tell me, though, that this is not at all uncommon.) Most of it, however, comes from false reporting regarding children. Recent IRS reforms make it somewhat easier to check up on this, but that has also added another layer of complexity and another set of government bureaucrats who have the right to pry into people's private affairs. While the fraud level has no doubt been lowered of late, and while it is dwarfed in any event by the routine fraud connected with business returns, it is still a problem.

In addition, although the evidence points to an overall positive contribution to work effort, the effect is not uniform. In their careful study, Hotz and Scholz note that "the predicted effects of the EITC are not all pro-work, especially with respect to hours and its labor market incentives for two-earner couples."[169]

Finally, there are practical limitations constraining how generous the program can become, for at some point the amounts paid out will trigger the same type of political backlash all means-tested programs do. It may be connected with the income tax rather than direct welfare payments, but that

---

169. Hotz and Scholz, "Earned Income Tax Credit," 2.

will not stop detractors from labeling those who receive the checks as dependent on the largesse of those who send in checks with their returns. Its work component will not shield it from the "But I work too" chorus.

At the end of the day, the EITC is far superior to other transfer programs in objectives, design, and effects. Nevertheless, it has some unintended consequences and is plagued by unfixable complexities. Moreover, if its payout rises much more, it will be beset by the political inflammation that sooner or later engulfs all means-tested transfer programs. The living wage, in contrast, suffers from none of these problems. It will achieve everything the EITC does with no disincentives of any kind, no policy tangles, and do it outside the government's budget.

Employment Subsidies

The proposal that comes closest to the living wage in desirability is Edmund Phelps' plan for employment subsidies.

> The essence of such a program is that the government makes periodic contributions to reward employment of workers in eligible low-wage jobs at qualified enterprises. In the scheme I favor, the periodic government disbursement goes to each qualified *enterprise* for every low-wage worker in its employ. All employees having the same wage are to bring in the same subsidy to the employer. The government contributes the same additional subsidy with every additional employee costing the employer a given hourly amount.[170]

This subsidy would alter the cost-benefit calculation each business makes (in principle, anyway) when considering hiring a new worker. Theoretically, firms hire workers up to the point at which their wage equals their contribution to marginal revenue. With a subsidy added in, it would be profitable to hire more workers. As for the financing, the subsidies would come from a flat, general payroll tax, estimated by Phelps to be 2 ¾%.

This plan has many virtues. It is based, first of all, on paid work at actual jobs. It makes the creation of more jobs at the low end of the wage scale and higher remuneration for those jobs its central objectives. This would put more people to work with beneficial impacts all around. The workers, their families, and their communities would all be better off. Furthermore, workers would begin to receive training that would qualify them for better jobs with higher wages. The financing would not be onerous. Moreover, Phelps has carefully

---

170. Edmund Phelps, *Rewarding Work: How to Restore Participation and Self-Support to Free Enterprise* (Cambridge, MA: Harvard University Press, 1997), 105-06.

traced out the likely economic impacts of the plan, and they are overwhelmingly positive.

However, the devil, as always, is in the details. Despite the plan's economic merits, its political and administrative dimensions present substantial stumbling blocks.

First, the rationale of the plan requires a gradual phasing out of the subsidy if it is to be limited to low-wage jobs. You could have, of course, a flat subsidy for all jobs. In that case, though, if it were significant it would entail huge financial outlays; on the other hand, if it were small, it would have little impact on low-end jobs. Consequently, to be effective it must be targeted to low-wage jobs. But that means we have to establish a cut-off point. Then, if we don't gradually phase out the subsidy, we create the classic trap, in which you are worse off right above the line than below it.[171] Phelps' plan is to begin the subsidy at $3.00 per hour for jobs carrying a market wage of $4.00 per hour. The subsidy then decreases smoothly through eight steps to a mere $0.06 per hour at a $12.00 per hour market wage.

This set up is eminently sensible from an economic and idealized policy design perspective. However, it is a political swamp. Setting the subsidy and its degree of graduation would cause endless political wrangling. Undoubtedly, economists and policy experts would be consulted, but there are no objective criteria to apply here. Why $3.00, rather than $3.25 or $2.75? Why eight steps rather than ten? Raw political calculations could, at any moment, make the whole program turn topsy-turvy. In general, the more complex a program and the softer the data and models upon which it is based, the more political havoc you can expect. Here we have both these elements suited out in their Sunday best.

Furthermore, there is that fund for paying the subsidy. Let us even suppose it were set up outside the regular budget, earmarked to go only for wage subsidies, in order to shield it from ordinary budget prowling. I fear that given what we know about the strength of business lobbies, they would nevertheless succeed in siphoning away part of this fund. "Why not give us the subsidy and let us provide the training?" "Why not give export businesses a portion of the subsidy so that they can sell more abroad and create more jobs?" Such a fund's future being restricted purely to the payment of the kind of employment subsidies Phelps envisages would be problematical, at best.

---

171. A simple example is the self-employment tax. If you make less than $400 from self-employment, you do not pay the tax. If you make $401 you trigger the 15.3% tax and end up with $339.65.

Then, there is the administrative quagmire. Phelps acknowledges two administrative problems, the paying of non-pecuniary benefits and phantom employees put on the payroll merely to obtain the subsidy. The latter is a far graver problem. He suggests attacking this type of fraud by allowing employers to take the credit only against their other taxes due. But this would merely be an invitation to more creative cheating. He also says that it might possibly be necessary "to restrict eligibility to good-sized firms in which such flagrant fraud might become known to non-owners."[172] This, though, fashions another severe political knot. How "good-sized"? In general, larger firms pay higher wages anyway; so the higher the eligibility line (whether in assets, sales, or profits), the less impact the program will have. The lower the line, the more administratively difficult policing the scheme would become. Further, wages are ordinarily the lowest in retail stores, restaurants, and such personal service industries as cleaning. All these sectors are dominated by small firms. If restricted to large firms, then, the subsidy would be unavailable where it is needed the most. If, on the other hand, the reach of the law were wide, we would need an army of inspectors to ensure compliance.[173]

Also, this plan does not escape the standard problems endemic to any proposal that uses the public purse to accomplish its goals. The identity of those who paid the payroll tax and those whose jobs were subsidized would be known, at the shop-floor level and in the society at large. Since payments would be one step removed from a direct government grant to an individual and since the payment to the recipient would be for actual work, it would mitigate those feelings of dependency, true enough. However, it would not abolish them entirely.

Let me say without reservation that of all the proposals surveyed so far, this one is by far the best. It is grounded in the benefits of work and is based on sound economic principles. However, it is not as good an alternative as the simple, straightforward living wage. If the economy can afford the $125 billion Phelps estimated the program would have cost in 1997, why can't it channel at least $125 billion to low-wage workers via the living wage? The 2 1/2% payroll tax-employment subsidy is simply a transfer system, a dressed-up one and a usefully dressed-up one, but a transfer system nevertheless. Why not effect the transfer (if that is what it would be) through the mechanism of a statutory living wage and avoid the possible mutilation of the program during future budget

---

172. Phelps, *Rewarding Work*, 115.

173. He also suggests limiting the subsidy to full-time workers, another area for endless definitional and enforcement problems.

negotiations? Altogether, I believe the shoals of politics would wreck this ship, desirable though it may be in the abstract.

CONCLUSION

In the end, although all these policies have certain advantages, none offers as much promise as a living wage, payable to all those who work. It would reinforce the values of civic republicanism by stressing both the inherent worth of work and work's deserved remuneration. It would remove a significant portion of social policy from the government's budget, transforming at once both the political process and how citizens view each other. Additionally, it has a far greater chance of attracting the political support necessary to secure its adoption, a topic to be explored in detail in a later chapter. This is not to say that the living wage does not suffer from its own problems and drawbacks; and I will attempt to provide a candid and dispassionate assessment of them. Before that, though, it will be helpful to examine precisely how a living wage measure might best be structured.

6. THE STRUCTURE OF A LIVING WAGE

Having put the case for the desirability of a living wage and demonstrating its superiority to a system of cash transfers, it is time to discuss the structure such a policy might take. Specifically, attention must be devoted to the coverage of the living wage, the possibility of differentials, and the level at which it should be set. I will argue that the coverage should be virtually universal, that there should be few if any differentials, and that the wage should be set as a percentage of what full-time workers in high income brackets enjoy.

COVERAGE

Coverage under national minimum wage laws has seldom been universal. Various groups of workers have been excluded based on gender (early American laws, for example, covered women only), age, disability, occupation, economic sector in which the work was carried out, and size of the employing firm. Furthermore, it has not been unusual for some covered workers (the young and those who receive tips, for example) to receive only a portion of the minimum wage.

As noted in the Introduction, the living-wage ordinances adopted by American localities have tended to cover only those workers employed by firms doing business with the governmental entity adopting the ordinance. Only a handful, chiefly that of Santa Monica, California, have extended the living wage to private employers, and even there its reach is limited.

The living wage being advocated here would be universal in scope. If you work — for whomever, under whatever conditions, whatever your characteristics, and whether you work full-time or part-time — you receive the living wage. Obviously, only the national government could enact such a policy, and that is assumed from here on out. Let me take up the various categories of workers who have in the past found themselves outside the umbrella of the minimum wage law, and show why in each case an exemption is generally a bad idea. There are a couple of instances in which a reduction in the living wage *might* be justified, but they are minimal.

Let us take the easy case first. There should be no exemption for occupations or sectors of the economy. The most common appeals are made on behalf of those who employ agricultural or domestic workers. The argument is either that the work is seasonal and/or irregular or that it will impose an undue burden on farmers or affluent households. From a civic republican perspective, neither of these arguments holds any weight. In fact, these workers are precisely those who most need a living wage. If it is uneconomic for large farmers to harvest their crops if they must pay a living wage, sell some of the land and let us have more small farmers. If you don't want to pay someone a living wage to clean your toilet, do it yourself.[174] An exemption here would be perverse.

It is sometimes alleged that small firms, the proverbial mom and pop operations, ought to be exempt from various regulatory enactments, including minimum-wage laws. The added burdens of governmental regulatory policy make success in a small business, especially a start up, particularly difficult. Much of the dynamism of the American economy comes from such firms, and anything that inhibits their growth is inimical to long-run economic health. There is some economic merit to this argument, and for many years the Fair Labor Standards Act, following this logic, contained a small firm exemption.[175] However, whatever benefits it may bring (and they are by no means clear) are outweighed by practical and policy concerns. The practical end is neatly illustrated by the enormous difficulty Congress had in coming up with an

174. We will discuss the argument about employment effects later. However, a note might be in order here. Would this not make the worker worse off since the employer would not create a job cleaning his/her toilet? The fallacy here is that what the affluent do not spend on toilet cleaners they will spend on something else. Those expenditures will then create other jobs. Certain luxury goods and services might indeed become more expensive, but that is hardly a loss.

175. The tortured history of this section of the Fair Labor Standards Act can be found in a brief version in Jerold Waltman, *The Politics of the Minimum Wage* (Urbana: University of Illinois Press, 2000), chap. 2 and in more detail in Willis Nordlund, *The Quest for a Living Wage: A History of the Federal Minimum Wage Program* (Westport, CT: Greenwood, 1997).

acceptable definition of a small firm (gross sales was the most satisfactory), and the inevitable difficulties and costs of policing it. The policy case is clearer, though. If our goal is to tie citizenship to the living wage, then it makes no sense to exempt those who toil in small firms.

The only general coverage exception should be for the legitimately self-employed. Starting a business is a risky venture, and most small businesses incur losses or low profits in their early years. Nothing should be done to discourage the launching of new enterprises; in fact, they should be encouraged, for, as noted, they foster much of the nation's economic innovation and job creation. If someone wants to work for less than the living wage in the hope of securing a bounty of future profits, she should certainly be allowed to do so.

The problem is that this exemption can be abused. In 1950, a Florida beer distributor employed a team of driver-salesmen and provided each with a helper. The latter were paid $5.00 for a ten-hour day. An investigator for the Department of Labor believed these workers were subject to the minimum wage (then 75 cents an hour). The company dutifully paid the back wages. The next day it released all the helpers and gave each driver a "bonus" of $5.00 per day to hire a helper. Now, the company said, the helpers were all self-employed. Fortunately, the Fifth Circuit Court of Appeals ruled that this was a "mere subterfuge and represented nothing more than a calculated attempt on the part of the employer to escape responsibility under the Act."[176] In short, when a "business" provides a service to wealthy individuals or large companies, there is the opportunity for the powerful to take advantage of the weak.

Since the living wage being proposed in this book would be much higher than the current minimum wage, the possibilities for this kind of underhandedness would surely increase. The statute would need a careful definition followed by diligent enforcement to police this area. If I want to take in laundry for less than the living wage, in order to build a customer base or just because I enjoy self-employment, I should be allowed to do that — as long as the choice is really mine. If my employer makes me a subcontractor merely to avoid paying me the living wage, significant penalties, clearly designed to deter, should be imposed on him.

---

176. *Stewart-Jordan Distributing Company v. Tobin*, 210 F. 2d 427 (1954).

DIFFERENTIALS

Arguments for three types of differentials from national minimum wage laws are often presented, and each would undoubtedly be floated if a genuine living wage were to be adopted: regional differentials, subminimums for youths or newly hired workers, and some type of sliding scale for tipped employees.

Regional differentials have been advocated by the Organization for Economic Co-operation and Development (OECD), largely on the grounds that economic conditions always vary by region.[177] This position makes some sense even from a civic republican perspective, since the cost of living varies from one area of the country to the other. The income it takes to live at the standard of a decent life, consequently, is not uniform throughout the country. Nevertheless, however much sense this might make from that angle, the sheer administrative and political difficulties of implementing such a scheme compel the putting of it to one side.

First, the regions would have to be demarcated, a daunting undertaking to say the least. How many regions would there be? Would they run contiguous with states? What would be the criteria for drawing the lines? Some already drawn administrative areas — say the Federal Reserve Bank regions — could be used. But would these necessarily relate to the variations in cost of living? In short, the regions would either have to be very large, such as the South, the Northeast, the Midwest, the Southwest, and the West, in which case they would be almost useless, or they would have to be very small and more economically homogenous, in which case the difficulties of the task would be multiplied almost beyond belief.

Furthermore, no matter how small the regions were, there would still be variations within them. Significant living cost variances, owing chiefly to housing costs, can occur within very short distances. No feasible "average" could realistically be calculated.

Then, there is the problem created by economic dynamics. Nothing is ever static in a constantly changing and growing economy. Some type of boundary commission would have to be set up to redraw the lines every so often, with all the attendant difficulties that would bring. One need only reflect on the problems and controversies encountered in the decennial drawing of congressional districts to get a grasp of the nature of the task.

---

177. OECD, *The OECD Jobs Study* (Paris: OECD, 1994), 46.

Finally, even if a satisfactory alignment of regions could be established, there would be the task of setting the differentials. By what formula would this be accomplished?

On top of all these considerations loom the political aspects. The lines would have consequences for various businesses, labor unions, and economic development offices of local governments. A great deal of effort would be put into getting the line drawn this way or that. Studies would be commissioned, data collected, and a lot of old-fashioned lobbying geared up whenever the regional lines were to be redrawn. A bigger waste of time and effort is hardly imaginable. It would produce nothing of value but jobs to replenish the nation's trees. In short, it would be a costly and useless political nightmare.

Therefore, the simplest and best solution is to set one national living wage. It would make for differences, yes. It would be worth more in certain areas than others, granted. But that is preferable to the alternative, a classic case in which the ideal has to give way to the practical in order not to destroy the good in the initial proposal.

A more difficult problem involves those just entering the labor market, especially young people with few skills. Britain, for instance, has a youth differential in its national minimum wage. When introduced, it was 83.3% of the adult level, and applied to people 18-21. We have a modest, but administratively difficult and only sporadically used, differential in the United States.[178] In the 1980s, Presidents Reagan and Bush sought to have a significant youth or training wage made a permanent part of the minimum wage law. In 1989 the controversy became intense, as President Bush insisted on the insertion of a "training wage" before he would sign the increase Congress wanted. In the end, he got a scaled back version of his original plan, a six-month subminimum wage for any newly hired worker regardless of age. The final bill only allowed for a three-month training wage that was limited to teenagers.

The argument for establishing differentials for youths and/or trainees usually consists of three points. First, most youths in the labor market, it is said, are not supporting families. They are merely part-time workers earning a little extra spending money for movies and CDs. Second, new workers, especially the young, need training in order to make them valuable to their employers, and a lower wage is justified in order to compensate the employer for the training

---

178. For an employee under 20, an employer may obtain a certificate from the Department of Labor to employ him or her for 90 days at $4. 25 an hour rather than $5. 15. No specific training is required during this period, and, legally, no other worker may be displaced. Department of Labor, Fact Sheet No. 032.

costs. Third, the lower wage will mitigate the supposed disemployment effects imposed by a minimum wage, disemployment effects which allegedly strike the young and unskilled with a special vengeance. With a lower wage, employers will hire more young, unskilled workers than they would if the full minimum wage applied.

The case against the differential, mounted mostly by unions, is that if focused on youths, employers will turn to young people over older workers. Finding them cheaper, employers will dismiss older workers and utilize large numbers of young people. If the lower wage applies to new hires, it will lead employers to have a revolving door, repeatedly laying workers off when the time limit expires.

There is some validity in the first of the pro arguments. Many young people are indeed not supporting a family on their earnings. According to a recent study by the Department of Labor, employment among 15 to 17 year olds during the school year ranges from 15% and 22% respectively for those in families in the lower two income quartiles to 30% in the top two quartiles.[179] Thus, a good number of these very young workers are indeed from more affluent families. However, at least some of the youths from the lower two quartiles do support families, and many others contribute substantially to the family's income. Moreover, if the data for 18- and 19-year-olds were added, the number of those who are fully self-supporting and those contributing heavily to family income would rise dramatically. Thus, while this argument for the differential is not wholly without reason, it is weak.

The second argument is completely bogus. The types of jobs new entrants to the labor force take, especially unskilled work, require little training. When I began working at a fast food restaurant, it took about half an hour to be trained, and I had one of the more skilled jobs. Later, when I moved up to retail sales at J.C. Penney, my training consumed about two hours. I was given a booklet on policies and procedures to read, then the manager walked me around the shoe department showing me where the various types and sizes were stacked. By mid-morning I was waiting on customers. Sure, training is good, and studies show that employer provided training is the most helpful to employees.[180] But employers are not more likely to provide the training to new, low-skilled workers if they are given a small differential from the minimum wage. In fact, very few employers make use of the current training wage.[181]

---

179. Bureau of Labor Statistics, Department of Labor, *Report on the Youth Labor Force*, 2000, chap. 4.
180. See Ruth Prywes, *The United States Labor Force: A Descriptive Analysis* (Westport, CT: Quorum Books, 2000), 71-77 for a survey of the various studies.

I will leave the third argument for the following chapter, where I will take up the disemployment effects arguments in more detail.

What of the unions' argument? It is highly unlikely that any rational employer would lay off experienced workers and replace them with an army of teenagers. At the entry level, though, it is possible that if an 18-year-old worker were markedly cheaper than a 30-year-old, then an employer might be tempted to go with the youth. Except in the most casual and temporary type of employment, though, unless the differential were really sharp, this would seem to occur most infrequently. Stability of employees is sought by virtually every employer, and the advantage older workers have here is well known. The same observation holds true for trainees. What sane businessperson would dismiss an otherwise reliable employee after ninety days or even six months in order to hire someone new and inexperienced? Whatever immediate gain were had would be more than offset by the costs of inexperience and the morale loss incurred. So, we might give this argument, a "some but not much" validity score.

On balance, the notion of a youth differential seems like a bad idea. For the youth who is on his or her own or who is supporting a family, for whatever reason, the costs of securing a decent livelihood are as great as for anyone else. Even if these young people are in a minority, their plight is enough to clinch the case.

One group of people who do pose a difficult case are the disabled. From the citizenship perspective, they should, of course, receive the living wage just like everyone else. Certainly, then, all except those with the most debilitating conditions ought to be paid the living wage. But the unfortunate nature of things might require a modest exception in certain cases. Currently, these workers can be paid a subminimum wage if the employer applies for a certificate from the Department of Labor. No floor is set here, with wages being set as "commensurate" with the employee's productivity compared to a regular worker.[182] Thus, the economic rather than the citizenship perspective rules. I would say that three conditions would have to be met for a disabled employee to be paid less than the living wage. First, the employing entity would have to be a nonprofit organization. Second, there would have to be a percentage of the living wage (say 75%) below which no wage could fall. Third, there would need to be a

---

181. Economist Alan Krueger estimated that between 1989 and 1993 only two per cent of firms with minimum wage workers, barely one per cent of all firms, utilized the 90 day training wage. See Jonathan Weisman, "Senate May Reprise 1989 Fight Over 'Training Wage,'" *Congressional Quarterly*, June 8, 1996, 1600-01.

182. Department of Labor, Fact Sheet No. 039.

tight administrative procedure to prevent abuse. For example, employers would have to apply for a waiver and accept the burden of proof (as they largely do now). Furthermore, ideally, the living wage would sit alongside an array of humane and quality public services (especially but not only health care) available to all and free at point of service.

Another category of workers for whom a differential is often sought are those in occupations where tips are frequent. Many people have made a relatively handsome income through tips. In one restaurant, for example, the waitresses paid the owner to work there because the tips were so good. Tipping is a well-established American custom, and it is not a bad practice in many ways. People share a little something extra to show appreciation for service well rendered.

In the United States, the minimum wage law has been rewritten several times to account for tipped employees. When Congress enacted the last minimum wage increase in 1996, tipped employees were one group that, sadly, those seeking a hike in the minimum wage had to sacrifice in order to win the increase. The 1989 law provided that employers of tipped workers had to pay 50% of the minimum wage (then $2.13) to a tipped employee, and then make up any difference if the total earnings did not reach the statutory minimum. Keeping the 50% provision would have moved the required pay up to $2.58, but opponents managed to retain the $2.13 floor. What this meant was that those who earn over the minimum level in tips loose forty-five cents per hour.

From the civic republican perspective, the problem is tipping itself. Even when the relationship is polite and cordial, the social differences are made manifest in the very act of tipping. Suppose an observer to the granting of a tip did not actually see the money change hands. Isn't it still true that the body language and nature of the eye contact between the two parties would make the disparity in social status obvious to all but the most obtuse? Because it carries with it this inevitable anti-egalitarian class differential, it is, at bottom, an unhealthy practice. It would be much better for everyone if it became archaic.

The best way to accomplish this is to pay baggage handlers, waiters and waitresses, doormen, and all other people a living wage. If these citizens were paid a living wage for performing the work itself, then tipping would be seen as an insult, not a gratuity. The dignity of the work I do, work that is valuable, should justify a living wage, not what I can gesticulate for and hope for at your discretion. Tipping could then disappear. To bolster this position, I cite the case of Australia. When the Basic Wage there was relatively high, tipping was rare. A self-respecting worker wanted a wage, not a tip. However, as the purchasing power of the country's basic wage (now called a "safety net wage,") has been allowed to fall and American businesses have expanded to the country, tipping has reared its head. The following note from a recent travel guide, though outdated in terminology, is instructive:

> Tipping is an excellent example of a practice where the Australian egalitarian attitude presents problems. One has to be very careful tipping. Many take it as an insult and refuse a tip with annoyance. "We don't do that sort of thing here," they will say. As American hotels spread throughout Australia, though, this practice is unfortunately changing. The main reason for the antagonism toward tipping is the egalitarian ethos, but there is also pride in the Australian basic wage, a minimum wage set by the Commonwealth Government.[183]

It is possible, therefore, to build an ethos in which tipping is a social *faux pas*. The civic republican rationale for eradicating it differs somewhat, it is true, from the traditional Australian justification for egalitarianism, but the effect is the same.

SETTING THE LEVEL OF A LIVING WAGE

No issue is more important, nor more vexing, than setting the level of a proposed living wage. The issues surrounding coverage are minor, even if a few adjustments are allowed at the margins, compared to the matter of how much the living wage should be. In the municipal ordinances enacted throughout the United States, the wage level is set in the ordinance itself, often with a differential if health benefits are provided or not. (The problem of health benefits will be ignored here, as we are working under the assumption that a public health system will be available to all.)

In setting the ideal living wage, we should first of all recall the rationale for it. A citizen's pay for a full-time job should provide enough so that 1) no one will be forced to live below a decent level, such level to be defined by the standards of contemporary society, and 2) the degree of economic inequality is not too great.

Vague though these standards admittedly are, they nonetheless should be kept ever in front of us. Furthermore, it would seem desirable that the basis for the wage should be readily understood and suitable for being adjusted easily. There are two general approaches to determining the amount of a living wage: 1)

---

183. Graeme and Tamsin Newman, *Hippocrene Companion Guide to Australia* (New York: Hippocrene Books, 1992), 52.

Calculate a "poverty level" and set the wage at or above that; 2) Set it as a percentage of some other variable. I will survey both of these, noting the advantages and disadvantages. In the end, I will argue that using mean individual income of the top five per cent of full-time year-round workers is the best approach.

Poverty Level

Traditional injunctions regarding "the poor," such as those in the Bible, left the term undefined. Presumably, it was self-evident to readers who the poor were. But when public policies were targeted at the poor, a precise definition had to be formulated. In the United States, that came in the 1960s.

American poverty thresholds were first developed by a civil servant at the Social Security Administration named Mollie Orshansky in 1963 and 1964.[184] The Department of Agriculture had previously developed four family food plans, the cheapest of which was "designed for temporary or emergency use when funds are low." A 1955 Department of Agriculture study had concluded that families of three or more tend to spend approximately one third of their disposable income on food. Thus, she took the cost of the basic food allotment and multiplied by three. Even though her calculations were based on after-tax income, the thresholds were announced as before tax income. With a few technical adjustments made in the following years, in 1969 the Bureau of the Budget (the predecessor of the Office of Management and Budget) declared that her figures, adjusted by the Consumer Price Index, to be the official method for measuring poverty in the United States; with a few other minor adjustments through the years, this remains the way we calculate poverty. In the popular press, it is regularly referred to as the "federal poverty line" for families of various sizes. Something similar is available for most advanced industrial countries, and usually utilized for various aspects of welfare policy.

Thus, a beginning point might be this line. A living wage could be one that lifts the worker out of officially defined poverty. However, this is an abysmal standard, comic if it were not so tragic. Ms. Orshansky, for starters, set up the standard not to measure how much was enough, but how much was patently inadequate. She was trying to "assert with confidence how much, on average, is too little." Moreover, the use of the most austere food budget available and the

---

184. The best brief summary of how the poverty lines are drawn is Gordon M. Fisher, "The Development and History of the U.S. Poverty Thresholds: A Brief Overview," *Newsletter of the Government Statistics Section of the American Statistical Association*, Winter 1997.

conversion of after-tax income to pre-tax income make the "poverty threshold" downright silly.[185]

A group of researchers at the Economic Policy Institute led by Jared Bernstein has built a much more realistic series of basic family budgets.[186] After an exhaustive review of both the technical and conceptual issues involved, they offer a sample budget for people living in Baltimore. But even this family, they note, "would have to give up many 'unnecessary' goods that most families take for granted, including restaurant (even fast-food) meals, vacations, movies, and savings for education, retirement, and emergencies."[187] Thus, improvement over the federal poverty level though it is, this figure is still measuring poverty.

For a living wage, in contrast, we want a measure of a "decent" standard of living, not one that will barely lift people out of poverty. Still, poverty lines could be used. For example, we could set the poverty level and then establish a reasonable multiplier. This has been done before; the food stamp program, for instance, uses 130% of the poverty level as its measure. We could use 150% or 200%, say, of Bernstein et al.'s data, or some such measuring rod.

Or, better, we could develop a realistic "decency standard" for someone living in the United States at the beginning of the 21st century. What would it take, bringing Adam Smith back into the picture, for someone to appear at the Mall of America in Minneapolis and be able to invite a random sample of shoppers there to one's home without shame? You might not need a wine rack stacked with upscale Chardonnay, but you would need a decent size home with reasonably good furniture and an inventory of working appliances, several changes of fair quality clothes, an automobile, some evidence of entertainments and at least modest vacations, and, of course, a stockpile of nutritious and varied foodstuffs.

The problem is that trying to construct such a "decency standard" is fraught with difficulties. There are a number of technical disputes involved, of course, with any such endeavor, but these pale compared to the political problems involved. We would be trying to draw a hard and fast line where ambiguity reigns. It could be done, but it would generate no end of controversy.

---

185. The National Research Council has developed a more defensible definition. The report was published as Constance Citro and Robert Michael, eds., *Measuring Poverty: A New Approach* (Washington: National Academy Press, 1995). Currently, the Office of Management and Budget is analyzing the possibility of using alternative measures.

186. Jared Bernstein, Chauna Brocht, and Maggie Spake-Aguilar, *How Much is Enough?* (Washington: Economic Policy Institute, 2000).

187. Bernstein, et al., *How Much is Enough?* Executive Summary, 3.

Even assuming we could come up with a satisfactory living wage level, it would have to be adjusted periodically. Both inflation and changing living standards would soon make any established wage level obsolete. One alternative would be to inaugurate a public body to adjust the wage. Both Australia and Britain currently utilize versions of this procedure for keeping their minimum wages up to date. In Australia, the Industrial Relations Commission, a quasi-judicial body, is charged with reviewing the safety net wage annually and making any adjustments. A variety of parties representing business, labor, and others are able to present briefs before the decision is taken. In Britain, the statutory Low Pay Commission continuously assesses the National Minimum Wage and suggests changes. The government (prime minister and cabinet) must then formally reply to the Commission's recommendations. While implementing the suggested changes is not mandatory, the government is, naturally, under heavy pressure to adopt the recommendations. Some body similar to either of these could, therefore, be set up in the United States to monitor conditions that would dictate a change in the living wage.[188]

However, there are two problems with this approach. The first is that the statutory guidelines under which such a body would work would inevitably be at best vague and at worst contradictory. This is certainly the case in both Australia and Britain. The Australian statute instructs the Commission to "provide fair minimum standards for employees in the context of living standards generally prevailing in the Australian community."[189] The Low Pay Commission was told in 2001 to propose a new wage level having "regard to the wider economic and social implications; the likely effect on employment and inflation; the impact on the costs and competitiveness of business, particularly the small firms sector; and to the potential costs to industry and the Exchequer [Treasury]."[190] Second, there would be a natural pull and tug of politics within the body. While this is not necessarily unhealthy, as important issues of public policy should be forcefully discussed and debated. Rather than informed debate, though, a sharp partisanship could quickly develop, as opponents of a minimum, and certainly a living, wage would most likely use the adjustment decisions to

---

188. A permanent commission to recommend periodic minimum wage increases was proposed in 1977 but not adopted by Congress. It was actually a compromise to President Carter's suggestion that the minimum wage be indexed to one-half the average manufacturing wage. In the end, a temporary Minimum Wage Study Commission was established to analyze the minimum wage and file a report, which it did four years later.

189. Workplace Relations Act, 1996, Part VI, Section 88B (2).

190. "Terms of Reference for the Third Report of the Low Pay Commission." Available at www. lowpay. gov. uk/lowpay/terms. htm.

attempt either abolition or emasculation of the entire policy. One need only witness the battles that erupt in Congress whenever minimum wage increases are debated to get a glimpse of how this would work. Naturally, this would also lead to a struggle over the appointments to the body, something again that occurs regularly in Australia and Britain.

If we are going to use the decency standard approach to setting the initial wage level, then it seems far preferable to automatically index it. One obvious way to do this is to tie the living wage to the Consumer Price Index (CPI). The CPI is now used for a variety of government programs, such as social security, and while not perfect, does allow the recipients to keep up with changes in the dollar's purchasing power. The disadvantages are two, however. First, the more government programs that utilize the CPI, the more controversial the technical basis of its computation becomes. More importantly, though, using the CPI would not take into account changed living standards. As economic growth occurs, the decency standard would rise also. A better alternative would be to index the living wage to productivity increases. This would have two distinct advantages. For one, it would allow workers to share in productivity gains, gains for which they are at least partly responsible. Second, it would make the public more aware of the importance of productivity. Business groups often complain that workers and the general public do not appreciate how vital productivity increases are to economic growth. Making the living wage sensitive to these gains would focus public attention as little else would.

Nevertheless, this whole approach has one serious and uncorrectable flaw. It has to be based on family size. Of course, various budgets can be calculated for different family sizes. But which one should be used to set the living wage? We could select something like a "typical family," say three or four people. Then we could argue that a full-time worker ought to be able to support that family at the decency standard. But this runs up against gender issues and changes in the typical nuclear family.

Do we want the "model" family of four to be one breadwinner, a stay at home adult, and two children? Do we want to encourage intact two parent families? If so, should the living wage be figured using two full-time earners? Is a married couple with no children to be considered differently from a married couple with two children. Is the latter couple to be considered differently from a single mother with three children?

Of course, during the late nineteenth and early twentieth century, when the living wage was first discussed, the model family was clear. The husband needed to earn enough to support himself, a stay at home wife, and several children. But the consensus over that has broken down. Trying to set a living wage by this method simply cannot proceed unless we make some arbitrary decisions. It is a labyrinth with no exit, for there is no agreement on even the basics. Given this ineluctable fact, it seems better to jettison the entire approach and turn to the percentage alternative.

The Percentage Method

Under this approach, we would select some readily available standard and set the living wage as a percentage of that amount. Not only would this avoid all the difficulties regarding the computation of family size, it would be easy to determine and change automatically. The challenge is selecting the appropriate standard.

American unions have sometimes suggested setting the minimum wage as a percentage of the average hourly wage. The chief problem with this standard is that it makes the base too low. In general, hourly workers are paid less than salaried workers; thus, tying the living wage to the average hourly wage leaves out a substantial pool of people against whom we are measuring adequate living standards. Furthermore, the changing structure of the economy has meant that fewer workers earn hourly wages than before. Establishing a living wage by this standard would more than likely see it shrink in value over the years, as the hourly work force decreases.

A better variation on this approach is to use average earnings, bringing the salariat into the pool. You could take average earnings for all full-time workers and divide out a per hour figure. This would allow us to measure the living wage by what people are actually earning. Unison, the British public service union, has advocated using median male earnings as the measuring rod since, overall, of course, males earn more than females. In the United States, for instance, average male earnings in 1998 (for full-time year-round workers) were 46% higher than those of females.[191] This would not be a bad standard. However, it would lead to a number of political fissures regarding the gender status of certain occupations. These matters need to be debated, but I fear cluttering up the discussion of the living wage with them would do more harm than good.

Another variation I like is tying the living wage to the salaries of certain public officials, such as members of Congress. Currently, a full-time minimum-wage worker earns 7.4% of what those who make our laws receive. Should anyone really make less than 20% or 25% of what these solons take home?

---

191. *Statistical Abstract of the United States, 2000*, Table 752.

The principal objection to all of these earnings based formulas, though, is that they omit unearned income. A good portion of the income of many people in the more comfortable strata of modern society is derived from dividends, interest, rents, and capital gains. These affect living standards every bit as much as earnings. Furthermore, at least a portion of these rewards are due to the exertions of ordinary workers. Of course, there should be an adequate return on capital and ample reward for risk taking. But it is only just to share this bounty with those who toil in fields, factories, and stores. We need, therefore, some kind of income based measure.

However, we must be careful. Individual income figures can include the underaged and the retired. We need a figure that represents the income of those in the workforce year-round and full time, for they are the most readily comparable to living wage workers. There are two different approaches here.

The first would rely on either the mean or the median income of all full-time, year-round workforce participants, whatever the source of that income. The mean would be a better figure to work with, since mean income is always higher than median income (a relevant matter for social criticism itself). After-tax mean household income in the United States, for example, is 23% above median household income.[192] This happens because a few huge income earners at the top pull up the mean but have no effect on the median. (Steve Forbes and nine minimum wage workers will have decidedly different mean and median income figures.) But there is the opposite problem, too. If we use the mean as our measure for a living wage, then the next calculation of the mean will be affected by the expected wage hikes. If we were to adopt this approach, therefore, it might be sensible to figure the living wage initially by comparison to the mean. We would simultaneously compute what percentage of median income the living wage is. From that point on, the living wage could be indexed to median incomes. There could also be a trigger that went into effect if the mean got too far above the median.

The second would be based on the incomes of those in the upper levels. Here, the civic republican command regarding the softening of harsh inequalities would be brought to the forefront. We could take some group of income earners — the top 1%, top 5%, top 10%, top 20%, or top 40%, for instance — and figure the living wage as a percentage of their average incomes. Personally, this is the approach I favor, and I lean to the top 5% category. The top 1%, of course, includes many who have inherited their wealth, but it also includes some like

---

192. *Statistical Abstract of the United States, 2000*, Table 739.

Bill Gates and Michael Jordan who have actually earned it, and some who weave in and out of the group. Overall, it is probably a bit too skewed a sample to be useful for policy purposes. But the top 5% are another matter. These people have regular incomes, which keep on rolling.

Before we do any calculations regarding this, let me issue two vital reminders: First, we are talking about a living *wage*. It is income that would only go to those who work. In general, no cash would be remitted to anyone without work. Second, the calculation only considers *incomes* in its attempt to mitigate inequality, not *wealth*. In 1998, *mean* family net worth was $282,500 while the *median* was $71,500.[193] Putting this in perspective, while disproportionately high incomes pull the mean *income* figure 23% above the median, disproportionately accumulated wealth moves the mean *wealth* figure 395% above the median. None of this wealth-based disparity is going to even be touched under a living wage policy.

Neither the Department of Labor nor the Department of Commerce keeps figures that provide the mean income of the top five per cent of all full-time year-round workforce participants. Consequently, for the moment we will have to obtain it indirectly for purposes of illustration. If this approach to setting a living wage were embraced, undoubtedly experts at the Department of Commerce could provide precise and reliable figures.

According to recent Department of Commerce figures, the top 5% of Americans receive 21.9% of all income. In 2000 (the latest year for which complete data are available), total personal income stood at $8,319.2 billion. (Personal income is incomes of individuals before taxes.) Therefore, the most fortunate five per cent of our citizens collectively claimed $1,821.9 billion in income in 2000. Five per cent of the population of 2000 is 14,071,000 people.

We cannot simply divide, however, because this figure includes children, most of whom obviously earn no income, the occasional child movie star aside. Let us assume that the age profile of each segment of the various income groupings mirrors that of the population as a whole. This is, admittedly, unlikely to be true; in general, more affluent people have fewer children. However, any skew introduced by making this assumption will be more than offset by the factors mentioned below. Overall, the Census Bureau reported that in 2000 21.4% of the population was 14 and under. Another 7.2% was 15 to 19. We may safely remove all the first group from full-time workforce participants. Let us next assume that 75% of those in the second category are also non-full-time

---

193. *Statistical Abstract of the United States, 2000,* Table 764.

workforce participants. This is surely an extremely generous assumption for the top 5%. It is probably closer to 100%. Further, another 6.7% of Americans are 20-24. Let us suppose that 50% of these people are in fact full-time workforce participants. I doubt that is true of the top 5% of the population, since so many are in college and graduate or professional school. These two assumptions would clearly more than compensate for the possibility of a differential in age profile.

In total, therefore, we will remove 30.2% from the 14,071,000, leaving us with 9,822,000 individuals. If we divide this number into the personal income these people enjoy, we obtain a per adult figure of $185,490. Even this is surely understated. For example, these households undoubtedly contain more stay at home spouses than the population at large. Furthermore, early retirement is more common, as is a longer life span. (Those over 85 are 1.5% of the population and those 75-84 4.4% overall.) In any event, I would contend that this is a very conservative estimate of the income of the top 5% of year-round full-time workforce participants. Moreover, as stressed above, it is purely for illustration.

Now, how much income should separate full-time participants in the economy? That is exactly what we should be debating. I will begin the discussion by offering 20% as a nice round figure. In a civic republic, should anyone have a house that is more than five times bigger than others', an automobile that is five times better, clothes that cost five times as much, stay in a five times better hotel on a vacation? I will even compromise at 15%, but that means that some people will get more than six times of these and other goods than their fellow full-time working citizens.

In 2000, using my income estimates would have meant a living wage of $17.84 and $13.38 per hour respectively.[194]

What percentage do you prefer?

---

194. This assumes a 40-hour week and 52 weeks per year worked.

7. Addressing the Arguments Against a Living Wage

No policy, of course, is without its costs and drawbacks, and a universal living wage is no exception. What follows is a careful and candid assessment of these costs and drawbacks. Some simply do not hold much water, while others need to be taken seriously. In the end, though, none of them is a strong enough objection to put the living wage prematurely into the grave.

Part of the problem in addressing the potential downsides of a living wage is that we have no experience with it, as least not at the levels I am proposing. Therefore, we have to turn to the various studies of national minimum wages, both in the U.S. and abroad, together with those connected to the recent spate of municipal living-wage ordinances. Reasonable conjectures from economic and sociological theory also need to be drawn, as a supplement to this empirical evidence. Opinions about how much weight to give to this or that factor will vary. What is important is that we should begin on a blank slate, not with some *prima facie* belief standing in our way.

In essence, there are five arguments against a living wage: that it will lead to unemployment; that it will cause inflation; that small businesses will be unable to absorb the costs and will fail in unacceptably high numbers; that there will be a shortage of jobs in a recession; and, finally, that it will work as a magnet for more illegal immigrants. The first three all turn out to be unproven by either the evidence or logic. The fourth is a genuine problem, but there are ways to deal with it. The fifth is unsolvable, but it should not stand in the way of adopting a living wage.

UNEMPLOYMENT

During the congressional debate on increasing the minimum wage in 1996, Republican Representative John Shadegg of Arizona unburdened himself of the opinion that the bill was "an unemployment act that hurts minority youth, and that is a shame," alleging that fully one out of every four minority workers between 17 and 24 would be out of work should Congress be so unwise as to enact the bill. Representative Mark Souder of Indiana added, "I understand it is called a minimum wage bill, but in fact it is a layoff bill. . . Kids will lose their jobs, minorities will lose their jobs, senior citizens will lose their jobs."[195] Despite these dire warnings, the measure was adopted, setting increases in the minimum wage effective October 1, 1996 and September 1, 1997. If Representatives Shadegg and Souder bothered to consult the unemployment rates in the months immediately before and after the increases went into effect, they found that they were identical: 5.2% in September and October of 1996 and 4.9% in August and September of 1997. Jared Bernstein and John Schmitt, two respected labor economists, later conducted a detailed, longer-term analysis of the impact of the twin increases. Their conclusion:

> Four different tests of the two increases' employment impact — applied to a large number of demographic groups whose wages are sensitive to the minimum wage — fail to find any systematic, significant job loss associated with the 1997-97 increases. Not only are the estimated employment effects generally economically small and statistically insignificant, they are also almost as likely to be positive as negative.[196]

This highlights two noteworthy features of the debate about the relationship between minimum wage increases and the level of employment: 1) The adamantly stated and uncompromising belief held by many people that the effects are direct, substantial, and debilitating; and 2) The absolute absence of any evidence that this is true.

The basic idea is built on the first chapter of any economics textbook, the "law" of supply and demand. On the demand side, echoing common sense, this proposition holds that the higher the price of a commodity, the less of it is purchased. If the price of ice cream goes up by 25%, the "law" would lead us to predict a decline in consumption. Correspondingly, if the price of labor goes up,

---

195. *Congressional Record*, May 23, 1996.

196. Jared Bernstein and John Schmitt, *Making Work Pay: The Impact of the 1996-97 Minimum Wage Increase*. Washington: Economic Policy Institute, 1998), Executive Summary.

less will be demanded. However, this "law" is one of those general propositions that, while broadly true, is subject to all kinds of caveats.

The first is that movements in the prices of substitutes must be taken into account. If the price of ice cream goes up by 25% but the price of candy shoots up by 50%, more ice cream may be bought, not less. The second is that the law is static, not dynamic. People adjust their behavior in all kinds of ways when prices change. The world is too complex to account for it by drawing crisscrossing lines on a graph and predicting what *must* happen if prices move along the vertical axis. The third is that the demand for labor is peculiar. Most goods and services are purchased because they fulfill a need or a want. I buy a house because I must have shelter and a backpack because I enjoy hiking. Perhaps somebody somewhere hires someone to, say, work in the garden because he enjoys just sitting in a chair and watching him.[197] Most labor, though, is purchased in order to make a product or a service to sell to someone. The demand for labor is therefore tied to the demand for the products and services the workers produce. In and of itself, labor has no inherent economic value.

The debate over the employment effects of minimum wage legislation is symptomatic of a deeper disagreement over the nature of economic knowledge. On the one side are those who develop models and deduce conclusions about how the world works from them; on the other side are those who study what is going on in the world and then try to fashion explanations.

Early labor economists tended to fall into the latter category. For example, when the British government imposed a minimum wage on the chain-making industry in 1909, the celebrated economist Roger Tawney was commissioned to study the policy's impact. He visited workplaces, examined payroll records, and interviewed business owners and employees. In the end, he found that the increased wages commanded by Parliament had had no impact on the level of employment.[198] Similarly, an American labor economist, Richard Lester, examined the case of textile mills in the South after the adoption of the minimum wage in 1938. He, too, found no evidence of reduced employment after the introduction of the national minimum wage.[199]

---

197. Of course, people pay to see entertainers and athletes "work." But that is because people are paying to watch them display a particular talent. Try selling tickets to, say, a cabinet-making shop.

198. Roger Tawney, *The Establishment of Minimum Wages in the Chain Making Industry under the Trade Board Act of 1909* (London: Bell, 1914).

199. Richard Lester, "Shortcomings of Marginal Analysis for Wage-Employment Problems," *American Economic Review* 37 (1946), 63-82.

In 1995, two Princeton University economists, David Card and Alan Krueger, published an influential book on the issue of minimum wages and employment levels.[200] They studied fast food restaurants in Pennsylvania and New Jersey in the same general labor market area. New Jersey had raised its state minimum wage while Pennsylvania was subject only to the lower federal minimum. Using a telephone survey, they compiled employment records for a good number of establishments. Their conclusion was that after the state minimum wage had gone up in New Jersey, there was actually an increase in the level of employment. Their work has been vociferously criticized by a number of economists, and there are some legitimate technical questions regarding the survey. No one, however, has been able to show that their conclusions are wrong.

Recent evidence from the U.K. supports the view that raising minimum wages has no effect on the number of people employed. Britain had no national minimum wage until 1997, but prior to 1986 there were a number of Wages Councils that set minimum wages in various industries. Using data reported by employers in the government's New Earnings Survey, three economists compared employment levels before and after wage hikes over several years. Their conclusion was that,

> [T]he specifications using our NES employment measures yield evidence that, counter to the conventional economic model, increases in Wages Councils minimum rates of pay were not associated with reduced employment. There is no evidence whatever for the notion that minimum wage effects on employment were negative.[201]

In 2001, Incomes Data Services, an independent research organization specializing in employment issues, published a report on the impact of Britain's new National Minimum Wage (predicted by market-infatuated ideologues when adopted, as usual, to bring about calamity). In the end, they argued that, "Overall, we can conclude that there continues to be no real negative employment effect from the National Minimum Wage."[202] Likewise, a 2002 survey by a manufacturers' group of small and medium enterprises found no evidence of declining employment associated with the minimum wage. Seventy-one per cent of the respondents said the introduction of the minimum wage had

---

200. David Card and Richard Krueger, *Myth and Measurement: The New Economics of the Minimum Wage* (Princeton, NJ: Princeton University Press, 1995).

201. Richard Dickens, Steahen Machin, and Alan Mourning, "The Effects of Minimum Wages on Employment: Theory and Evidence from Britain," *Journal of Labor Economics* 17 (1999), 16-17.

202. Incomes Data Services, "The Impact of the National Minimum Wage in 2001," IDS Report No. 844, November 2001.

no effect on their business, while 13 per cent said it had actually had a positive effect.[203]

Another study by American labor economists Jared Bernstein and John Schmitt, focusing on the impact of the minimum wage, especially on young workers, over a long time-span, offered several conclusions. Two of them were:

> No evidence exists that teenagers or less-than-high-school-educated adults lost work as a result of the 1996-97 minimum wage increases....

> Historically, analyses of the minimum wage's impact on young workers have never shown the predicted large job-loss effects.[204]

Then, there have been a series of studies of municipal living-wage ordinances and state minimum wage laws. The Economic Policy Institute conducted a study of Baltimore's living wage measure by interviewing employees and employers. The Institute's team found no evidence of job losses or reductions in the number of hours worked.[205] In 1996, Oregon raised its state minimum wage substantially through a statewide referendum (making it the highest in the country in 1998 and 1999). A study released in 2001 by the Oregon Center for Public Policy found that not only did workers at the lower end of the income distribution achieve real income gains, but also that, "The employment rate for young workers with low education, generally thought to be most affected by the minimum wage, grew faster than the rate of the workforce as a whole subsequent to the minimum wage increase."[206]

Finally, in 1998 Oren Levin-Waldman conducted a survey of small businesses (those with fewer than 500 employees) asking whether the 1997 minimum wage hike had affected their hiring practices.[207] Only 6.2% replied that it had, and only one-third of one per cent said they had laid anyone off as a result of the increase. Among those firms hiring minimum wage workers, a full 87.9% said their hiring plans were not affected at all by the change.

To be sure, there are some studies that purport to find negative employment effects associated with minimum wage increases, but often they

---

203. "Minimum Wage Has Had No Impact Say SME's," Manufacturing*talk*.com, March 4, 2002. Available at http://www. manufacturingtalk.com/news/sgs/sgs100. html

204. Jared Bernstein and John Schmitt, "The Impact of the Minimum Wage," Economic Policy Institute Briefing Paper, 2001, 1.

205. Christopher Niedt, *et al., The Effects of the Living Wage in Baltimore*, Working Paper No. 119 (Washington: Economic Policy Institute, 1999).

206. Jeff Thompson and Charles Sheketoff, *Getting the Raise They Deserved: The Success of Oregon's Minimum Wage and the Need for Reform* (Silverton, OR: Oregon Center for Public Policy, 2001), 1.

207. Oren Levin-Waldman, "The Effects of the Minimum Wage: A Business Response," *Journal of Economic Issues* 34 (2000), 723-30.

turn on some controversial technical method of analyzing the data. For instance, one recent study of Ireland's new minimum wage found when the data were run one way that there was no difference in employment growth between businesses affected and not affected by the law. When the authors changed methodology, though, they found a slight effect on a few firms.[208] Likewise, David Neumark, using data provided by the Bureau of Labor Statistics' Current Population Survey, conducted an analysis of cities that have adopted living-wage ordinances. He concluded that while some workers' wages did go up, there were negative employment effects for others, posing an unpleasant trade off.[209] However, three University of Massachusetts economists raised serious technical questions about his methodology; when they reworked his data, the correlations disappeared.[210] Of course, too, it is entirely possible that there would be disemployment effects if a living wage were set high enough. For example, during a 1995 congressional hearing devoted to discussing the relation between minimum wages and unemployment, Representative James Saxton of New Jersey fulminated that if the doubters were correct, "Why, then, don't we just raise the minimum wage to \$300 or \$400 an hour and pay everyone lawyers' wages?"[211]

Such outbursts aside, the point remains: At any level seriously suggested, and certainly at the level I am proposing, there is simply no evidence that a statutorily mandated living wage would have any negative employment effect whatsoever. In short, the textbook-based assertion is unproved.

---

208. Donal O'Neill, Brian Nolan, and James Williams, "Evaluating the Impact of a National Minimum Wage: Evidence from a New Survey of Firms in Ireland," University of Dublin, Department of Economics, September 2002.

209. David Neumark, "How Living Wage Laws Affect Low-Wage Workers and Low-Income Families," Public Policy Institute of California, Report No. 156, 2002.

210. Mark Brenner, Jeannette Wicks-Lim, and Robert Pollin, "Measuring the Impact of Living Wage Laws: A Critical Appraisal of David Neumark's 'How Living Wage Laws Affect Low-Wage Workers and Low-Income Families,'" (Amherst, MA: Political Economy Research Institute, 2002), Working Paper No. 43. To demonstrate how the results can turn on arcane methodological issues, one paragraph is worth quoting:

> Our overall conclusion is that Neumark's findings are neither methodologically sound nor robust statistically or substantively. To begin with, Neumark's econometric model relies on a truncated sample of workers that excludes higher-wage workers from the data pool. While Neumark's approach is correct in focusing its attention on low-wage workers, the particular manner in which he does so, through truncating the full sample, is vulnerable to sample selection bias. This diminishes the reliability of his results, since they are subject to both bias and inconsistency. We show that Neumark's results are not robust when one takes an alternative approach to truncation, that is, utilizing quintile regression. (p. 2)

211. U. S. Congress, Joint Economic Committee, *Evidence against a Higher Minimum Wage*, part 1, February 22, 1995, 86.

WHY THE TEXTBOOK MODEL IS WRONG

If there is no evidence to support the textbook model, and if in fact the data sometimes point to the relationship being the opposite of what the model predicts (higher minimum wages produce more jobs), why should this be so? Actually, there are two perfectly plausible reasons: efficiency, and the role of demand shifts.

Efficiency gains

At first blush, businesses faced with a higher wage bill seem to have three options: reduce the number of hours employees work, to hold labor costs constant; raise prices; or reduce profits. But there is a fourth alternative: increase efficiency. That is, producing the same product or service at a lower cost.

Higher wages can actually contribute to efficiency in several ways. The first is that it enables a firm to hire more skilled workers, who are likely to be more efficient. The second is that it reduces turnover, which can be extremely costly to production schedules. Several studies of businesses that pay high wages have indeed found them to reap enormous benefits from these two facts. Borealis Breads, for instance, is a profitable Maine bakery known for its high wages, a policy that generates a skilled and loyal work force.[212] The White Dog Café in Philadelphia has a similar story to tell. In an industry notorious for low wages and high turnover, the owner of this establishment pays very well and also earns a steady profit. Numerous other examples could be cited as well.[213]

Much of the advantage these firms enjoy, granted, is because the wages they pay are *relatively* high. They get the best workers because their competitors pay so much less. If there were a universal living wage, this advantage would disappear. Nevertheless, we need to think this through a little further.

For example, a group of labor economists surveyed by the University of New Hampshire said that the main reason the less skilled would lose their jobs if a living wage were adopted is that businesses would hire more people with higher skills.[214] The underlying assumption is that higher wages call for higher skills. Let's concede that point, but look at it this way: higher skills come from

---

212. All these examples are highlighted in "Choosing the High Road: Businesses That Pay a Living Wage and Prosper," Center for Responsible Wealth, 2000.

213. A number are provided in Robert Pollin and Stephanie Luce, *The Living Wage* (New York: New Press, 1998).

214. Survey Center, University of New Hampshire, "The Living Wage: Survey of Labor Economists," August 2000. (Survey conducted for the Employment Policies Institute.)

training and require more sophisticated equipment to make the skills useful. Therefore, if a higher wage is prescribed, the cost calculus of training workers and investing in better equipment will change. With higher wages, businesses will find it worthwhile to develop better and more intensive training programs for their workers (gaining, meanwhile, an added incentive to keep them) and invest in more productive facilities. If wages stay low, they can make do with unskilled workers and less efficient equipment.

Eric Schlosser has written a distressing description of the modern U.S. meat-packing industry.[215] Thousands of low skilled workers are herded into huge facilities with fast-moving conveyor belts and assigned routine tasks. The industry itself sees rapid turnover as a good thing, since the workers are expendable. Suppose, though, the firms were forced to pay a higher wage. They are surely creative enough to find ways to build better packing plants and train their workers in new techniques.

At this point, we often hear the old Luddite cry of technological unemployment. A few workers may get the better jobs running the new equipment, at packing houses and elsewhere, but what about the others? Michael Lind has eloquently addressed this point.

> Here is a heretical thought: What's wrong with technological unemployment? The substitution of technology for human and animal labor is the basis of the prosperity of advanced societies like the United States. In 1800, almost everybody in the U.S. was a farmer. Today almost nobody is, even though the U.S. produces more food per capita, thanks to tractors and other devices. . . In every generation, all the way back to when the first industrial revolution produced the first anti-industrial revolution, . . . there have been predictions of mass unemployment caused by technology. Certainly the transitions have frequently been painful, but the children of displaced workers — albeit not all of their parents — have usually obtained more comfortable and often more intellectually demanding employment. A case can be made, then, that the replacement of labor by machinery as a result of a higher minimum wage (or anything else that increases labor costs) is a positive step, not an evil to be avoided.[216]

In short, just as the displaced farmers got jobs producing the tractors, the displaced meat packers would get jobs making the newly needed equipment. And, surely, we could do a better job than our nineteenth-century predecessors

---

215. Eric Schlosser, *Fast Food Nation: The Dark Side of the All-American Meal* (New York: Houghton Mifflin, 2001), chaps. 7-9.

216. Michael Lind, "The Case for a Living Wage," *New Leader*, September/October 2001, 13.

in easing the transition. The point is that a living wage could have a beneficial effect on production and efficiency.

There is still another element to efficiency. It is the way people feel and the extra effort they make when they have a sense of dignity and feel treated with respect. This is intangible, to be sure, but it is real, as anyone who has worked in any type of organization can testify. There are many facets to dignity, of course, but compensation is definitely one of them. When people are repeatedly told that their wages are set solely by some impersonal "market" force, they feel no better than a commodity, in a word, debased. But people are not commodities. Even work that is rote and routine, even dirty and unpleasant, can be given a certain dignity by making the compensation decent. Joan Fitzgerald attended some meetings in Massachusetts nursing homes after new training and wage policies were put into effect. She reports that the employees were eager to obtain the training and had a decidedly better attitude about their jobs, which in this case means better care in nursing homes.[217] When I was conducting research on the minimum wage at a local employment office, one young man said to me, "When you are paid more, you are motivated. You are motivated to work and you feel better about yourself. When you get $5.15 an hour [the then prevailing minimum wage] you just don't feel worth very much." The social consequences contained in this sentiment are worth pondering; for the present point, though, it is the work motivation that needs stressing. Hal Taussig runs Idyll, Ltd. in Philadelphia, a specialized travel business. Taussig pays exceptionally high wages for his industry and reports an "esprit de corps" among his people as well as active efforts to help the company keep its costs low.[218] There is every reason to believe that people in general would respond, for the most part anyway, the same way.

Purchasing Power

Discussions of higher wages often focus exclusively on costs. But the other side of the equation should be of equal concern. What people earn has a decided effect on consumer spending, a major motor of business prosperity. A high level of consumer spending is obviously good for business, and that in turn creates more jobs.

We sometimes forget that one of President Franklin D. Roosevelt's major goals in proposing the minimum wage was to boost purchasing power to fight

---

217. Joan Fitzgerald, "Better-Paid Caregivers, Better Care," *The American Prospect*, May 21, 2001.
218. Cited in "Choosing the High Road," p. 17.

the Depression *and* to build a permanent cushion against future recessions by putting a floor under a precipitate fall in consumer spending. During the 1938 debate over the minimum wage, Roosevelt argued that:

> To raise the purchasing power of the farmer, however, is not enough. It will not stay raised if we do not also raise the purchasing power of that third of the Nation which receives its income from industrial employment. Millions of industrial workers receive pay so low that they have little buying power. Aside from the undoubted fact that they thereby suffer great human hardship, they are unable to buy adequate food and shelter, to maintain health or to buy their share of manufactured goods.[219]

This view has the support of both economic theory and common sense. Aggregate demand is admitted by virtually all economists, even those not inclined to give it the weight disciples of John Maynard Keynes do, to be a key element in how the economy functions. Increases in aggregate demand can come from either higher government expenditures or higher consumer spending. Consequently, higher wages are not only a path to better living for the affected workers, but for many businesses and their workers as well.

Edward Filene, a prominent Boston businessman of the 1930s, made the common sense case. Filene, in many lectures and articles, pointed out that each individual business, left to its own devices, views wages as a cost.[220] Hence, firms seek to keep wages as low as they can. However, it is in the *collective* interest of business to have high wages. Moving products off business' shelves depends on people having money in their pockets. In an individualized market, though, businesses which try to pay high wages, as Filene's department stores did, find themselves at a competitive disadvantage. Therefore, it would make all businesses better off if government set a high wage.[221] With higher wages, there would be ample consumer dollars to compete for. Filene saw clearly that, in essence, wage costs were not like other costs. The costs of materials and supplies do not re-enter the business as demand; wages do.

A recent study of San Francisco's living-wage ordinance supports this notion. It found that the living wage had added $20.8 million of additional

---

219. Franklin D. Roosevelt, Public Papers of the President, Annual Message for 1938, 5.

220. A compilation of Filene's speeches and essays can be found in Edward Filene, *Speaking of Change* (New York: Privately published, 1939). Some earlier thoughts are contained in his *The Way Out: A Forecast of Coming Changes in American Business and Industry* (Garden City, NY: Doubleday, 1924).

221. This is similar to the familiar "problem of the commons." If everyone in a village has the right to graze his or her livestock on the commons, it is in everyone's long-run interest to keep grazing moderate. Any one individual, however, has the short-run interest to let his stock graze as much as he can. Hence, everyone's short-run interest is at war with his/her own long-run interest. It takes, therefore, a coercive mechanism to make everyone behave as a truly "rational actor."

spending to the economy, considering the multiplier effect.[222] Every one of those dollars got rung up in a cash register somewhere, padding thereby a business's bottom line, and at the same time creating a demand for workers.

Consider: Isn't it perfectly plausible that when the minimum wage goes up, workers at Pizza Hut spend a portion of their increased income at Wal-Mart, and vice versa? If so, both companies still need as many workers as before — as they would with the adoption of a living wage.

INFLATION

There are two different prongs to the argument that higher minimum wages lead to inflation. One is that increases in costs are inevitably reflected in price increases; the other is that the additional spending resulting from higher incomes provides excess demand.

Any time a business incurs additional costs, the immediate reaction is to attempt a price increase. If many businesses try this and it is successful (that is, if consumers keep on purchasing the product), then there is simply more being paid for the same product, a classic instance of inflation. Logically, it would seem, therefore, that a legally-imposed wage increase would lead to price increases across many sectors of the economy.

The evidence for this outcome, though, is shaky. William Alpert conducted a study of the restaurant industry, a sector heavily affected by increases in the minimum wage, before and after the December 1979 increase in the minimum wage. In a survey he undertook, a full 61% of managers and owners stated that they had or would raise prices. However, when he did his aggregate analyses of restaurants, he failed to uncover any actual movement in prices. Using data from both the Bureau of Labor Statistics and the Chamber of Commerce on restaurant food and apparel prices, Madeline Zavodny examined the period from 1987 to 1992 in an attempt to isolate any price increases connected with the minimum wage hike of 1989. Her inspection did indeed find a very small upward movement in some, but not all, restaurant prices (1.0% to 1.5%); however, there were no increases at all associated with retail apparel.

The first key to understanding how this works is to appreciate the role of labor costs in overall costs. For most businesses, labor costs are only one factor

---

222. Michael Reich, Peter Hall, and Fiona Hsu, "Living Wages and the San Francisco Economy: The Benefits and the Costs" (Berkeley: University of California Institute of Industrial Relations, 1999).

in the total cost picture, and as a percentage of selling prices or a percentage of total costs, it is ordinarily rather small. For example, according to IRS data, for American corporations as a whole, total salaries and wages (counting, that is, management compensation) are 8.8% of receipts and 9.6% of total costs.[223] For general merchandise retail stores, those figures rise only to 10.5% and 10.9% respectively and for eating and drinking establishments to 19.5% and 20.8%. Thus, even for eating and drinking places, a 10% rise in *total* wage and salary costs would only raise both figures to around 22% and 23% respectively, assuming no efficiency gains. I acknowledge, though, that raising the base wage to levels I am advocating could have a material effect on costs, and hence on cost pressures.

Nevertheless, there are two other factors to consider. The first is the role of efficiency gains, as noted above. Without question, there would be substantial pressure on businesses, particularly on those employing low-wage workers, to search for efficiencies. Better equipment, enhanced training regimens, better organizational methods and so forth would undoubtedly be the order of the day.

But there is also the second factor — the role of other products, which needs to be considered in a dynamic business model rather than a static one. Suppose fast food prices did rise somewhat; but price increases face a ceiling called "what consumers will pay." Suppose that consumers do indeed stop buying as much fast food as they did before. Would they stop spending? Of course not. They would simply buy more food at grocery stores and prepare it themselves. Economically, just as much would get done (and new jobs would be created at supermarkets); there would just be a shift in how it was done. (In fact, more people eating at home might not be a bad outcome, on several fronts.) The general point is that consumers' dollars don't just disappear. New economic opportunities and new jobs are created whenever the cost and price structure of given industries change. Thus, inflation in the industries that employ large numbers of minimum wage workers might not lead to any inflation at all in the economy considered as a whole.

The other reason some people argue that minimum wage increases are inflationary is that they shift purchasing power down the income ladder, increasing consumption over saving. Put simply, the rate of saving over spending is higher in higher income brackets. If the net effect of a minimum wage increase is to take some income away from people who live in houses with swimming

---

223. Internal Revenue Service, Corporation Returns with Net Income: Balance Sheet, Income Statement, Tax and Selected Other Items by Major Industry, 1999. October 2002.

pools and give it to those who live in mobile homes, then in the economy as a whole there will be a rise in spending. Such an infusion of purchasing power will then create inflationary pressures.

This argument, of course, falls over the same stumbling block as the employment argument. It takes no account of how wage increases might improve productivity. Besides, if people's wages begin to rise to comfortable levels, they might begin to save, too. When every dollar does not have to go for rent, food, clothing, and transportation, you can begin to think about laying something aside.

But there is an even more infuriating aspect to this argument. When was the last time you read an article about Wall Street bonuses or CEO pay that mentioned the possible inflationary effects? For instance, in one of the last great go-go years of the recent stock market boom, 1999, the *New York Times* ran a front-page end-of-the-year article on Wall Street bonuses.[224] They were expected to reach $13 billion that year. True, some of that was undoubtedly saved, but a lot of it went for additional homes, expensive vacations, and new luxury cars. Not one word was said in the article about how inflationary this might be, nor did economists direly issue such warnings. Incidentally, at the levels at which I suggested setting the living wage in Chapter 5, those bonuses would provide either 36,435 or 48,580 people with a *yearly* income at the living wage.

There is still another perversion here. In the spring of 2003, President Bush's economic spokespeople were arguing that we needed a tax cut, largely for the wealthy, to "stimulate" the economy. One of their arguments was that if the stock market goes up, people will feel more confident about their financial security and begin spending. Inflation? Deafening silence. Besides, you cannot have it both ways. If low-wage workers would indeed spend more, why not just provide them the money (as Keynes, of course, suggested) to stimulate the economy?

In short, the chain of causation between an increase in the take home pay of low-wage workers and inflation is nebulous and unproven.

BUSINESS FAILURES

In 1995, Herman Cain, president of the National Restaurant Association, told Congress's Joint Economic Committee that raising the minimum wage was

---

224. *New York Times*, December 14, 1999, 1.

unwise in part because "When you raise the cost of doing business for many thousands of businesses that are just making it — and there are thousands of small businesses that are just barely making it — you risk shutting their doors permanently."[225] While I have no doubt that Mr. Cain sincerely believes this, once again, there is simply no evidence that it is true.

William Alpert's 1985 study of the minimum wage's impact on the restaurant industry also examined this issue. He built a model of projected restaurant failures based on the increased costs that minimum wage hikes supposedly generate. He then compared his predictions to the actual rate of failures. "While the differences between actual and predicted failures are not statistically significant, the predicted failure rate is usually below the actual failure rate. . . We find no evidence that the minimum wage has lowered restaurant . . . profits."[226]

Two colleagues and I examined the overall failure rate among businesses in the years between 1949 and 1984.[227] We compared normal failure rates with those in the year of and the year following a minimum wage increase. In neither the year of the actual increase nor the following year was there any rise whatsoever in the normal rate of business failures. We then ran a second test concerning the size of the minimum wage increase; again, though, we found no relationship.

Madeline Zavodny took a slightly different tack. She counted the total number of eating and drinking establishments, firms most affected by minimum wage increases, before and after the 1991 minimum wage hike.[228] She found that there were actually more establishments after the increase went into effect.

David Card and Alan Krueger studied the stock price movements in 110 publicly-traded firms affected by minimum wage increases.[229] For the firms in their sample, when minimum wage increases were seriously floated in Congress (a more important time than the actual increase, since investors react to future events), there were only minute effects on stock prices, about one or two per cent.

---

225. U.S. Congress, Joint Economic Committee, *Evidence against a Higher Minimum Wage*, part 1, February 22, 1995, 22.

226. William Alpert, *The Minimum Wage in the Restaurant Industry* (New York: Praeger, 1986), 93.

227. Jerold Waltman, Allan McBride, and Nicole Camhout, "Minimum Wage Increases and the Business Failure Rate," *Journal of Economic Issues* 32 (1998), 219-23.

228. Madeline Zavodny, "The Minimum Wage: Maximum Controversy over a Minimal Effect," (Ph. D. Dissertation, Massachusetts Institute of Technology, 1996), 36-39.

229. Card and Krueger, *Myth and Measurement*, 52-56.

Finally, Small Business Administration data show a *decline* in business closures after the minimum wage increases of 1991, 1996, and 1997.[230] The rate of closures was 10.8% in 1991 and 10.3% in 1992. The figure stood constant at 9.7% in 1996 and 1997 and then fell to 9.4% in 1998.

As with unemployment and inflation, then, there is no evidence whatsoever to support the idea that a rash of business failures would befall the country upon the introduction of a living wage.

A POSSIBLE SHORTAGE OF JOBS

If, as hinted at in Chapter 4 and argued more fully in the final chapter, the living wage should replace most non-work based cash transfer programs, then maintaining an adequate supply of living wage jobs is essential. Suppose, therefore, that the supply of willing workers were to exceed the supply of available jobs. A serious living wage proposal cannot merely gloss over this possibility. There are basically three answers to this query: 1) the economic effects a living wage itself would have; 2) suggestions — and a hope — for better macroeconomic management; and 3) a concrete program to be put in place should the first two still not produce enough jobs.

First, we must consider the economic ramifications of having a living wage in place. For one thing, it would surely be a buffer against the fall in purchasing power which occurs early in an economic downturn. The usual scenario is that as a recession begins some firms lay off workers. A decline in aggregate purchasing follows, not only because of the job losses but also because many people still with jobs curtail spending as they become fearful about their own future. This leads to lower sales for retailers, with a resulting excess inventory buildup all along the production chain. Affected firms lay off more workers, which accelerates the downward spiral.

Unemployment insurance, public assistance programs, and increased government spending (whether through actual spending or tax cuts is immaterial) are the modern correctives to this situation, and generally seem to work reasonably well, at least to the extent that we have not had another 1930s-style depression. However, we should take note of the fact that President Franklin D. Roosevelt's first policy to fight the moribund aggregate demand of the 1930s and serve as insurance against a future rapid fall in demand was to

---

230. Reported in Holly Sklar, Laryssa Mykytz, and Susan Wefald, *Raising the Floor: Wages and Policies That Work for All of Us* (Boston: South End Press, 2001), 74.

institute a minimum wage.[231] It seems plausible that a living wage would serve that purpose also. In fact, since it would require no transition for many workers (that is, no filing for unemployment benefits or applying for public assistance) and no policy tinkering, the economic benefits of the enhanced aggregate demand would flow more smoothly. There is no reason, therefore, to think that a living wage policy would not be as good as and perhaps superior to the current bevy of programs to maintain adequate consumer demand when the business cycle starts downward.

It has been said that managing the economy is more like gardening than programming a computer. We still do not understand exactly how the economy works, and are unable to predict precisely what effects will flow from what policies. Nonetheless, we do know much more than ever before, and we continue to learn. The government's full employment tool-kit, while it will never be perfect, can be made better. One thing seems clear, and that is that low long-term interest rates are very important. On one front, they make the effective price of big-ticket consumer items, such as homes and automobiles, cheaper. On another, they make it easier for businesses to borrow for new plant and equipment, the engines of greater productivity. If, therefore, we strive to keep long-term interest rates low and add other effective techniques of economic management, we can accomplish a lot.

Nevertheless, neither the adoption of a universal living wage nor the emergence of an economic Solomon is going to repeal the business cycle. For the foreseeable future, we are going to have hills and valleys of economic activity, even if they are relatively modest ones in a general trajectory of long-term growth. As a result, there will be times when there will be people who want to work but find no job waiting for them at the employment office.

The best answer to this problem is to follow Mickey Kaus' suggestion of a modern-day WPA-style public works program.[232] Kaus' program could be tweaked a bit (in part because he was addressing problems related to long-term welfare recipients), but he and I are advocating basically the same thing.

There would be federally operated job centers in all cities above a certain population level, say 50,000. State and local governments would submit requests either for service provision — cleaning parks, collecting garbage, etc. — or

---

231. Although the federal minimum wage was not enacted until 1938, one of the central components of the administration's first anti-Depression policy, the National Industrial Recovery Act, was minimum wages. See George Paulsen, *A Living Wage for the Forgotten Man: The Quest for Fair Labor Standards, 1933-41* (Selingsgrove, PA: Susquehanna University Press, 1996).

232. Mickey Kaus, *The End of Equality* (New York: Basic Books, 1992), chap. 8.

capital projects — schools, bridges, hospitals, etc. — to the agency operating the center. Every day the center would send all those who show up to the work sites, where supervised real work would be done. Any adult who showed up (even, say, Barbara Streisand or Tiger Woods) and presented documentation of citizenship could work, and be paid for the hours he or she worked. Attached to each work center would be a public day care center that would care for any child brought by a worker.

Of course, there are problems with this program, but they are not crippling. The first is that you do not want these jobs to become more attractive than work in the private sector. A huge army of public workers would be unhealthy for all concerned. Rather than operating some kind of expensive placement scheme, though, the simplest expedient would be to pay these public workers 85% of the living wage. Presumably, then, they would seek out private sector jobs whenever they could. Yes, this violates the principle of paying everyone a living wage, and that by the government itself; but the administrative efficiency to be gained has to take priority here. It is the best among unpleasant alternatives. These jobs are fallbacks, not sinecures. In the real world, you sometimes have to give a bit, and here is one of those times.

Wouldn't the projects, especially the building projects, be terribly inefficient? Absolutely. Kaus quotes an estimate by a WPA administrator from the 1930s who admitted that its building operations were only 60% as efficient as comparable private efforts.[233] The program set out here would probably be even less efficient, as the WPA had many trained workers, worked steadily on given projects, and had semi-permanent supervisors. Here you would have many workers with few skills, erratic work assignments, and a need for heavy supervision costs. But we are not trying to get the maximum building for the buck here; we are trying to provide people with jobs. They could be made to march around the city shouting slogans, but getting something done is better than getting nothing done. Even if it takes five years to erect the new playground at the park or ten years to build the new courthouse, we would eventually have the playground and the courthouse, and we will have provided a barrier on the fall of purchasing power, which should in turn stimulate jobs in the private sector.

Another objection is that such a program would or at least could take jobs away from regular public service workers. Public sector unions are, therefore, bound to object. It is possible, even very likely in some jurisdictions, that local

---

233. Kaus, *End of Equality*, 134.

governments will substitute the labor of those from the work center for that of public employees. This would be especially true for low-skill tasks such as garbage collection and park landscaping. However, first, these losses should be minimal because the number of people showing up for work would be unpredictable. It is unlikely the citizens would let their city council make the garbage pick up routine dependent on the vagaries of the federal work program. Going to the work center any given day would be voluntary, after all. Second, if there were some job losses, surely a transition program could be set up. For example, most losses could be handled by attrition. But, in the end, the objections of public sector unions are not as important as achieving a living wage for every American. I would think, in fact, that union leaders would see it as a good tradeoff: gaining a living wage for everyone, including their members, in exchange for a few possible job losses in the local and state government sector.

INCREASED ILLEGAL IMMIGRATION

According to the Census Bureau, approximately 500,000 illegal immigrants enter the United States each year.[234] Despite locating and deporting about a million a year (nearly half of whom are caught at the border), the government estimates that there are about eight million currently in the country. The Center for Immigration Studies puts the likely numbers at between 700,000 and 800,000 annual entrants and perhaps as high as 11 million resident.[235] Some of these, unquestionably, are fleeing repression of one sort or another or are on the run from criminal prosecutions in foreign countries. However, the vast bulk of them are drawn by the economic opportunities available in the United States. According to one study, even at the very low wages offered, some Mexican workers in an American meat-packing plant can make in an hour twice what they could make in a day in Mexico.[236]

There is little doubt that a living wage would make the United States an even stronger magnet for the economically impoverished of the world, especially those from nearby countries. Furthermore, by boosting the demand for being smuggled into the United States, we would automatically increase both the

---

234. The data can be found at www. census. gov/dmd/www/ReportRec2. htm, Appendix A of Report 1.

235. These numbers have to be considered in light of the fact that the Center is opposed to large-scale immigration. See the organization's website for more information.

236. Schlosser, *Fast Food Nation*, 161-62

number of human smugglers and the prices they could charge. It is also likely we would elevate the level of ruthlessness with which the smugglers pursue their trade. At the same time, the economic incentive to hire illegal workers at illegally low wages would rise, and there is no reason to believe that there would not be a ready supply of unscrupulous operators who would do exactly that.

However much our heartstrings are pulled by the plight of these desperate people, and no matter how much our history compels us to lay out the welcome mat for immigrants, we would have to take steps to stem this tide. Devotees of the free market, of course, constantly push for vastly increased if not virtually unlimited immigration. The reason is obvious: a horde of immigrants will drive the price of labor down. Consider this bit of policy analysis from a recent op-ed piece in the *Wall Street Journal*:

> American immigration laws are colliding with economic reality, and reality is winning. Migration from Mexico is driven by a fundamental mismatch between a rising demand for low-skilled labor in the U.S. and a shrinking domestic supply of workers willing to fill those jobs. . . . Current immigration law has made law breakers out of millions of hardworking, otherwise law abiding people — immigrants and native employers alike — whose only "crime" is a desire to work together in our market economy for mutual advantage.[237]

Turning to another country's history for a moment, Australia's "White Australia" policy (allowing only white immigrants, ended in the 1970s) is often seen as sheer racism, and there is ample evidence that that was part of it. But the high basic wage dictated by Australian industrial relations policy could not work if Australian businesses were allowed to import foreign, in their case mostly Chinese, workers eager to work in dangerous jobs at low wages. Consider what the wage level on the western section of the transcontinental railroad would have been if the massive import of Chinese workers had been banned.

Consequently, if a living wage policy is to work, we must, sadly, restrict immigration. Yet, frankly, there are no good options for doing this.[238] We would have to try to do more of the same and do it better. This means more rigorous border policing, stiffer penalties for smugglers, and heavy fines for firms that

237. Daniel Griswold, "Mexican Workers Come Here to Work: Let Them!" *Wall Street Journal*, October 22, 2002. See also the articles in *The Economist*, October 5, 2002 and November 2, 2002.

238. A good discussion of the administrative problems inherent in dealing with immigration is Shannon Barrios, "Is the Immigration and Naturalization Service Unreformable? Past Experience and Future Prospects," *Administration and Society* 34 (2002), 370-88. Nothing about the agency's new name or home in the Department of Homeland Security addresses the issues Barrios raises.

knowingly hire illegal aliens. Perhaps a national identification card system should be considered. But in the end, any of these steps will mean that the smugglers will become even more dangerous than they are now, because their risks will go up; that being the case, not only will they become more violent to their "customers," but also their attempts to circumvent the law by bribing border guards and other law enforcement personnel will intensify. We need only ponder what has happened every time we have tried to increase the risk of drug smuggling.

Naturally, the best solution is to encourage economic development in the poor countries of the world. Such propositions are often a way merely to provide a sop for U.S. consciences while doing nothing, and even if we dedicated ourselves to it we would not know exactly how to do it. Nonetheless, we certainly know a good bit more than we did a generation ago about the roots of economic development.[239] We have a few usable ideas. Encouraging markets rather than state-led development is far more likely to succeed, and encouraging indigenous economic activities is better than erecting giant development "projects." Surely, therefore, if we seriously attack this problem we can do something to help, and reduce thereby, somewhat at least, the number of people desiring to flee to the United States. But even if that works, it will take some time.

Let us grant, then, that, at least in the short run and intermediate run, we will face even more illegal immigrants attempting to sneak into the country, and that the accompanying scale of human tragedy is likely to escalate the day after we adopt a universal living wage. Nevertheless, that is not a sufficient reason not to do it. The stark truth is that material conditions in America make it appealing to people the world over, and anything we do to make it a better place makes it more so. But that is fulfilling our history, from the Puritan wish to "build a city on a hill" forward. Should we reject expanding freedom of speech or building better schools because that might attract more immigrants? No. And we need to adopt a living wage for everyone who works in this country because it is the right thing to do. We will simply have to cope with the illegal immigrant problem as best as we can.

---

239. See David Landes, *The Wealth and Poverty of Nations: Why Some are So Rich and Some So Poor* (New York: Norton, 1998).

Conclusion

In 1999, the Employment Policies Institute sponsored a study of the possible economic impact of the then-pending living-wage ordinance in Chicago.[240] (Like most other living-wage ordinances, this one would have applied only to city contractors.) The study's authors concluded that the annual cost to the city would be close to $20 million, that labor costs to affected employers would go up by $37.5 million, and that "at least" 1,300 jobs would disappear. If these figures withstood scrutiny, then a national, universal living wage would be an unmitigated disaster.

Fortunately, if we unpack the study we get a different picture. First, the entire effort rests on the tired static model. According to the authors, "Each dollar that is paid to a worker in additional earnings must come from someone else."[241] Methodologically, the study is based on a sample survey of 133 employers, with the results generalized to the total number of firms in the city. To obtain the $37.5 million labor cost rise, for instance, they ask the respondents how many employees would be eligible for a pay increase should the ordinance go into effect. They then estimated the costs of granting these raises and multiplied that by the number of employees reported. Next, they took this figure and multiplied it by a citywide conversion factor to get an estimate for all contractors. The survey respondents reported a total of 3,930 workers eligible for a raise. The authors estimated that it would take $14.4 million to accomplish this. The conversion factors yielded 9,807 similarly situated workers citywide, and applying the same ratio, we get $37.5 million. Not one mention is made of productivity increases. Similarly, when the costs to the city are being totaled up, no allowance is made for productivity gains. On another front, when the job losses are summed, no provision is made for enhanced purchasing power. In short, there may well be some additional costs to a city when a living wage goes into effect, and, who knows, there may even be some job losses (though it is equally likely there may be job gains), but a study that takes no account of the dynamism of business enterprises is not only suspect but it also shortchanges the capabilities of the ordinary business person. The economist Roger Tawney,

---

240. George Tooley, Peter Bernstein, and Michael Lesage, *Economic Analysis of a Living Wage Ordinance* (Washington: Employment Policies Institute, 1999). The Employment Policies Institute should not be confused with the Economic Policy Institute. The former is a more free-market oriented think tank, while the latter generally has a progressive orientation. The Employment Policies Institute has published a compilation of its opposition to the living wage, *Living Wage Policy: The Basics* (2000).

241. Tooley, *et al.*, 7.

who did the first empirical studies of the impact of a minimum wage, mentioned above, provides the best corrective: "The ingenuity of employers and workpeople so greatly exceeds that of economists that discussions of what 'must' happen, unsupported by evidence as to what has happened or is happening, are usually quite worthless."[242]

At the end of the day, therefore, there are two potential drawbacks to a universal living wage: the difficulty of providing jobs when the business cycle drops to the negative side and the heightened attractiveness of the United States to illegal immigrants. Neither, though, is enough of a reason to jettison it. As for the other widely-touted ill effects — employment losses, inflation, and business failures — until more actual evidence is presented, they rest on too speculative a foundation to be a barrier to establishing a policy that would make life better for millions of Americans and at the same time make our political order more robustly healthy.

---

242. Tawney, *Establishment of Minimum Wages in the Chain Making Industry*, 105.

8. PUBLIC SUPPORT FOR A LIVING WAGE

We might agree that poverty and gaping inequality are scars on the body politic, and, further, that they are remediable scars. Additionally, we might agree that a universal living wage is the most appropriate policy to address these twin ills, and that it will do far more good than harm. It is still a fair question, though, whether it is a policy that can win the support of a significant portion of either the American or the British public. Many commendable policies are viewed by the public as unworkable or unwise for a variety of reasons; discussions of them are therefore "academic" in the most ivory-towerish sense of the term. Are there other strategies for attacking poverty and inequality, it is fair to ask, that might stand a better chance of adoption because they are more congruent with public values and attitudes?

I hope to show that the majority of Americans already back the living wage, and, additionally, that it is the policy most likely to win public approval for an assault on poverty and inequality. Although British data are a bit more sketchy, particularly because the minimum wage is so new but also because the context and the contours of welfare reform are so different, at least a presentable case exits that a living wage would enjoy considerable public backing there as well.

PUBLIC ATTITUDES REGARDING POVERTY AND INEQUALITY IN THE UNITED STATES

Americans clearly believe that poverty is a major social problem. As shown clearly in Table 8-1, an overwhelming 88 per cent see poverty as a problem, 55 per cent as a "big" problem and 33 per cent as "somewhat" of a problem.[243] Only a minuscule two per cent believe that it is not a problem. (Eight per cent thought it a small problem and one per cent did not know. From this point forward, unless they are significant, I will omit the "don't knows.") In another poll "about the United States and its government," one of the propositions was: "As long as so many Americans are poor or homeless, our nation has failed to live up to its ideals."[244] The wording may have been a bit leading, but still, 57 per cent agreed (39 per cent strongly agreed) while 41 per cent (17 per cent strongly) disagreed.

TABLE 8-1 POVERTY AS A PROBLEM IN MODERN AMERICA	
How big a problem	Percentage response
A big problem	55%
Somewhat of a problem	33%
A small problem	8%
Not a problem	2%
Don't know	1%

Note: Percentages do not add to 100 in all tables because of rounding.
Question: How big a problem is poverty in our society today? Is it a big problem, somewhat of a problem, a small problem, or not a problem at all?

Furthermore, U.S. citizens are not satisfied with the efforts made so far to eradicate poverty. In the latest poll, the largest number, 37 per cent, said they were "very dissatisfied" when asked how they felt about the "state of the nation in . . . efforts to deal with poverty and homelessness?"[245] An additional 34 per cent replied that they were "somewhat dissatisfied"; only 23 per cent said they were "satisfied," and a mere four per cent were "very satisfied." Even more disturbing, people seem to feel that the nation is moving backward. When asked, in 2002, "Do you think the problem of poverty, hunger, and homelessness is about the same as it has been, that the country is making progress in this area, or that the country is losing ground?," 42 per cent said the country was losing

---

243. National Public Radio/Harvard University Kennedy School of Government Poll, February 2001. Hereafter cited as NPR Poll.
244. Public Agenda, 2002. Available at www. publicagenda. org.
245. Gallup Poll, January 20, 2004.

ground.[246] Thirty-three per cent said it was about the same and 20 per cent believed progress was being made. The respondents here could have been responding more to homelessness than poverty, but that is uncertain.

Turning to the public's beliefs regarding the causes of poverty, it is certainly not a shortage of jobs. Only a third think that, as depicted in Table 8-2.[247] However, 54 per cent are convinced that part-time and low-wage jobs are a major cause of the problem. Further, of the six causes that command a majority, four of them are personal attributes rather than social causes. Only medical bills and the lack of good jobs can be attributed to societal failings. Similarly, in another poll, people were asked whether the fate of children in poverty was traceable to "social and economic problems or . . . the failure of their parents as individuals." Half said the parents as individuals were at fault, while only 31 per cent said social and economic conditions were more to blame.[248]

TABLE 8-2

THE MAJOR CAUSES OF POVERTY ACCORDING TO THE PUBLIC

Causes	Percentage citing this item as a "major" cause
Drug abuse	70%
Medical bills	58%
Decline in moral values	57%
Too many part-time and low wage jobs	54%
Too many single parents	54%
Poor people lacking motivation	52%
Poor public schools	47%
The welfare system	46%
A shortage of jobs	34%

Question: For each of the following, please tell me if this is a major cause of poverty, a minor cause of poverty, or not a cause at all.

Buttressing the proposition of Table 8-2 that Americans believe that inadequate pay is central to the plight of the poor are the results of another poll that asked people whether they thought "poor people in the United States are people who work but can't earn enough money, or people who don't work?"[249]

---

246. Princeton Survey Research Associates Poll, March 2002.

247. NPR Poll. Another question in the poll asked "Do you think there are jobs available for most welfare recipients who really want to work? Yes = 78 per cent. In a separate poll, people were asked: "Do you think that every willing and able person can find work if they try hard enough or is this not really doable right now?" Here, 73 per cent said people can find work.

248. Pew Research Center, *Pew Forum on Religion and Public Life*, February 25, 2002.

Sixty-one per cent indicated they thought it was lack of earnings, while only 34 per cent thought not working was at the root of the problem. Interestingly, when the poor are asked, they also point to low earnings as a cause of their plight. When quizzed why people in the United States are poor, they most often cited a lack of education (73 per cent), but a high second was "lack of a living wage," coming in at 59 per cent.[250] "Unjust laws and social policies" garnered 38 per cent, the third highest amount. (Respondents were asked to choose three from a list.) Then, when asked what their major concerns were, a general category "unemployment, jobs, low wages," topped the list. It outstripped racial bias, poverty, housing, education, health care, and a variety of other items.

It seems clear that Americans in general and the poor themselves both believe that inadequate pay is the major source of poverty. To be successful in the public's eyes, therefore, any policy to fight poverty must address this central fact.

Much less survey data is available on the public's views on inequality.[251] What there is, though, shows that people are rather concerned about economic inequality and see it as on the rise. In a 2003 poll, Americans were asked whether they felt "the distribution of money and wealth in this country today is fair, or do you feel that the money and wealth in this country should be more evenly distributed among a larger percentage of the people?"[252] More than double the number, 63 per cent to 31 per cent, thought it should be distributed more evenly. Then there is the outrage, although it admittedly may be only temporary, felt at the pay packages of CEOs. When asked to rate various problems on a 1-10 scale, with 10 being "an extremely serious problem," 64 per cent of respondents placed the matter of "Corporations paying huge salaries to CEOs" in the 8-10 bracket.[253] Another poll asked how angry people were at CEOs who received large salaries while their companies were "losing money and laying off workers." As might be expected from the question's wording, three out of four were very angry.[254] While exaggerated perhaps, the sentiment is still real.

More directly relevant is a comparison of Gallup Poll data from 1988 and 1999; in twelve years, the number who said we are a "have/have not" society

---

249. NPR Poll.

250. Catholic Campaign for Human Development, *Low Income Poverty Pulse*, December 4, 2003.

251. Some helpful polls, although almost of them only indirectly addressing the issue, are discussed in Everett Carll Ladd and Karlyn H. Bowman, *Attitudes toward Economic Inequality* (Washington: American Enterprise Institute, 1998).

252. CNN/USA Today Poll, January 10, 2003.

253. Peter D. Hart Research Associates, conducted for the AFL-CIO, August 29, 2002.

254. Public Interest Project, June 17, 2003.

climbed from 26 per cent to 39 per cent. By 2001, a Pew Research Center Study found that 44 per cent felt that way. In percentage terms, therefore, in the thirteen years between George Bush, Sr.'s winning of the presidency and the year of the September 11 terrorist attacks, the number of people who think we are divided into haves and have nots grew by 69 per cent.[255] Moreover, in 1999, 69 per cent thought that the gap separating the rich and the poor would only grow worse,[256] and economic data show that indeed it has.

GOVERNMENTAL RESPONSIBILITIES

A chorus of spokespeople on the right seem to never tire of telling us that Americans are hostile to "big" government and, indeed, to government in general. The reigning ideology among political elites seems to be that governmental responsibilities should be kept to an absolute minimum. However, ironically, the public does not seem to share that attitude. For example, an overwhelming 86 per cent agreed, and 64 per cent strongly agreed, when asked, "Do you agree or disagree that the federal government has a responsibility to try to do away with poverty in this country?"[257] Then, when asked, "Should the government do more to help working families, or should the government not do more?," a rather striking 76 per cent said "more."[258] A further glimpse into how far people are willing to have government go can be gained from a 1999 poll that asked how much people agreed or disagreed with the proposition that: "It is the responsibility of the government to take care of people who can't take care of themselves."[259] Twenty per cent completely agreed, 42 per cent mostly agreed, 14 per cent disagreed, and 21 per cent mostly disagreed. Further, when asked to choose between the two statements — "The government in Washington, DC should make every possible effort to improve the social and economic position of the poor" and "The government should not make any effort to help the poor, because they should help themselves," 65 per cent opted for the former and only 29 per cent for the latter.[260]

---

255. Pew Research Center for the People and the Press, *Economic Inequality Seen as Rising*, June 21, 2001, 1.
256. Pew Research Center for the People and Press, May 6, 1999.
257. Ms. Foundation for Women Poll, Conducted by Lake Snell Perry and Associates, 2002. Hereafter cited as Ms. Foundation Poll.
258. Ms. Foundation Poll.
259. Princeton Survey Research/Pew Research Center Poll, October 1999.
260. Gallup Poll, May 31, 1998.

In sum, it seems rather obvious that Americans view poverty as a serious problem for their society, and that they are willing, even eager, to have government take steps to alleviate it. Feelings on inequality may be more muted, but they are definitely in the mix.

POLICIES TO FIGHT POVERTY

Let us go straight to the heart of the matter. In 2000, Americans were asked pointedly: "Do you agree or disagree that as a country we should make sure people who work full-time are able to earn enough to keep their families out of poverty?"[261] Almost everyone, a full 94 per cent, agreed. In fact, 80 per cent strongly agreed. Surely, people understood that the phrase "make sure" can only mean governmental action. And the lopsidedness of the response shows, to put it bluntly, that the living wage likely enjoys more public backing than any policy in U.S. history. Although it was confined to Maryland, a similarly worded poll there found identical results. The question was, "Government should ensure full-time workers can earn enough to keep their families out of poverty?," with a strongly agree to strongly disagree response option.[262] Ninety-three per cent agreed, with 75 per cent strongly agreeing. Importantly, the support crossed income levels and partisan lines. Ninety per cent of those making over $50,000 a year agreed, as did 85 per cent of Republicans. Moreover, this is nothing new. Asked in 1989 whether they favored "a minimum wage high enough so that a family of four could live above the poverty line if the father worked and the mother stayed home," 75 per cent of Americans said yes and only 17 per cent no.[263]

This stentorian backing for a living wage is not surprising, given the consistent high level of support for raising the minimum wage. Between 1945 and 1996, 39 polls were taken seeking to find out whether the public favored raising the minimum wage.[264] In all save one (in 1952), a substantial majority, usually in the 75-80% range, responded in the affirmative. Polls taken since then report the same results. A 2002 poll asked whether people favored raising the minimum wage to $8.00 per hour (from $5.15, a whopping 61 per cent increase);

261. Jobs for the Future Poll. Conducted by Lake Snell Perry and Associates, October 2001.
262. Lake, Snell Perry and Associates Poll, Conducted for Annie E. Casey Foundation, the Open Society Institute-Baltimore, and Jobs for the Future, November 6, 2000.
263. Parents Magazine Poll, May 1989.
264. These polls are discussed in detail in my *Politics of the Minimum Wage* (Urbana: University of Illinois Press, 2000), chap. 3.

77 per cent (55 per cent strongly) agreed.[265] Other recent polls are equally enlightening, and equally lopsided. One from 2001 utilized the "strongly favor" to "strongly oppose" format, with the statement "An increase in the minimum wage from $5.15 an hour to $6.45 an hour." This was favored by 87 per cent (49 per cent strongly) and opposed by only 12 per cent (four per cent strongly).[266]

Then there are the general issue polls, in which respondents are read a series of issues and asked their views, either how much they favor or oppose each point or how important it is for the president and Congress to act on the measure. In one 2001 poll employing the "relative importance for the president and Congress to address" approach, with the choices ranging from extremely important through very important and moderately important to not important,[267] the question, "How about raising the minimum wage?" found that to 31 per cent it was extremely important and to another 32 per cent it was very important. In addition, 25 per cent said it was moderately important and only 11 per cent that it was not important.

Going still further, a poll taken during the 2000 presidential campaign asked people how they would vote on 20 different issues if they could do so.[268] A full 82 per cent said they would vote to raise the minimum wage, the third highest support level for any proposal. Furthermore, in a different poll, 79 per cent thought indexing the minimum wage to inflation would be a good idea.[269] Finally, in January of 2004, the public was asked about their political priorities for the year. "Should increasing the minimum wage," they were queried, "be a top priority, important but lower priority, not too important, or should it not be done?" Thirty-eight per cent thought it should be a top priority and thirty-nine percent important but lower. Only five per cent thought it should not be done. In short, Americans consistently and overwhelmingly register their approval for a higher minimum wage.

Other polls show that Americans overwhelmingly believe that an increased minimum wage would be more effective than most policies in fighting poverty. Table 8-4 reports the results of one such inquiry.[270] Increasing the minimum wage comes in at a tie for first place. Moreover, the public thinks raising the minimum wage would also be good for the economy overall. One poll, for

---

265. Ms. Foundation Poll.

266. Princeton Survey Research/Pew Research Center Poll, June 2001.

267. CNN/USA Today Poll, June 2001.

268. Gallup Poll Monthly, November 2000, 30.

269. Ms. Foundation Poll.

270. NPR Poll.

TABLE 8-3
HOW AMERICANS WOULD VOTE ON SPECIFIC ISSUES IF THEY COULD

Issue	% For	% Against	% Unsure
Mandatory teacher testing in public schools	95	4	1
Hate crime legislation	83	14	3
Raising the minimum wage	82	16	6
Across the board tax cuts	78	19	5
National standardized tests for schools	75	21	4
Licensing of new handguns	72	22	6
Prayer in public schools	69	29	2
Privatizing part of Social Security	66	30	4
Ban on "partial birth " abortions	63	35	2
Reducing government agencies	62	30	8
Assault weapon ban	59	39	2
School vouchers	56	39	5
Re-establishing relations with Cuba	56	35	9
Targeted tax cuts	52	43	5
Exploration of Arctic Wildlife Refuge in Alaska	44	50	6
Stop legal immigration	43	51	6
Legalization of civil unions	42	54	4
Overturn *Roe v. Wade*	30	67	3
Racial preferences in jobs/schools	13	85	2
Gender preferences in jobs/schools	11	86	3

Question: Suppose that on Election Day this year [2000] you could vote on key issues as well as candidates. Please tell me whether you would vote for or against each one of the following propositions.

instance, asked about "some proposals that have been suggested to stimulate the economy."[271] Queried about raising "the income of low-wage workers by increasing the minimum wage" as a stimulus, 84 per cent (59 per cent strongly) were in favor.

Americans continue to stand up for minimum wage increases even when told they will have to pay the costs. A 1989 poll, for example, asked those who favored a minimum wage increase if they would "still favor raising the minimum wage even if businesses passed the increased salary costs along to the American consumer in the form of higher prices on some goods and services."[272] A full 82 per cent said yes.

When Americans go to the polls, they usually vote for minimum wage increases as well. In 1996, three states, California, Oregon, and Missouri, had measures on their ballots that called for increasing their state minimum wages. In California, the proposition passed by a 61 per cent to 39 per cent margin, while in Oregon the vote was 57 per cent in favor and 43 per cent opposed. In Missouri

271. Ms. Foundation Poll.
272. ABC News/Washington Post Poll, April 1989.

156

TABLE 8-4

SUPPORT FOR PROPOSALS TO FIGHT POVERTY

Proposal	Percentage Supporting It
Expanding subsidized day care	85%
Increasing the minimum wage	85%
Spending more for medical care for poor people	83%
Increasing tax credits for low-income workers	80%
Spending more for housing for poor people	75%
Making food stamps more available to poor people	61%
Guaranteeing everyone a minimum income	57%
Increasing cash assistance for families	54%

Question: Here is a list of things the government could to to directly help the poor in America. Please tell me if you support or oppose each.

---

the increase failed, 29 per cent to 71 per cent. It could be that the scope of the Missouri proposal, though, affected the vote. It not only called for a healthy hike, to $6.75 by January 1, 1999 ($2.00 above the prevailing federal minimum wage), but also made a fifteen-cent raise mandatory each year thereafter. In addition, it expanded the coverage of the statute and allowed local governments to add even higher minimum wages. In 1998, Washington state voters approved a similar measure by a 66 per cent to 34 per cent margin, providing for the state minimum wage to keep up with inflation in the future.[273] Several local elections have also shown dramatic support for higher minimum wages through local living-wage ordinances. In St. Louis, for instance, the "for" vote was more than three to one. In New Orleans, 63 per cent registered their approval while in San Francisco, 60 per cent did.

There are two qualifications that must be acknowledged when using voting results as an indicator of public support for higher minimum wages. First, not all of them pass, as in Missouri. Second, the states and cities where they have passed are not typical of the country as a whole. However, regarding the second item, it at the very least indicates attitudes there, and in California's case, that accounts for a lot of people. Ballots are important barometers for two additional reasons. People voting yes in these referenda know that the policy is actually going to be adopted, which is different from responding to a hypothetical question from a survey taker. The response is, therefore, taken more seriously.

---

273. William Quigley, *Ending Poverty as We Know It: Guaranteeing a Right to a Job at a Living Wage* (Philadelphia: Temple University Press, 2003), 121.

Moreover, the voting public is different from the general public. They are more attentive to politics, they are generally better off economically, and they are older. In other words, they share the fewest traits possible with minimum wage workers. Thus, their support for increased minimum wages when they enter the voting booth is more than a little significant.

This does not imply that a higher minimum wage is the only policy Americans support to fight poverty. Every survey taken points to a wide variety of other policies that win the public's endorsement. More education and training always attract almost universal support. Nine out of ten people support "helping low-income Americans develop skills they need to compete in the global economy" and an equal number are willing to see tax dollars spent to "pay for education and job training for people leaving welfare."[274] Support for subsidized day care, public employment programs, and help with medical care all likewise enjoy enormous public support. However, taken alone, these data paint a seriously misleading picture, for they sidestep at best and ignore at worst, the role of work.

THE ROLE OF WORK

Many people on the political left continue to read the data summarized in the foregoing paragraph as indicative of a large, if latent, public sympathy for their position. Two by no means unique examples illustrate the point. A progressive California organization called the "California Budget Project" conducted a poll of Californians in 2002. The press advisory announcing the results begins by saying that, "A new survey finds that nearly two-thirds (62 per cent) of California voters believe that the principal goal of federal welfare law should be moving people out of poverty, instead of into a job where they will not earn enough to support their families."[275] It then listed as "key findings" the following: Voters believe that the principal goal of TANF should be moving families out of poverty; Voters believe limits on the length families can receive TANF should be flexible because they understand that each family's circumstance is unique; Voters support government programs that help the working poor make ends meet; Voters support benefits for legal immigrants; and Voters support maintaining welfare spending during a recession.

---

274. *Jobs for the Future*, April 30, 2000.
275. Available at http://www. cbp.org/2002/pr020417. html.

The public does support all these things; however, they do not support them *instead of* work, as the California Budget Project implies. They support them *along with* work. The other example comes from a similar poll conducted for the Oregon Center for Public Policy.[276] It too shows how strongly people support more child care, education, and training. "The findings reflect clear support for focusing attention and money on strengthening opportunities for TANF recipients to move from welfare to good jobs. A plurality of those who had an opinion felt in general that too little money is being spent on child care programs for working families (39 per cent), job training (39 per cent) and TANF (35 per cent)." This survey did address work, but only indirectly. It asked respondents whether they thought the current requirements (calling for 20-30 hours of work per week) should be increased. We learn that 69 per cent oppose increasing them for all recipients of TANF and 78 per cent oppose increasing them for mothers with children under six. The clear implication is that there is far more support for education and training than for a work requirement. No question was asked about whether a work requirement of any kind is a good idea.

These results are encouraging to those who opposed TANF reform in the first place, especially when they are coupled with poll results showing the public's willingness to pay higher taxes to help the poor. To cite just one example, 69 per cent support "providing additional assistance to working poor families with children even if it means providing less tax relief to people like themselves."[277] There is ample data, in short, to support the oft-heard statement that Americans will support all manner of welfare measures as long as they are not called that.[278] What the left largely remains oblivious to, however, indeed almost pathologically hostile to, in spite of occasional lip service, is the American public's deep and abiding attachment to work and the values they believe accompany it.

In his excellent pre-reform study of the politics of the Aid to Families with Dependent Children program, Steven Teles summed up decades of survey research:

---

276. Oregon Center for Public Policy, *DHM Survey Report: OCPP-TANF Reauthorization, Conducted by Davis, Hibbitts, and McCaig*, August 12, 2002.

277. Cited in David and Lucile Packard Foundation, *Public Views on Welfare Reform and Children in the Current Economy*, February 20, 2002, 4.

278. This literature is reviewed in Stanley Feldman and Marco Steenbergen, "The Humanitarian Foundation of Public Support for Social Welfare," *American Journal of Political Science* 45 (2001), 658-77.

The public knows . . . how it would choose to deal with the problem of poverty: with jobs. There is no finding as consistent or as overwhelming in all of the survey data I have seen than the support the public gives for guaranteed government jobs programs and other efforts to expand employment. The public is willing to have inflation rise in order to expand employment, thinks government should do more to expand employment, and agrees that 'the government in Washington ought to see to it that everybody who wants to work can find a job,' all by very strong margins. . .

[Americans] believe that work is of supreme importance, both for its own sake and because of its connection with upward mobility. Work is the primary means through which the public desires to help the poor. Americans oppose welfare because they believe it represents the negation of the work ethic. A number of polls taken across a range of years and worded in a variety of ways suggest that the public wishes to narrow the difference between work and welfare by transforming the current welfare program into one that pays people for work. The margins are staggering.[279]

Post-welfare reform data underscore Teles' point. A recent poll asked those who were aware of welfare reform, "All in all, do you think the new welfare law is working well, or not?"[280] Over six in ten, 61 per cent, thought it was working well and only 23 per cent felt it was not working well. (Both = 2 per cent; Don't Know = 15 per cent). In other words, 73 per cent of those with an opinion thought it was working well. Then, those who thought it was working well were asked why they believed it was successful. The unmistakable conclusion is that the American people are pleased that public policy now requires work, as reported in Table 6-6. How could it be more clear? Another poll produced almost identical results. When asked to identify the "very important" and "most important" factors in judging the success of welfare reform, moving people into work outstripped all other factors, racking up an 85 per cent score as "very important."[281] Nearly two and a half times more people designated the work requirement as the "most important" factor than any other item. When interrogated about future reform in 2002, the public evidenced the same values. When asked how important it is for government programs like welfare to pursue various goals, 96 per cent rated "require recipients to work" as important, with 82 per cent indicating that it was "very important."[282] Again, this was the highest response both overall and in the "very important" category.

---

279. Steven M. Teles, *Whose Welfare? AFDC and Elite Politics* (Lawrence: University Press of Kansas, 1996), 53-54.

280. NPR Poll.

281. Future of Children Poll.

282. Future of Children Poll.

TABLE 8-5
PERCEPTIONS REGARDING HOW WELL WELFARE REFORM IS WORKING

Degree to which welfare reform is working	Percentage
Working well	61%
Not working well	23%
Don't know	15%
Both	2%

Question: All in all, do you think the new welfare law is working well, or not? [Asked of those who knew of the reform.]

TABLE 8-7
FACTORS IN JUDGING THE SUCCESS OF WELFARE REFORM

	Percentage citing it as a very important factor	Percentage citing it as the most important factor
People off welfare into work	85%	46%
Fewer families in poverty	74%	19%
Fewer families on welfare	68%	9%
Children in low-income families better off	61%	15%
Government welfare spending reduced	50%	4%

Questions:
In judging how successful welfare reform has been, how important do you personally feel each of the following factors should be. In your opinion, should this be a very important factor, somewhat important, not too important or not an important factor at all in judging the success of welfare reform.

And which of these should be the most important factor in judging the success of welfare reform?

TABLE 8-6
MAJOR REASONS WELFARE REFORM IS WORKING WELL

"Major" reason	Percentages
Law requires people to go to work	87%
Law has substantially cut welfare rolls	64%
Welfare departments now doing more to help poor people	52%
Now less stigma attached to welfare	28%

Question: Please tell me whether each is a major reason you think the new law is working well. [Asked of those saying the new law is working well.] Multiple responses allowed.

The reasons for and the depth of these feelings can be gleaned from two other polls, the first conducted in 1995 (before welfare reform) and the other in

2000. The first posed this question: "Some people feel that the most upsetting thing about welfare is that it costs too much in tax money. Others feel that the most upsetting thing about welfare is that it encourages people to adopt the wrong lifestyle and values. What is your opinion?"[283] Nearly two out of three, 65 per cent, cited the "wrong lifestyle" as what upset them most, while only 14 per cent were concerned most about the costs of the program. Even more revealing, perhaps, is the 2000 poll, administered only to parents of children five and under. It asked: "It's important for kids whose families are on welfare to see their parent working or going to school, even if it means the kids must be in child care. Do you agree or disagree? Is that strongly or somewhat?"[284] A resounding 86 per cent agreed (53 per cent strongly).

This does not mean, as some have tried to argue, that Americans are hostile to the poor. Sharon Hays contends, for instance, that Americans think women should stay home with their children, but they don't care about poor women doing so.[285] The cultural message, she believes, is: "You and your children don't count as much as everyone else." True, many Americans harbor doubts about day care, and think that a mother being at home is often helpful for children. But they also value work. They have to make a choice, and they believe that given what they think are the causes of poverty — worklessness and the behaviors it leads to — they opt for work. They would prefer it to be different, but it is not. Thus, there is no real contradiction here; rather, it is a hard choice and the public chooses intelligently. It is well to recall that Americans believe the poor are basically like themselves, with essentially the same values. Eighty-two per cent say that the poor share most or some of the same values as themselves; in contrast, incidentally, only 61 per cent believe that of rich people.[286] And, it should be stressed, it is often those closest to the poor who want more stringent work requirements. Even in the Oregon survey quoted above, those with less than a high school education were more in favor of moving the work requirement upwards than the public as a whole.

The poll data on welfare reform, therefore, must be read alongside the data from before regarding why the public thinks poverty persists. A lack of access to and the costs of health care arise again and again (which is a subject for another

283. Public Agenda, December 1995.

284. Public Agenda, June 2000.

285. Sharon Hays, *Flat Broke with Children: Women in the Age of Welfare Reform* (New York: Oxford University Press, 2003).

286. Washington *Post*/Kaiser Family Foundation/Harvard University Poll, National Survey of American Values, August 1998.

day, especially since the public seems willing to pay for this); but the central and overriding point for the present endeavor is that ordinary Americans strongly believe that work is an absolutely essential component of a healthy life. It is both a route out of poverty and a ticket to membership in the civic community.

The study of American attitudes regarding poverty and values commissioned by the Ford Foundation summed it up this way:

> Hard work is the litmus test for how we feel about the poor and those on welfare. The working poor are generally respected — they are working hard and we as a society want to do everything we can to help them succeed.[287]

SUMMING UP AMERICAN SUPPORT FOR A LIVING WAGE

Americans are often presented as being of two minds when it comes to poverty and social welfare policy. Tamara Draut, Director of the Economic Opportunity Program of Demos, a progressive-leaning organization, to choose only one example, speaks of the Fair American and the Tough American.[288] The Fair American is concerned about poverty, wants governmental action to address it, and is willing to pay for a variety of social programs. The Tough American believes in self-reliance, individual responsibility, hard work, and the basic fairness of market outcomes.

The truth, however, is that there is not nearly as sharp a dichotomy as Draut and others like her believe. Americans are deeply moved by the persistence of poverty amidst plenty. They view it, realistically, as rooted in a combination of social forces and personal shortcomings, with decided leanings toward the latter. They believe that work — actual, regular, disciplined work — is the surest, in fact the only, permanent path out of poverty. Consequently, everyone who is physically able to do so should work. Simultaneously, they believe that those who work should be fairly and adequately rewarded for that work.[289] This seems (to me, anyway) perfectly logical and thoroughly consistent.

Rather than being divided between the Fair American and Tough American, public attitudes actually reflect the Realistic American and the Civic

---

287. Ford Foundation Study, 6.

288. Tamara Draut, "New Opportunities? Public Opinion on Poverty, Income Inequality and Public Policy: 1996-2002," New York: Demos, 2002.

289. They are also willing to fund programs to aid work, such as child care, training programs, and relief from medical expenses.

American. They are realistic in that they recognize the prevalence of poverty and the causes of it. At the same time, they are civic in that they feel that none of their fellow citizens who work should live in poverty. They believe that work is part of the fulfillment of citizenship duties and is the way to enhance one's own quality of life. When a fellow citizen works, they want him or her to be fairly compensated. What they want is a living wage for everyone who works, which, with rare exceptions, should be every adult.

Some polls, after they ascertain how people feel about poverty, turn to several other social programs, such as job training programs, food stamps, housing subsidies, and selective tax cuts. For instance, the list of items from the Jobs for the Future poll: "Tax cuts to businesses that train low-skill workers," "Increasing funding for education and training to prepare the jobless," "Expanding child care assistance for low-income workers," "Tax cuts for workers to stay out of poverty," and "Helping low-income workers pay for career-related college programs." All of these recorded between 82 per cent and 90 per cent approval. However, the American public is emphatically not going to lend its support to any anti-poverty policy mix that does not have work at its center. Sure, they back those other policies, but not standing alone. A renewed push for governmental expenditure programs, no matter how "popular" in the short-run, is a formula for the marginalization of progressive politics, not its renewal.

One more number from the polls is worth citing. When asked about "creating temporary government work programs for the unemployed in needed areas like school and road construction," 90 per cent of Democrats, 83 per cent of Independents, and 82 per cent of Republicans would support such a policy.[290] Coupled with the reasons the American public thinks welfare reform is succeeding and the consistent support for a living wage and sharp minimum wage increases, it seems crystal clear that the public would back a living wage along the lines laid out in Chapter 5, with jobs provided by public authorities, if need be.

Draut says in her essay that "Finding ways to communicate progressive ideas that resonate with public values about work, individual responsibility and fairness is a significant challenge facing advocates."[291] I wholeheartedly endorse that position, and I maintain that a universal living wage, and only a universal living wage, will meet that challenge.

---

290. Jobs for the Future Poll.
291. Draut, "New Opportunities?" 21.

Attitudes Regarding Poverty and Inequality in Great Britain

As with Americans, British citizens also believe that there is a good bit of poverty in their country. In the 2002 British Social Attitudes Survey (BSA), 62 per cent said "there is quite a lot of poverty" in Britain today.[292] Only 35 per cent thought there was "very little." This is consistent with past polls, as a majority ever since 1986 has opted for the "quite a lot" statement. Moreover, the public also believes that the presence of poverty is a problem for society. The Department for the Environment asked people in 2002 how important a number of matters were "for the quality of life, both now and in the future."[293] "Poverty and social inequality" was rated as "very important" by 62 per cent and "fairly important" by 29 per cent. True, these numbers were lower than those recorded for health, education, crime, employment, and air quality, but were higher than for a vast array of other issues.

As for the causes of poverty, British attitudes seem to fall closely in line with those in the United States. Oxfam, the international aid charity, offered this summary:

> The public in the U.K. has tended to be more judgmental about those living in poverty than people in many countries — being more likely to say, for example, that poverty is due to "laziness and lack of will power" rather than to "injustice in our society."[294]

Inequality strikes an even greater chord. In the 2002 BSA, people were asked, "Thinking of income levels generally in Britain today, would you say that the gap between those with high incomes and those with low incomes is too large, about right, or too small?" A full 82 per cent chose "too large." Moreover, the sentiment crossed occupational groupings and political party affiliation. For instance, 79 per cent of the top occupational class (managerial and professional) said the gap was too large. While 88 per cent of Labour supporters thought the

292. The British Social Attitudes data are analyzed in Alison Park, John Curtice, Katrina Thomson, Lindsey Jarvis, and Catherine Bromley, *British Social Attitudes: The 20th Report* (London: Sage, 2003). The raw are available from the UK Data Archive at the University of Essex. All subsequent poll data are from the various BSAs unless otherwise noted.

293. Department for the Environment, Food and Rural Affairs, Survey of Public Attitudes to Quality of Life and the Environment, 2002. The poll was restricted to England, but 83 per cent of the UK population live there.

294. Oxfam, "The Facts about Poverty in the UK." Available at oxfamgb.org/ukpp/poverty/thefacts. htm#8. See also Peter Golding, "Poor Attitudes" in Saul Becker, ed., *Windows of Opportunity: Public Policy and the Poor* (London: Child Poverty Action Group, 1991).

gap was too large, it is important that 71 per cent of those who identify with the Conservatives thought so, as well.

Another BSA question from 2002 was, "How much do you agree or disagree that ordinary working people do not get their fair share of the nation's wealth?" Over six in ten, 62 per cent, agreed with this proposition. Two questions from the 1999 survey provide another window into popular attitudes. Table 8-8 shows what categories people think are underpaid and overpaid. Pay for skilled factory workers attracts almost universal disapproval, but that for unskilled factory workers is not far behind. Conversely, corporate chairmen's compensation finds little approval with the public. These patterns, incidentally, held constant when the same question was asked in 1987 and 1992. Also in 1999 people were asked what they thought an unskilled factory worker and the chairman of a corporation actually earned and then what they thought each should earn. Unskilled workers were believed to average £10,000 a year and the chairman £125,000. On the preference side, people thought unskilled workers should receive £12,000 and the corporate chair £75,000. Two things are noteworthy. First, the public would raise the pay of the unskilled but lower that of the corporate chairs. Second, they believe a gap of 12.5 to 1 exists, but they would lower that to 6.25.

TABLE 8-8

WHO IS OVER-AND UNDERPAID IN BRITAIN, 1999

Occupation	% who see it as underpaid	% who see it as overpaid
Unskilled factory worker	76	3
Skilled factory worker	99	1
Doctor (GP)	42	20
Cabinet minister	12	67
Chairman of a corporation	5	80

GOVERNMENTAL RESPONSIBILITIES

British political culture has always supported stronger governmental interference in the economy than would find favor in the United States. Also, general levels of trust in government are always higher in Britain than in the United States.[295] Thus, when people view something as a problem, there is less mistrust of governmental efforts to redress it than in the United States. There is little survey data, therefore, about governmental efforts to alleviate poverty per se; since at least the first decade of the twentieth century a legitimate role for government in this area has largely been assumed. Inequality, though, is more problematic, and here there are specific data.

British people do not see inequality as inevitable or good for Britain. In the 1999 BSA, 54 per cent disputed the idea that "large differences in income are necessary for Britain's prosperity." Mrs. Thatcher and her acolytes have obviously not carried the day, here. Further, 73 per cent of those queried in the 1998 survey agreed that it was "definitely" or "probably" government's responsibility to reduce inequality. Only 17 per cent thought it was not. In 2000, 58 per cent agreed with the statement, "It is the responsibility of the government to reduce the difference in income between people with high incomes and those with low incomes." (In 1999, 65 per cent agreed.)

ATTITUDES TOWARD THE CURRENT SYSTEM

While Mrs. Thatcher repeatedly attacked the postwar consensus that surrounded the welfare state, she did not manage to destroy the political backing it enjoys. Most likely this is because the British system has always had a broader scope than the American one. A much larger percentage of the population, consequently, enjoys the benefits of welfare state programs, insulating them from the type of political hostility routinely mounted in the past against AFDC. However, there has been a growing disquiet among the public, with clear signs that all is not well. Many people seem to feel that the system, at least the cash benefits parts of it, are not administered fairly.

For example, an enormously high 81 per cent agreed (in 2002) that "large numbers of people" were falsely claming benefits. Only 14 per cent disagreed, down from 25 per cent in 1983. A MORI poll asked in 2002, "To what extent do you agree or disagree that other people seem to get *unfair* priority over you when it comes to public services and state benefits?" Eighteen per cent definitely agreed, 22 per cent agreed and 23 per cent tended to agree. (Asylum-seekers and immigrants were seen as the chief culprits when these respondents were asked who was getting the priority.) Then, in 2002 the public were asked whether they agreed or disagreed that, "Most people on the dole are fiddling in one way or another." Thirty-eight per cent of the public registered their agreement while

---

295. In 1998, 57 per cent of UK citizens said they basically trusted the state whereas only 40 per cent of Americans did. Philip Norton, *The British Polity*, 4th ed. (New York: Longmans, 2001), 31.

only 28 per cent disagreed. Previously, the plurality had been the other way around. Most likely the awareness of attitudes such as these is what led the Labour government to take several well-publicized steps to fight benefit fraud.

Three other questions shed more light on the public's attitudes. There are, the public believes, important disincentives built into the benefit system. When asked to estimate the benefits for the unemployed, most respondents gave an inflated figure; however, even when told the actual amount, a majority still said recipients were poor or very hard up. The sheer monetary amounts paid therefore do not seem to elicit hostility. But when asked whether or not "If welfare benefits weren't so generous, people would learn to stand on their own two feet," a strong 44-30 per cent plurality agreed. Finally, people believe that there is no shortage of jobs and that the unemployed could find one if they looked very hard. Nearly two-thirds, 65 per cent, agreed that, "Around here, most unemployed people could find a job if they really wanted one," three times the number that disagreed.

Historically, there has not been much conflict in Britain over work versus staying home regarding lone parents who are benefit recipients. The unemployed were usually seen as male breadwinners while women were viewed as playing the more traditional role. Thus, it is not surprising that the New Deal for Lone Parents does not have a compulsory work requirement. However, these attitudes may be in the process of changing. For example, in 1989, 28 per cent agreed that, "A man's job is to earn money; a woman's job is to look after the home and family."[296] By 2002, though, that had dropped to 17 per cent. In a similar vein, in 1989, 64 per cent agreed that "Women should stay at home when there is a child under school age." But by 2002, that had fallen to 48 per cent. Interestingly, too, in the MORI poll cited earlier about people receiving unfair advantages in public services and state benefits, lone parents came in third when people were asked who was receiving unjust priority (although the number was still only eight per cent). It may be, then, that political pressure will soon build to force more benefit recipients, including lone parents, who are mostly women, into paid work.

---

296. Rosemary Crompton, Michaela Brockman, and Richard Wiggins, "A Woman's Place . . . Employment and Family Life for Men and Women," in Park, *et al. British Social Attitudes*, 164.

POLICIES TO FIGHT POVERTY AND INEQUALITY

Support for the minimum wage has not been measured nearly as long as in the U.S., obviously. However, the British results that we do have are strikingly similar to those found in the U.S. In 1999, 88 per cent of the public said they agreed that, "It is right that the law should set a minimum wage so that no employer can pay their workers too little." More than half, 53 per cent, strongly agreed, while a paltry six per cent disagreed. People simply do not believe what the economists cited in Chapter 6 continue to say regarding job losses. The statement that "There should be no minimum wage because it will mean that too many low paid workers will lose their jobs" got the assent of only 16 per cent, with a resounding 61 per cent disagreeing.

While we have no question regarding the living wage that is parallel to that asked in the United States, other survey data can be coupled with this overwhelming support for a minimum wage to make a good case that the British public would stand behind a living wage proposal. The argument is indirect, but I believe convincing.

Look, first, at attitudes toward expenditure. The British public is patently not opposed to paying higher taxes for public services. They were asked in 2002, "Suppose the government had to choose between the three options on this card. Which do you think it should choose? 1) Reduce taxes and spend less on health, education and social benefits; 2) Keep taxes and spending on theses services at the same level as now; 3) Increase taxes and spend more on health, education and social benefits." In line with past surveys, 63 per cent selected the third option.

However, another question — "The government should spend more money on welfare benefits for the poor, even if it leads to higher taxes" — provides one glimpse into which of the three priorities of the first question fall by the wayside. Only 45 per cent favor this. Moreover, examining where people would want extra public spending to go, welfare state benefits fare badly, as shown in Table 8-9. Additionally, when asked: "Would you like to see more or less government spending on benefits for the following groups," it is clear that single parents and the unemployed are at the bottom of the list. Note, though, that people with children who work but receive low incomes still command wide respect and trigger a willingness to do something about their plight. It seems clear, in short, that the British public is becoming exasperated with the benefit system, and are unwilling to pay increased taxes to support it — unless the magic word "work" is used.

TABLE 8-9
FIRST AND SCEOND PRIORITIES FOR THE ALLOCATION OF EXTRA GOVERNMENT SPENDING, 2002

Spending category	% who want more spent here as first or second priority
Health	79
Education	63
Police and prisons	14
Public transport	13
Housing	10
Roads	6
Social security	5
Help for industry	4
Defense	3
Overseas aid	2

Note: "Social security" connotes the entire benefit system, not only old age pensions.

TABLE 8-10
GROUPS FAVORED FOR MORE GOVERNMENT BENEFITS SPENDING, 1998

Group	% who believe government should spend more on their benefits
People who care for the sick or disabled	82
Disabled people who cannot work	72
Retired people	71
Parents who work on very low incomes	68
Single parents	34
Unemployed people	22

Public attitudes on government-sponsored redistribution can be read several ways. The assertion, "Government should redistribute income from the better-off to those who are less well-off," won the endorsement of only 39 per cent. However, that was more than opposed it, 36 per cent. A trend line, though, demonstrates that since 1994 the percentage support has been falling steadily. Any direct redistribution, therefore, is on thin political ice. In fact, Labour ministers had studiously avoided using the term, despite its respectable party lineage, until 2002. In September of that year, Tony Blair said that the party's goal "must be a Britain in which we continue to redistribute power, wealth, and opportunity to the many, not the few, to combat poverty and social exclusion, to deliver public services people can trust and take down the barriers that hold people back."[297] This seems to be something of a catch-all phrase, and uttered as it was in the days before the annual party conference, it was probably designed to be a bit of a "something for everybody in the party" line.

While it is doubtful there is much public support for direct redistribution, two other questions provide some important clues as to what people do think. In 2000, 75 per cent said it was definitely or probably "government's responsibility to provide a job for everyone who wants one." This is not to say they believe such a task would be simple. Only 15 per cent thought that it would be easy "these days for any government . . . to ensure that everyone who wants a job" to have one. Sixty-seven per cent acknowledged that it would be difficult. On another front, if we look at public willingness to fund the new tax credit for low-income workers, we see the value attached to work as well as the concern the public has for children. Table 8-11 makes it clear that lone parents who work have a special place in the public's estimation, and its desire to put that support into financial terms. Couples without children come nowhere close.

TABLE 8-11	
PEOPLE WHO DESERVE TO HAVE THEIR WAGES "TOPPED UP" BY GOVERNMENT, 2000	
Group	% who believe they should have their wages "topped up"
Lone parents	70
Couples with children	61
Couples without children	27

297. *Guardian*, September 18, 2002.

SUMMING UP BRITISH ATTITUDES

If we piece all these bits together, the following propositions can be defended:

1. The British public has a growing skepticism about the current bene-fits system, and is unwilling to see more funds poured into it.

2. They believe most of the unemployed could find a job if they looked hard enough.

3. Work is highly valued.

4. A minimum wage commands extremely high backing.

Now, if these are all correct, and especially given the willingness to spend more for those on low income who work, is it not reasonable to believe that a living wage would enjoy very strong backing from the public? Until we have a survey asking that question directly, this will have to do.

9. THE RISE AND FALL OF THE MINIMUM WAGE

As industrialization spread throughout the west in the late nineteenth century, it created deplorable conditions along with vastly increased wealth. Though poverty had long existed, of course, the new economic order seemed especially harsh. Moreover, by concentrating many of the poor in the new sprawling cities, it gave a renewed urgency to their circumstances. Social reformers everywhere took up their cause, and in the end fashioned three strategies to alleviate poverty and misery: public assistance, social insurance, and higher wages.

Public assistance had a lineage dating from England's experience with the Elizabethan Poor Law. In time, English public authorities focused on "classification."

The historian of the British welfare state, Derek Fraser, put it this way:

> Essentially the Elizabethan Poor Law identified three main groups to be dealt with. The impotent poor (the aged, the chronic sick, the blind, the lunatic), who really needed institutional relief, were to be accommodated in "poor houses" or "almshouses." The able-bodied were to be set to work on hemp or some other appropriate material and for this a "house of correction" (really a workhouse), not at first residential, was to be established. As a corollary to this, children in need of relief were to be apprenticed to a trade so that they would become useful, self-supporting citizens. Finally, the able-bodied who absconded and preferred the open road or the persistent idler who refused to work were to be punished in this "house of correction." In other words the ideal was for three different sorts of treatment for three different sorts of pauper.[298]

The second category was at the heart of the policy, for they were felt to be the "deserving poor," temporarily in poverty through some circumstance beyond their control. Developing the criteria for eligibility, though, determining the amount to be paid to approved claimants, and developing administrative machinery proved no less vexing than similar programs today. Whatever its defects, the outlines of the policy — locating the deserving poor and providing them with some minimal assistance — remained in place for over two hundred years, and were transported to the American colonies. Into the nineteenth century, most American states had some form of "outdoor relief" designed to accomplish the same objectives.

Social insurance, pioneered in Bismarck's Germany, was modeled on private insurance. People — either everyone or some targeted group — would pay into a government-operated insurance fund. When a particular malady, usually unemployment, sickness, or old age, befell someone, he or she could then "draw" on the fund. This had the great advantage of not adding to general tax levies, being relatively simple to administer (since eligibility was usually established), and removing the stigma often associated with public assistance. Since it covered the major causes of income reduction, it would at least ease poverty temporarily.

Inasmuch as wages were the chief source of income, though, securing adequate wages was an inherently promising way to attack poverty. When wages were so low that subsistence was barely, or perhaps not even, possible, workers and their families would remain destitute. One obvious route to higher wages was the promise of collective bargaining through unions. In many industries, however, organizing unions was well nigh impossible. Female workers, disdained by the male union ethos, unskilled workers, and immigrants posed special problems when it came to developing viable unions. A legally mandated minimum was the only practicable route to securing a wage base for these workers.

In the later nineteenth and early twentieth centuries social insurance and minimum wage legislation held a high place in reform efforts in both the United States and the United Kingdom. For many, in fact, minimum wages were thought to be the centerpiece of what came later to be called "social policy." Over time, however, more quickly in Britain than in the United States but eventually in both, social insurance and public assistance — and more the latter than the former — replaced minimum wages as the major components of social policy. In

---

298. Derek Fraser, *The Evolution of the British Welfare State* (London: Macmillan, 1973), 30.

the 1940s in Britain and the 1960s in the United States, minimum wage policy slipped to the bottom shelf of efforts to address poverty. In its place, only partially by design, arose a vast system of public assistance. By the 1990s this system of public assistance had become all but indefensible, as its glaring defects were painfully obvious. In both Britain and the United States, far-reaching reforms were enacted that substantially cut back on a variety of social assistance programs. Critics wielded too broad a brush, however, equating public assistance with all efforts to alleviate poverty, thereby delegitimizing social policy in general. What is needed now is a return to the original Progressive program and a resurrection of the living wage as the central anti-poverty strategy.

This chapter tells the story of the rise and then the decline of the minimum wage. The following one turns to the fate of "welfare reform" in the 1990s.

THE AMERICAN MINIMUM WAGE: BIRTH TO THE GREAT SOCIETY

If we want to reach back to the taproot, the American minimum wage can be traced to the era before the Civil War. Nascent working-class reformers argued that the slow destruction of the independent artisan and his replacement by workers drawing wages from an employer was creating a stratum of "wage slaves." Since the producer, the owner of the firm, was gaining a profit from each hour the employee worked, the latter was being denied the full fruits of his labor. He was, therefore, some fraction a "slave." Not only was this inherently unjust, the refrain went, it undermined the personal independence necessary for republican politics.

After the Civil War, according to historian Lawrence Glickman, a consumerist view replaced the emphasis on the producer side of the equation. "The defining concept was the notion of 'just reward,' rather than 'exact equivalence.'"[299] Workers needed, according to this view, adequate compensation for their toils, adequate being defined as that which would secure a decent life for them and their families. Economic self-sufficiency, and its concomitant, political independence, was now to be measured by the standard of living that the worker's wage could purchase. "It was only a short leap," Glickman says, "from the concept of the 'just reward' to 'just wages,' and from 'just wages' to 'living wages.'"[300]

---

299. Lawrence Glickman, *A Living Wage: American Workers and the Making of Consumer Society* (Ithaca, NY: Cornell University Press, 1997), 26.

The idea of a living wage as the appropriate strategy of avoiding, as befitted the vocabulary of the time, destruction of the role of family breadwinner for men and prostitution for women, merged easily into the Progressive movement.[301] Although a broad movement with many countercurrents, its central thrust was a search for ways to soften the ill effects of late nineteenth-century industrialization. Merging religious indignation — Protestant, Catholic, and Jewish — with careful analysis of political economy, the Progressives argued for a significant number of reforms.

On the social welfare front, charitable activities and public assistance were certainly not ignored by the Progressives. Indeed, private charities grew to record levels and the system of public, state and local that is, relief expanded as well. In 1913, Kansas City became the first city to consolidate disparate relief programs under a Board of Welfare, and it was not long before other cities did likewise.[302] Much of the emphasis during this period, as is often the case, was driven by a concern for the fate of children. A White House Conference on Dependent Children was held in 1909, and while its immediate impact was slight, it did raise the profile of children's issues, and historians generally credit it with leading to the creation of the United States Children's Bureau in 1912.[303] Citing the needs of children, Missouri planted an important seed in 1911 when it enacted the first "widow's pension" statute, allowing counties to make cash payments to widows who were "full-time mothers."

Nevertheless, public assistance was less important to the Progressives than social insurance and minimum wages. After Bismarck led newly-unified Germany into the social insurance field, agitation for similar programs spread elsewhere. Isaac Rubinow (an actuary) and Henry Seager (a Columbia University economist) penned the two most comprehensive American treatises on the subject, while the American Association for Labor Legislation (AALL), founded in 1906, provided much of the lobbying. Rubinow's treatise, entitled *Social Insurance: With Special Reference to American Conditions*,[304] advocated workmen's compensation, health insurance, old age pensions, and

300. Glickman, *Living Wage*, 26.

301. The literature on Progressivism is vast. A good introduction, emphasizing the transnational character of the movement, is Daniel Rodgers, *Atlantic Crossings: Social Politics in a Progressive Age* (Cambridge, MA: Harvard University Press, 1998).

302. Michael Katz, *In the Shadow of the Poor House* (New York: Basic Books, 1986), 154.

303. Walter I. Trattner, *From Poor Law to Welfare State: A History of Social Welfare in America*, 5th ed. (New York: Basic Books, 1994), 216.

304. Isaac Rubinow, *Social Insurance: With Special Reference to American Conditions* (New York: Holt, 1913).

unemployment insurance. Seager's work, *Social Insurance: A Program for Social Reform*,[305] covered identical themes, and urged a broad-based, integrated program. The AALL enjoyed early successes in the workmen's compensation field, with 43 states adopting programs between 1909 and 1920. A campaign for state health insurance programs faltered, though, when opponents successfully labeled it "Made in Germany" as World War I approached. Securing old age pensions and unemployment insurance at the state level proved equally difficult, but the discussion never died out. When the Roosevelt administration began laying the groundwork for the Social Security Act of 1935, the seasoned advocates of social insurance played a major part in hashing out the details of the policy proposals.[306] Both unemployment insurance and old age pensions now bore a national stamp (although the unemployment insurance program was to be administered, as it still is, by the states). Sadly, though, Roosevelt decided to omit health insurance proposals from the bill.

Australia is the home of minimum wage legislation, with Victoria adopting the first ever law in 1896. It applied to only a limited number of industries and its level was set by separate boards for each industry. Nevertheless, its scope steadily expanded, and it was made national when the Australian states became a nation in 1901. Its influence on reformers in others countries was huge.

American Progressives put great stock in the possibility of a statutory minimum wage lifting most families out of poverty. Take Father John Ryan, for example, a Catholic priest and economist. He wrote a much-discussed book in 1906 entitled *The Living Wage: Its Ethical and Economic Aspects*.[307] He spoke of both the excess profits that firms accumulated which would enable them to pay a higher wage and Christian, mostly Catholic, social teachings. After establishing the economic practicability and the moral necessity for a living wage, he turned to how it might be brought about. Showing the defects in any kind of voluntary plan, he contended that only a governmentally enforced minimum wage would work.

Even Henry Seager, who put such great hope in social insurance, thought a minimum wage would buttress his program.

---

305. Henry Seager, *Social Insurance: A Program of Social Reform* (New York: Macmillan, 1910).

306. The best brief book on this episode is still Roy Lubove, *The Struggle for Social Security* (Cambridge, MA: Harvard University Press, 1967).

307. John Ryan, *The Living Wage: Its Ethical and Economic Aspects* (New York: Macmillan, 1906).

Any program of social reform for wage earners may be analyzed into two parts. One part aims to protect them in the continued enjoyment of their present standards of living. The other endeavors to assist them to advance these standards to even higher levels. The proposal to establish minimum, or living, rates of wages by law for individuals and classes that are now so unfortunate as to fail to secure them is the link which connects these two parts into a consistent and comprehensive program.[308]

A minimum wage was expected to accomplish a great deal. Learned Hand's 1915 essay is only of many that could be cited:

It is a means of education, a step forward in the standard of living. Much will depend upon the way the increase is used, but it has been long recognized that a sudden rise in the standard of living may alone be enough to raise the class which gets it, since it reacts upon their own mental attitude towards life. Some relief from the oppression of physical privations, some security for a future, some provision against disease and unemployment, may so change the workman's approach to his daily routine as to make the increased wage a cheap expedient, even when viewed in the most mechanical way. The result stands in trial, not in dialectic; but we must insist upon the reasonable expectation of those who view it hopefully, and we must seek to advance it, at least until it has been demonstrated to be false.[309]

When advocates of the minimum wage turned from theory to political action, they faced several severe constraints. A major one was the coolness of unions to the idea.[310] While workers had long argued for a living wage to provide them with an "American standard of living," they were suspicious of governmental wage fixing. Their fear was that a legal minimum would become a maximum. It was not an entirely baseless worry, inasmuch as even some reformers had not been clear about the differences among "minimum wages," "living wages," and "subsistence wages." Plus, there were subtexts, some historians believe. White male unions harbored substantial prejudice, so the argument goes, against women, African-Americans and other ethnic minorities (such as the Chinese), and recent immigrants. Whatever the real reason, minimum wage proponents were denied a significant potential ally.

Furthermore, those who would gain from a minimum wage were hardly in a position to exert political influence, even if they had been so inclined. They were by definition the worst off among the population, limiting any possibility

---

308. Henry Seager, "The Minimum Wage as Part of a Program for Social Reform," *Annals of the American Academy of Political and Social Science* 38 (1913), 3.

309. Learned Hand, "The Hope of the Minimum Wage," *The New Republic*, November 20, 1915, 67.

310. The only major exception was John Mitchell of the United Mine Workers.

they would devote time or resources to political activity. Moreover, they had no way to secure access to the political system: no campaign contributions to make, no network of connections to the seats of power, no organizations to mobilize voters.

Another obstacle was contemporary constitutional jurisprudence. The Supreme Court had deployed a two-pronged approach to making laissez-faire economics very nearly synonymous with constitutional law. The commerce clause, which grants Congress the power to regulate interstate commerce, was construed in such a way that production was not a part of commerce.[311] Factory conditions, then, were beyond the reach of Congress, lying within the jurisdiction of the states. Then, using the Fourteenth Amendment's due process clause,[312] the Supreme Court had created a "liberty of contract," which severely restricted state action. People had not just a general legal right, but a constitutional right, to enter into any contract they wished. Any state regulation of this "right" was therefore invalid. Minimum wage backers and law professors spent many pages searching for a way around these barriers. The very number of these articles is, at the same time, one testament to how much attention minimum wage policy received.

Then, of course, there was the vociferous opposition of many employers. Not only were they opposed to minimum wage policies specifically, but to what they represented. If government could regulate the wage bargain struck between employers and employees, by implication it could regulate virtually any aspect of business operations. Consequently, any proposal for minimum wage legislation served as a lightning rod for attack.

It is somewhat surprising, therefore, given the usual models of politics that grant such power to established interests, that minimum wage advocates did as well as they did.[313] It is a tribute, in the end, not only to their dedication and political acumen, but to the backing, even if largely latent, that the policy must have enjoyed among the public at large. As one indication of such public support, when in 1912 a constitutional convention in Ohio submitted a proposal authorizing a minimum wage to a referendum, it passed 354,588 to 189,728.[314]

---

311. The case was *U. S. v. E. C. Knight Co* 156 U. S. 1 (1895).

312. No State ... shall deprive any person of life, liberty, or property, without due process of law.

313. David B. Robertson has argued that the fragmentation of American political institutions also aided business interests in checkmating labor legislation. David B. Robertson, *Capital and State: The Battle for American Labor Markets from the Civil War to the New Deal* (Lanham, MD: Rowman and Littlefield, 2000).

Who supplied the political energy for the minimum wage movement? In common with most of Progressivism, the minimum wage coalition's sociological profile was almost entirely upper middle class. Academics, religious figures, leaders of women's organizations, and assorted reformers combined to press the issue, mostly in the states. One of the major pillars in this effort was the National Consumers League.[315] Born in New York City in 1890, it was composed of relatively well-off women who were concerned about conditions in the city's sweatshops. Workers toiled exceedingly long hours in these facilities in unsanitary conditions for dismal wages. Their first strategy amounted to a consumer boycott of firms which marketed products made in sweatshops. Finding the enforcement of their standards impossible, they fished about for alternative approaches. A legally set minimum wage was the obvious answer, especially inasmuch as Australia and then New Zealand had proved the program practicable.

Reformers began a determined effort in several states. In 1912, they convinced the Massachusetts legislature to enact the first American minimum wage statute. Its coverage was limited to women, not only as a practical concession to union opposition, but in hopes that it might allow the measure to pass constitutional muster. Louis Brandeis had recently convinced the Supreme Court that Oregon could regulate the hours worked by women in the interest of protecting their health. The measure was an example of the exercise of a state's "police power," the authority to protect its citizens' health, morals, and safety. If the minimum wage could therefore be sold as a method of helping women lead a more healthy life, then perhaps the judges would not void it under the "liberty of contract" doctrine.[316] The law also had limited scope, in that it applied to only selected industries. The wage level was to be set by tripartite boards, which were ordered to consider both the needs of the employee and the financial condition of the business firms involved. Finally, its enforcement mechanism was merely the publication of the names of firms which *complied* with the minimum wages established by the boards. Although manifestly weak and largely incapable of being enforced, it was a first step.

---

314. Willis Nordlund, *The Quest for a Living Wage: A History of the Federal Minimum Wage Program* (Westport, CT: Greenwood Press, 1997), 13.

315. The work of the League, and of women generally, is ably covered in Viven Hart, *Bound by Our Constitution: Women, Workers, and the Minimum Wage* (Princeton, NJ: Princeton University Press, 1994), especially chapters 4 and 5.

316. See Thomas Reed Powell, "The Constitutional Issues in Minimum Wage Legislation," *Minnesota Law Review* 2 (1917), 1-21.

Reform movements in other states managed to obtain stronger laws. By 1919, thirteen states — Oregon, Utah, Washington, Nebraska, Minnesota, Colorado, California, Wisconsin, Kansas, Arkansas, Arizona, North Dakota, and Texas — and Congress acting for the District of Columbia had adopted minimum wage laws. Only Nebraska copied the anemic publicity enforcement strategy of the Massachusetts law. In the remaining states, a variety of fines and prison terms for violators were adopted, along with an occasional right for the employee to bring a suit for illegally denied back wages.

Oregon's statute is especially interesting in that it shifted the ground for determining the wage level. Rather than considering the needs of both employers and employees, it focused exclusively on the latter. The statute provided that, "if [the employer] chooses to take the benefit [the worker's labor], he must bear the burden," and later defined the "benefit" as the cost of the woman producing her labor. While the central goal of the minimum wage legislation was protecting the worker from debilitating conditions, the state legislature said it was also to protect ethical employers from their unscrupulous competitors. The state hoped, in the words of the law's defenders in court, to act "in the interest of the fair employer."[317]

Although it has to be discounted to the same degree as all government proclamations, the 1916 report of the chair of Oregon's Industrial Welfare Commission (which administered the minimum wage law) provides an interesting glimpse into the range of problems the policy was designed to address. They included "economic evils," such as "diminished" powers of production and consumption, along with inefficient workers; "social evils," such as disease, low educational standards, and substandard morals; "domestic evils," such as family disintegration and parental neglect; "individual demoralization," including the lowering of ambition and "deterioration of physique"; and "national weakness," such as the "sapping and decay of patriotism," and leaving citizens unfit for national defense.[318] Hyperbole aside, it is safe to say that reformers expected the minimum wage to be a significant policy innovation that would contribute markedly to a more healthy economy and society.

As World War I drew to a close, minimum wage advocates were confident new advances could be made. South Dakota was added to the states with a statute in 1923. However, the minimum wage soon ran into a judicial roadblock in the case of *Adkins v. Children's Hospital*, handed down also in 1923.[319] The case

---

317. Nordlund, *Quest for a Living Wage*, 15.
318. Quoted in Nordlund, *Quest for a Living Wage*, 15.

successfully challenged the constitutionality of the District of Columbia's minimum wage law; but, decided as it was on the basis of "liberty of contract," its shadow fell over state minimum wage laws as well. Criticism of the decision echoed across the Progressive field. Arizona's governor said that the court's reasoning "comes close to bordering on the ridiculous."[320] Henry Seager felt that given "the present trend of opinion and teaching in the law schools of the country and . . . the gradual revival of progressive thinking . . . in every section there is good ground for hoping that the next appointees to the Supreme Bench will share the enlightened views" of the dissenters rather than the court majority.[321] This, it should be noted, was during Calvin Coolidge's presidency. Interestingly, though, only a few direct challenges were made to the state laws in wake of the decision, probably since most were being emasculated by not having the level raised significantly, if at all.

Dismayed but not silenced by this setback, minimum wage advocates continued to work.[322] The proposal never died out, therefore, and when the Depression struck in 1929, its backers returned to the public arena.

Agitation for challenging the Supreme Court's excessively narrow interpretation of the Constitution by passing new state minimum wage laws spread. This policy was pressed even during the crisis of relief set off by the onset of the Great Depression. Probably few supporters of minimum wages opposed public assistance payments to the unemployed. However, they continued to press minimum wage legislation at the same time. In 1932, the National Consumers League drafted a model bill, supported by the incoming president and his secretary-of-labor-to-be, Frances Perkins. Seven states soon adopted the measure. (Incidentally, Perkins also supported a wage and hour bill and social insurance, and obtained Roosevelt's backing for both of these before she took the labor post.)

By the time Franklin D. Roosevelt convened his "Brain Trust" to plan for economic recovery, the role of a minimum wage in pumping new purchasing power into the economy was placed alongside its role in lessening want. George Paulsen, in his careful study of the origins of the federal minimum wage, writes that,

---

319. 261 U.S. 525 (1923). An interesting and informative contemporary analysis of the case is John Ryan, *The Supreme Court and the Minimum Wage* (New York: Paulist Press, 1923).

320. Quoted in Nordlund, *Quest for a Living Wage*, 24.

321. Henry Seager, "The Minimum Wage — What Next?" *Survey* 50 (1923), 216.

322. This period is covered in Rodolf Brodha, "Minimum Wage Legislation in the United States," *International Labour Review* 17 (1928), 24-50.

Roosevelt and his advisers looked upon labor as a key element in any recovery program. For both economic and humanitarian reasons, they accepted the need to improve the purchasing power and living standards of poorly paid workers.[323]

The president's first initiative was the National Industrial Recovery Act (NIRA). As finally enacted by Congress, the statute provided for business groups to draft codes of fair competition, which would then be promulgated by the president and have the force of law. A central part of each of the codes, at the insistence of the White House, was to be the President's Reemployment Agreement, which set a minimum weekly wage of $12-15.

The Supreme Court declared the NIRA unconstitutional in 1935 on two grounds: that it exceeded Congress power under the commerce clause, and that it delegated too much legislative power to the executive branch.[324] Nevertheless, two important points need to be made. First, the minimum wage was the first anti-poverty policy adopted by the New Deal. In fact, the 1938 Fair Labor Standards Act, the federal minimum wage law, simply re-enacted the minimum wage section of the NIRA's framework code. Second, the minimum wage provisions were by far the most popular parts of the NIRA. Indicatively, in 1936, 70 per cent of the public supported a constitutional amendment allowing minimum wages.[325] But it is the comments made by workers that are most telling. Two examples point to not only the economic side of the NIRA's minimum wages, but the more intangible social and political aspects as well.[326]

Our life is no bed of roses because that ain't the way it is for workers yet but it's better for us than ever I seen it and I been in a factory 9 years since I was 15.

The most surprising day ever seen in this place was yesterday when the boss was ordered to pay us the code rate. . . You can guess the money is handy. But there is something more than the money. There is knowing that the working man don't stand alone against the bosses and their smart lawyers and all their tricks. There is a government now that cares whether things is fair for us. I tell you that is more than money. It gives you a good feeling instead of all the time burning up because nothing is fair.

---

323. George Paulsen, *A Living Wage for the Forgotten Man: The Quest for Fair Labor Standards, 1933-41* (Selingsgrove, PA: Susquehanna University Press, 1996), 36.

324. *Schechter Poultry Corporation v. United States*, 295 U. S. 495 (1935).

325. Gallup Poll, July 12, 1936.

326. These and a number of other quotations can be found in M. D. Vincent and Beulah Amidon, "NRA: A Trial Balance," *Survey Graphic*, July 1935, 333-37 and 363-64.

The demise of the NIRA led the Roosevelt administration to turn to other strategies. Some were designed to provide immediate relief and some, largely the social insurance programs, were to provide a more stable long-term social policy. The most important social insurance legislation was, of course, the Social Security Act of 1935. Its chief components were old-age pensions and unemployment insurance. Buried within it, though, were some small public assistance programs, one of which, Aid to Dependent Children, would eventually become all but the equivalent of "welfare" in the public mind.

Daniel Patrick Moynihan has argued that the assumption of the New Dealers and most subsequent analysts until the 1960s was that these public assistance programs would decline, if not disappear altogether.[327] That is, social insurance, and improved wages (guided I would add, for the New Dealers at least, by a minimum wage), would obviate the need for them. For several of the programs, experience seemed to support this supposition, as the numbers enrolled declined steadily well into the 1960s.

Meanwhile at the state level, reformers continued to push for minimum wage laws. By 1935, fully one third of the states had minimum wage statutes on the books. Some were carry-overs from the earlier spate of adoptions, others more recent. Constitutional challenges continued to come from opponents, however. In 1935, the Supreme Court responded by invalidating New York's new minimum wage law in *Morehead v. Tipaldo*.[328] It was the last judicial victory for minimum wage opponents. In 1937, the justices shifted ground and upheld the Washington minimum wage law (applicable only to women) in the landmark case of *West Coast Hotel Company v. Parrish*.[329] The decision signaled the end of the "liberty of contract" basis for voiding minimum wages, as well as any number of other regulations. It is significant that this major change in judicial outlook regarding a state's ability to regulate commercial life came in a minimum wage case.

Despite focusing effort on social insurance, the Roosevelt administration never retreated from the desire to set a floor on wages (and establish maximum hours as well). As early as 1933, the Department of Labor had sponsored two "Conferences on the Minimum Wage," which pulled together a wide variety of interested parties. These continued even with the end of the NIRA. A sixth conference followed the Supreme Court's ruling in *Tipaldo*, and issued a report

---

327. Daniel Patrick Moynihan, *The Politics of a Guaranteed Income: The Nixon Administration and the Family Assistance Plan* (New York: Random House, 1973), 20.

328. *Morehead v. New York, ex rel. Tipaldo*, 298 U. S. 587 (1936).

329. *West Coast Hotel Co. v. Parrish*, 300 U. S. 379 (1937).

arguing that: "The strong public support of minimum wage legislation testified to by the storm of protests which has arisen against the New York decision strengthened the administrators in their determination to preserve and extend the great social gains made under these laws."[330] A seventh conference, convened after the *West Coast Hotel* decision in 1937, seemed to demonstrate that the administration was finally prepared to move toward recommending a comprehensive federal law.

On May 24, 1937, Roosevelt sent one of his most important messages to Congress, asking for a minimum wage law, accompanied by a restriction on hours and a ban on child labor. Although these latter two items were obviously important, most historians agree that the proposed Fair Labor Standards Act was always primarily a minimum wage law. It was in this message that Roosevelt uttered some of his most oft-quoted lines: "One-third of our population . . . is ill-nourished, ill-clad, and ill-housed." "[A] self-supporting and self-respecting democracy can plead no . . . economic reason for chiseling workers' wages or stretching workers' hours."[331]

The proposal unleashed an intense debate in Congress, as both proponents and opponents rightly viewed it as a landmark in social legislation.[332] The administration continued to press hard for the measure, Roosevelt giving it high priority in his State of the Union address for 1938. Although the Senate passed the bill fairly soon, it took an unexpected victory in a special election in Florida to finally secure the House's approval. Clearly, the administration's partisans did not get all they had hoped for in the new law. The necessary political compromises led to a more restricted coverage than they had wished, and the level of the wage was the same as that of the NIRA codes. Nonetheless, the United States now had in place a national, uniform minimum wage that applied to both men and women.

The Truman and Eisenhower administrations saw little movement in the area of social policy.[333] The minimum wage, however, was never far from the few discussions that were held. Truman badly wanted an increase in the minimum wage (which in the original act had been slated to increase slowly but regularly

---

330. Quoted in Nordlund, *Quest for a Living Wage*, 46.

331. Quoted in Paul Douglas and Joseph Hackman, "The Fair Labor Standards Act I," *Political Science Quarterly* 53 (1939) 493.

332. There are several studies of the passage of the FLSA. A brief and readable one is Jonathan Grossman, "Fair Labor Standards act of 1938: Maximum Struggle for a Minimum Wage," *Monthly Labor Review*, June 1978, 22-30.

333. A brief history of subsequent minimum wage amendments can be found in Jerold Waltman, *The Politics of the Minimum Wage* (Urbana: University of Illinois Press, 2000), chap. 2.

until 1945). During the 1948 presidential campaign, he called for a major increase and expanded coverage. His Secretary of Labor, James Tobin, in his first testimony to Congress put the case for an immediate increase. In the end, Truman won his increase, but he was forced to swallow a bitter pill to get it: an actual reduction in coverage. At the same time, he did obtain approval for a better enforcement regimen, allowing the Department of Labor to bring a suit on the employee's behalf for back wages. The Eisenhower administration, although it is usually portrayed as generally conservative, did push for both an increase in the minimum wage and expanded coverage. The president won an increase in 1955 but expressed disappointment that no new coverage was adopted. Every year after 1955, he proposed new coverage, but secured none.

Enter John F. Kennedy. He is a pivotal figure in the development of the minimum wage, an aspect of his political career that has not received the attention it deserves. In early 1959, he introduced a bill in the Senate to expand coverage even more than the administration's bill of that year did and to simultaneously raise the level of the wage. In the ensuing battle in Congress, Kennedy took the lead for the Democrats. When matters reached a head in the conference committee during the summer of 1960, the issue became entangled in presidential politics. Offered a compromise on the wage level but with no expanded coverage, Kennedy balked. He promised to make his case during the upcoming election, which he did. On several occasions, including the famous televised debate with Richard Nixon, he argued for a higher minimum wage and substantially more coverage.

In December 1960, Kennedy gathered his top aides to lay out his initial legislative program. Five items emerged, and near the top of the list was a higher minimum wage with greater coverage. (The others were federal aid to public schools, hospital insurance for the elderly, housing legislation, and aid to depressed areas.) Notably, no cash-based public assistance program was on the list. Kennedy submitted his minimum wage bill in February 1960, calling for 4.3 million workers to be brought under the law's umbrella and the level of the wage to be increased significantly. The commitment of the president to the bill can be gleaned not only from its prominent place on his agenda, but his intense reaction, reportedly sticking a letter opener into a desk, for example, when a key section on coverage failed in the House by one vote. In the end, Kennedy had to abandon his hoped-for coverage for about 500,000 people (mostly laundry workers) to obtain it for the other 3.8 million. These amendments constitute a watershed, for now the minimum wage reached truly into the mainstream of the American workforce.

Some modest changes were indeed made in public assistance programs during these years. In a 1961 executive order, Kennedy increased food assistance to the poor and with another in 1962 he extended the school lunch program. Modest changes were also made to the ADC program, which had been renamed Aid to Families with Dependent Children. The Public Welfare Amendments of 1962, as they were known, added two-parent families to the eligibility rolls if one was unemployed.[334] Initiated elsewhere, the measure received only half-hearted support from the White House. Clearly, public assistance was not the central poverty fighting strategy of the New Frontier; more jobs at better wages was. In early 1963, Kennedy was devoting more serious attention to poverty, and asked Walter Heller, chairman of the Council of Economic Advisers, to look into the question of poverty and come up with ideas on how to address it. According to one careful study of Kennedy's presidency, in the autumn of 1963 the administration was set to propose new programs for jobs and human services, but not more cash assistance.[335]

Soon after he assumed office, over Christmas week of 1963, Lyndon Johnson began to think about launching a major anti-poverty effort.[336] The term "war on poverty" was coined at a meeting at his Texas ranch during that week. In the State of the Union address on January 8, 1964, he uttered the famous "This administration today, here and now, declares an unconditional war on poverty in America." Soon after, and especially after the resounding Democratic electoral victories that November, a variety of bills were sent to Congress. A plethora of new programs, many grouped under the new Office of Economic Opportunity, spewed forth. Most of them funneled money to state and local governments for various purposes (improved housing, more educational opportunities, and so forth). Medicare was the only new social insurance program, but several of the older ones were made somewhat more generous. While a minimum wage increase eventually passed in 1966, it was a decidedly secondary concern.

In the end, though, events outside government were eclipsing the efforts of both the Kennedy and Johnson administrations. In part, this was tied to the success of the civil rights movement in reaching its legal goals. Under Martin Luther King's leadership, the movement was turning increasing attention to

---

334. Technically, the unemployed parent provision had been added earlier. The 1962 law extended its life. See Charles Noble, *Welfare as We Knew It: A Political History of the American Welfare State* (New York: Oxford University Press, 1996), 92.

335. James N. Giglio, *The Presidency of John F. Kennedy* (Lawrence: University of Kansas Press, 1991), 119-20.

336. Vaughn D. Bornet, *The Presidency of Lyndon B. Johnson* (Lawrence: University of Kansas Press, 1983), 54.

economic issues; when he was assassinated, King was planning the poor people's march on Washington. In larger part, though, it was a change in intellectual orientation among reformers. On the left, there was a growing idea that somehow payments from the public treasury ought to be treated as a "right." Law professor Charles Reich had laid the intellectual foundations for this approach, arguing that such payments were akin to property, and his proposal was quickly picked up by others.[337]

This framework found an agreeable reception among two important groups of people. The first were African-American militants, who were impatient with the pace of reform. The second was professional social workers. Naturally sympathetic to the needs of the poor, they could now feel that they were on "their side" rather than that of the state. A social worker's role, the new ethos held, should be trying to help their "clients" get the maximum benefits "due" them rather than focusing on protecting the public purse and imposing middle-class moral standards. Comfortingly, the approach seemed to march in step with the times, as radicalism became chic.

A book, an organization, and an event are indicative. The book is Frances Fox Piven and Richard Cloward's *Regulating the Poor*. The central thesis of this work is that anti-poverty programs historically and now are really designed not to help the poor but to keep them under control. Given this, the poor must fight back. How?

> In the absence of fundamental economic reforms, therefore, *we take the position that the explosion of the rolls is the true relief reform*, that it should be defended, and expanded. Even now, hundreds of thousands of impoverished families remain who are eligible for assistance but who receive no aid at all.[338] (Emphasis in original.)

The organization was the National Welfare Rights Organization, founded in 1966. Although middle-class reformers formed the organization's leadership cadres, according to Michael Katz "poor black women formed the movement's backbone."[339] Its actual policy successes were modest; however, it is important for what it demonstrates about the new attitude, and how the organization in turn affected the sentiments of public assistance recipients. Katz believes that

---

337. Charles Reich, "The New Property," *Yale Law Journal* 73 (1964), 733-63.
338. Frances Fox Piven and Richard Cloward, *Regulating the Poor: The Functions of Public Welfare* (New York: Vintage, 1971), 348.
339. Katz, *Shadow of the Poor House*, 253.

As an assertion of the strength and competence of poor women; as a demonstration of the potential power in the fusion of race, class, and gender; as a channel for helping poor women transform *their ideas of welfare into entitlement* — aside from its part in expanding welfare benefits and increasing the AFDC rolls — NWRO remains a remarkable and significant episode in American social history.[340] (Emphasis added.)

The event occurred in 1970, when the Senate Finance Committee killed Richard Nixon's Family Assistance Plan (FAP). An interesting amalgam of public assistance and work incentives with a guaranteed income, Nixon had proposed the FAP in 1969. It passed the House, though not without some opposition, and seemed headed for passage in the Senate. While many conservatives in the Senate and elsewhere opposed the plan, in the end it was liberals who destroyed the plan in the Finance Committee. Their grounds were that the payments were inadequate and that it contained work provisions.

The result of the change in outlook is easily demonstrated. In New York City, in 1965 there were 531,000 people on the welfare rolls; by 1970 that number had climbed to 1,165,000.[341] Lest it be believed that New York City was unique, Figure 9-1 depicts the rapid rise in the number of people nationally on the AFDC rolls during the 1960s and early 1970s. Figure 9-2 shows the same trend as a percentage of the population. This, it should be remembered, occurred during a period of low unemployment and strong economic growth. Furthermore, the minimum wage reached its highest level ever in 1968, measured in constant dollars. Daniel Patrick Moynihan put it this way: "The number of persons classified as poor in the span 1959 to 1968 decreased by 36 per cent. The number of public-assistance recipients rose 41 per cent."[342] Public assistance was now the policy of choice for reformers, and its relative place in the budget demonstrates how much success they had. Speaking of the Kennedy-Johnson years, Vaughn Bornet notes that, "While increases in social insurance were relatively modest, public assistance more than doubled during prosperous times. The [AFDC] program expended $1.5 billion at the outset, but $3.6 billion at the close."[343] From then until the 1990s, public assistance was, in the public's mind, identical to social policy.

In broadest terms, the history of American social policy had, up until the 1970s, three phases. The first, stretching from the colonial era to the late nineteenth century, saw only public relief to the "deserving poor" accompanied

---

340. Katz, *Shadow of the Poor House*, 254.
341. Cited in Moynihan, *Politics of a Guaranteed Income*, 26.
342. Moynihan, *Politics of a Guaranteed Income*, 39
343. Bornet, *Presidency of Lyndon Johnson*, 233.

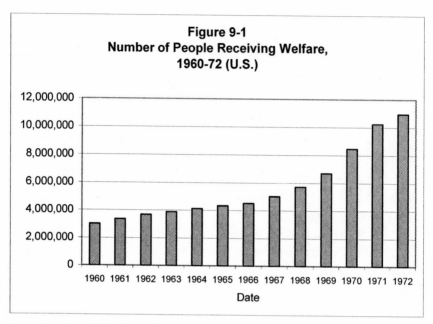

Source: Department of Health and Human Services

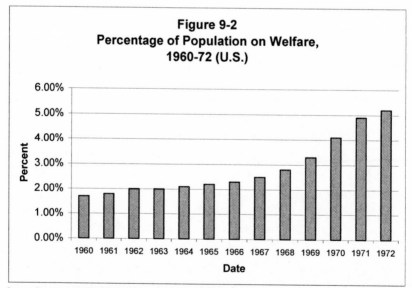

Source: Department of Health and Human Services

by the efforts of private charities. The second, from the late nineteenth century to roughly the late 1950s, saw reformers push hardest for a combination of a minimum wage and social insurance. During the third, from the early 1960s to the early 1990s, public assistance was the centerpiece of social policy, complemented by social insurance. The minimum wage was, at best, an afterthought.

Piven and Cloward and the NWRO thus won the war, temporarily at least. But they also assured the ultimate demise of America's largest public assistance program, for what they preached was neither morally, logically, nor politically tenable.

THE MINIMUM WAGE IN BRITAIN: FROM BIRTH TO *Beveridge*

The operation of the Elizabethan Poor Law waxed and waned through the years. Administratively, the statutes placed most of the actual decisions under the control of the haphazard English system of local governments. The local justices of the peace (a combination administrative and judicial official) appointed boards of overseers, who both levied the necessary taxes on property and distributed the funds to the poor. Since each area was only responsible for its local paupers, much effort was spent trying to send claimants elsewhere. A special act had to be passed in 1662 to establish uniform rules for residency, but these were widely evaded. In 1795, local authorities began a policy of supplementing low wages in order to bring the destitute up to subsistence level (called the Speenhamland system). Although much criticized later, it can be viewed as an early form of minimum wage and family allowances.

In 1832, a Royal Commission was appointed to inquire into the operation of the Poor Law and make recommendations. Its 1834 report laid the groundwork for the Poor Law Amendment Act of 1834. Aimed chiefly at reducing the rate of local property taxation, it established the workhouse system. Workhouses were to be built in which conditions would be so draconian that people would do anything to avoid them. Indeed, the number of claimants for assistance immediately fell, as hoped. Supposedly, a central government body was to ensure that certain bare minimum conditions were maintained in the workhouses, but they were unable to secure much co-operation, as local boards refused to spend the money (which had to be raised from local taxes) required for even these modest ameliorations. Small wonder that fear of the poor house permeated English working class life throughout much of the nineteenth century.

As industrialization quickened, critics began making their voices heard. The mid-Victorian middle classes had, it is true, a strong attachment to self-help. At the same time, though, the presence of poverty elicited a good bit of attention.[344] The number of charities and the funds they gathered from the public grew exponentially. Simultaneously, writers reporting on the condition of the poor attracted a reasonably large audience. Thus, there was, by the last two decades of the nineteenth century, a fertile ground for reform proposals. And it was social insurance and a minimum wage that came to dominate the reform agenda.

How attenuated the place of public assistance had become in the early twentieth century can be glimpsed from the fate of the Royal Commission on the Poor Law, which reported in 1909. A majority report stressed the need for a few minor changes in the current system. For example, they wished to further centralize control and make greater use of charitable organizations. A minority report, however, advocated abolishing the system entirely. In its place would be specialized departments dealing with pensions, health, and so forth. They proposed, also, a system of labor exchanges and a permanent countercyclical public works program to fight unemployment. David Lloyd George, the government's point man in social policy, gave the report a cool reception, and only pushed for the labor exchanges, a measure which passed parliament in 1909. Already, Derek Fraser contends, Lloyd George "was drawn towards insurance" as a way to address the problems of poverty.[345]

The spadework on social insurance had been done earlier. Joseph Chamberlain, a prominent member of the Liberal Party, suggested old age pensions as early as 1878, and workmen's compensation was enacted in 1897. Unemployment insurance, along with health insurance and old age pensions, dominated the political discussions, though.[346] The Liberal Party was clearly the main conduit for reform in that day, although the presence of the new Labour Party, many historians believe, created some pressure on them. Put firmly into power in the election of 1906, the Liberals embarked on a broad program of social reform, including several important pieces of social insurance legislation as well as Britain's first minimum wage law.

---

344. A fascinating look at how the Victorians viewed poverty is Gertrude Himmelfarb, *The Idea of Poverty: England in the Early Industrial Age* (New York: Knopf, 1984).

345. Fraser, *Evolution of the Welfare State*, 149.

346. The development of social insurance is covered in Helen Fisher Hohman, *The Development of Social Insurance and Minimum Wage Legislation in Great Britain* (Boston: Houghton Mifflin, 1933), chaps. 1-5.

Although Herbert Asquith sat in the prime minister's chair, it was Lloyd George who as Chancellor of the Exchequer, stood as the major figure of the administration, at least in domestic policy. Interestingly, Winston Churchill, as president of the Board of Trade, also played a key role in this spate of reform legislation.[347] One of the government's first achievements was an expansion of the workmen's compensation system passed in 1906. This was followed by an old age pensions law in 1908. Then the National Insurance Act 1911 created both unemployment and health insurance. Something of the tenor of Lloyd George's feeling can be seen from a speech he gave defending his famous budget of 1909 (The "People's Budget"):

> This is a War Budget. It is for raising money to wage implacable warfare against poverty and squalidness. I cannot help hoping and believing that before this generation has passed away we shall have advanced a great step towards that good time when poverty and wretchedness and human degradation which always follow in its camp will be as remote to the people of this country as the wolves which once infested its forests.[348]

The parallel with Lyndon Johnson's 1964 battle cry could hardly be more pronounced.

The minimum wage was seen as being just as important as social insurance. Striking miners had called for a living wage in 1893. The noted economist J.A. Hobson had advocated a general living wage in 1896.[349] A Select Committee on the Sweating System said in 1889 that local governments should mandate that fair wages be paid in all firms with which they contracted. "Sweating" was the term used in this period to refer to the working conditions that prevailed in many factories: long hours, an unhealthy environment, and low wages.

Sidney and Beatrice Webb, two of the leading theorists of reform, fleshed out much of the idea for a minimum wage in 1897. They tied a minimum wage to a general "national minimum," covering hours, working conditions, and wages. In the Webbs' words

---

347. According to Bentley Gilbert, Churchill was almost alone responsible for the British unemployment insurance system being even broader than its German counterpart. See Bentley Gilbert, "Winston Churchill versus the Webbs: The Origins of British Unemployment Insurance," *American Historical Review* 71 (1966), 846-62.

348. Quoted in Fraser, *Evolution of the Welfare State*, 145-46.

349. J. A. Hobson, "A Living Wage," *Commonwealth* 1 (1896), 128-29; 165-67.

When any European statesman makes up his mind to grapple seriously with the problem of the "sweated trades" he will have to expand the Factory Acts of his country into a systematic and comprehensive Labor Code, prescribing the minimum conditions under which the community can afford to allow industry to be carried on, and including not merely definite precautions of sanitation and safety, and maximum hours of toil, but also a minimum of weekly earnings.[350]

Agitation to address sweating grew throughout the early years of the twentieth century. In 1906, George Cadbury, a wealthy chocolate magnate, sponsored an exhibition on sweating in London. Visitors walked through displays of sweated factories and viewed the workers, young women mostly, toiling at their tasks. Low wages were a constant theme of the exhibits. By all accounts, it created a sensation, attracting over 30,000 people.

In the exhibition's aftermath, hoping not to lose political momentum, a National Anti-Sweating League was established which attracted a broad cross-section of backers. Its major proposal, its only proposal really, was a minimum wage. Its goal, the League said, was "to work towards the setting up of machinery to deal with sweating on lines of a compulsory minimum wage in specified industries."[351] It held a large conference on the minimum wage at the Guildhall in late 1906, attended by 341 prominent people and covered widely in the press. The Fabian Society soon joined the effort, issuing one of its famous tracts, entitled *The Case for a Minimum Wage: A Detailed Proposal for the Abolition of Sweating.*[352]

Charles Dilke, a Liberal M.P. who had married a tireless advocate of the minimum wage, had been introducing minimum wage bills in parliament since the 1890s, but had watched each one die. Now he was joined by the leaders of his party. The government hastily dispatched a representative to Australia to investigate the operation of the minimum wage law there. A House of Commons Select Committee on Home Work (the term for farming out assembling products to workers in their homes) was established in 1907, but under the

---

350. Sidney and Beatrice Webb, *Industrial Democracy* (London: Longmans, 1897), 767. It should be noted in passing that the Webbs spoke only of a "minimum wage," and conceded that it would be far from a "living wage."

351. National Anti-Sweating League, *Report of a Conference on a Minimum Wage Held at the Guildhall, London, October 24-26, 1906*, 3. On the anti-sweating movement in general, see John Sheldrake, "The Sweated Industries Campaign," *Socialist History* 3 (1993), 37-54 and Jenny Morris, *Women Workers and the Sweated Trades: The Origins of Minimum Wage Legislation* (Aldershot: Gower, 1986).

352. Fabian Tract No. 128, 1907.

guidance of the Home Secretary, Herbert Gladstone, it assumed a much broader writ.

That some type of minimum wage was going to be introduced by the government was certain, but its structure and coverage were matters of dispute. Churchill argued for a national minimum wage covering about one-third of the entire workforce. Others wished for more restricted coverage and separate wage levels for various industries. In the end, the government opted, cautiously, for the second approach, and its bill encountered very little opposition. The Trade Boards Act 1909 created four trade boards, for the paper box, machine-made lace, ready-made and wholesale bespoke tailoring, and chain-making industries. With the exception of chain making, all employed a predominantly female workforce. In fact, chain making had been included only after public outcry erupted over a report on the working conditions women endured in these facilities, pointing to "the glare of the fire and hot irons [with] women bare-armed, bare-chested, perspiring and working with feverish eagerness."[353] Altogether, the act covered approximately half a million workers. Despite its limited reach, one contemporary called it "the most advanced scheme of social reconstruction which the Government has as yet brought forward."[354]

Although several Labour M.P.s wanted to use the Trade Boards Act as a springboard for a universal minimum wage, reformers concentrated most of their efforts on expanding the number of trade boards. Five others were added before the First World War, and a separate statute established minimum wages in mining.[355] During the war, additional trade boards were created and other legislation extended minimum wage policies to munitions work and agriculture.

A critical turning point in the history of the minimum wage in Britain occurred at the end of the First World War. The government convened a National Industrial Conference composed of employers and trade union representatives. Its initial report, in 1919, recommended "the establishment by legal enactment of minimum time rates of wages, such rates to be universally applicable."[356] To carry out this project, the Conference urged the appointment of a commission empowered to suggest within three months both the level of the

---

353. Quoted in Hart, *Bound by Our Constitution*, 57.

354. Quoted in Sheila Blackburn, "Ideology and Social Policy: The Origins of the Trade Boards Act," *Historical Journal* 34 (1991), 44.

355. The most complete coverage of wage regulation is Rodney Lowe, "The Erosion of State Intervention in Britain, 1917-24," *Economic History Review* 31 (1978), 270-286, especially 272-81.

356. Quoted in Lowe, "Erosion of State Intervention," 273. On the Conference more generally, see Rodney Lowe, "The Failure of Consensus in Britain: The National Industrial Conference, 1919-21," *Historical Journal* 21 (1978), 649-75.

wage and how it could be best administered. The proposal was accepted in principle almost immediately by the cabinet at a private meeting. Lloyd George, now prime minister, drafted a letter to the executive committee of the Conference including the endorsement:

> Every worker should be ensured a minimum wage which will enable him or her to maintain a becoming standard of life for himself and his family. Apart altogether from considerations of humanity it is of the highest interest to the State that children should be brought up under conditions that will make them fit and efficient citizens.[357]

The Minister of Labour, however, wished to delete this portion, since he feared committing the government to too much. In the end, he convinced his cabinet colleagues that the more prudent course was to establish a commission to study "the expediency" of a universal minimum wage and "the basis on which the requisite rates should be fixed."

The authority of the proposed commission quickly became a political football between the Conference's leaders and the cabinet. Further, it became embroiled in the broader dispute of whether or not a permanent National Industrial Council, favored by the Conference, should be established. Citing constitutional problems, the handing over of policy making to an extra-parliamentary body, the government refused to even countenance such a proposal. In the end, even the watered-down minimum wage commission was never established. As a "compromise," the government pressed for the creation of more trade boards. By 1921, as a result, the number of trade boards had grown to 63, covering about three million workers. Although at one point fully another 100 were suggested, no more were added after 1921.

The idea of securing a minimum wage as part of a guaranteed national minimum for all citizens did not die out, however. At the 1918 Labour Party conference, a resolution was approved calling for a legal minimum wage to be "extended and developed so as to ensure to every adult worker of either sex a statutory base line of wages (to be revised with every substantial rise in prices) not less than enough to provide all the requirements of a full development of body, mind and character." When the party turned to writing its manifesto for the 1918 election, the link between "better pay" and a "national minimum" certainly points to a minimum wage.

---

357. Quoted in Lowe, "Erosion of State Intervention," 274.

> In industry Labour . . . works for an altogether higher status for labour, which well mean also better pay and conditions. The national minimum is the first step, and with this must go the abolition of the menace of unemployment, the recognition of the universal right to work or maintenance, the legal limitation of hours of labour, and the drastic amendment of the acts dealing with factory conditions, safety, and workmen's compensation.

In 1919, the party published one of its most celebrated documents, *Labour and the New Social Order*. It set forth four central objectives: universal enforcement of a national minimum, democratic control of industry, a revolution in national finance, and the use of the nation's surplus wealth for the common good. The first of these was to be accomplished through a living wage combined with a robust full employment policy. In 1924, the Labour Party briefly came to power and drew up a bill to establish a National Minimum Wage Commission along the lines of the 1919 proposal. However, the government's parliamentary majority evaporated before the bill could be acted on.

The more radical wing of the Labour Party, the Independent Labour Party (ILP), took up the minimum wage issue, in their rendition a "living wage," in the mid 1920s. Not only did they view it as the best prescription for the alleviation of poverty, it would also address unemployment for it would "create a vast new internal market. It would make a demand that would set every factory busily working to supply the needs of the home population. It would cure the disease of under-consumption which makes unemployment."[358] At the 1927 conference of the Labour Party, the ILP introduced a resolution calling for a living wage. Labour leader Ramsay MacDonald, however, was opposed, largely on the ground that it might scare away voters. He and the party elders maneuvered the conference toward a compromise, setting up a joint committee of the party and the Trade Union Congress to study both the living wage and family allowances as ways of reaching a national minimum standard. The committee's 1930 report focused entirely on publicly funded family allowances and ignored the living wage. Meanwhile, in 1929, the conference was presented with a new motion to make the living wage the main mechanism for achieving the national minimum, with family allowances merely a complementary policy. The motion was voted down, however, and a different one was approved that called for stand-alone family allowances. Still, the 1929 manifesto affirmed that "workers should have a minimum wage." Its place had begun to slip, though, from centerpiece to

---

358. From *The New Leader*, May 22, 1925, Quoted in Robert Dowse, *Left in the Centre: The Independent Labour Party, 1893-1940* (London: Longmans, 1966), 131.

afterthought. After 1929, the proposal fell from the party's manifestos entirely, not to appear again until 1987.

Public assistance re-entered the mainstream of British social policy through necessity and intellectual ferment. The necessity was the near bankruptcy of the unemployment insurance fund engendered by the continuing high levels of unemployment that plagued the interwar economy.[359] Haltingly at first, then wholeheartedly, the government began subsidizing the unemployment insurance fund from general revenues. In the process, payments to the unemployed became the dole, demolishing the distinction between social insurance and public assistance. The most important figure in the intellectual discussion of social policy during these years was of course William Beveridge.[360] Long concerned with poverty policy, first when he worked among the poor in East London and then as an academic and public commentator, in his early years he worried a good bit over low pay. By the 1930s, though, he thought that conditions had changed, and that at least five-sixths of modern poverty was attributable to unemployment, sickness, old age, and the death of a family breadwinner.[361] To Beveridge, therefore, social policy was best composed of a combination of social insurance and public assistance.

Without question, of course, the most important milestone of mid-century social policy was the 1942 report on *Social Insurance and Allied Services*, which, although it was technically the product of a committee, Beveridge largely wrote. Accordingly, it is more commonly known simply as *The Beveridge Report*.[362] Commissioned by the government to set the framework for postwar social policy, it fulfilled this function admirably.

The report begins by stating that the "aim of the Plan for Social Security is to abolish want by ensuring that every citizen willing to serve according to his powers has at all times an income sufficient to meet his responsibilities." It then listed eight primary causes of need: unemployment, disability, loss of livelihood by someone not employed, retirement, marriage needs of women, funeral expenses, childhood, and physical disease or incapacity. In line with Beveridge's assessment of the roots of poverty, low pay is not on the list. The title of the report contains what he considered to be the cure.

---

359. This episode is recounted in Bentley Gilbert, *British Social Policy, 1914-1939* (Ithaca, NY: Cornell University Press, 1970), chap. 2.

360. An excellent biography of Beveridge is Jose Harris, *William Beveridge: A Biography* (Oxford: Oxford University Press, 1977).

361. Beveridge was relying on two studies conducted by Seebohm Rowntree, one in 1899 and one in 1941. See Howard Glennerster, *British Social Policy since 1945* (Oxford: Blackwell, 1995), 31-33.

362. An American edition was published by Macmillan in 1942.

The report called for a "national minimum," and then developed a two-pronged "social security" strategy to meet it. First, there would be national insurance, financed by universal contributions. The insurance fund would provide an array of universal benefits, including children's allowances. This system would be supplemented by national assistance, need-based and means-tested payments to those who fell through the cracks of the insurance net. At no point does the report mention a minimum wage, and there is no evidence Beveridge or his committee ever even considered it. Minimum incomes were to be maintained for all, but through the mechanism of the public treasury.

Within the Labour Party during these years, energies were devoted mainly to fashioning policies for nationalization of industry and for fighting unemployment. Although its 1945 manifesto called for "good wages," its guideposts for postwar social policy were the proposals contained in *The Beveridge Report*. The historian of the 1945-51 government, Kenneth Morgan, writes that: "The 1945 election manifesto was largely a reaffirmation of key sections of Beveridge, with added emphasis on such old Labor themes as a national health service and a big housing drive."[363]

The Family Allowance Act 1945 was the first measure the new Labour government pushed through parliament. It called for flat-rate payments for all, beginning in 1946. The most complex of Labour's postwar statutes was the National Insurance Act 1946, which the Minister of National Insurance, James Griffiths, said would create a "National Minimum Standard." Combining several extant plans with a number of new ones, it was based, Griffiths said at the time, explicitly on Beveridge's proposals. Following Beveridge again, Griffiths then drafted the National Assistance Act 1948. It abolished the old Poor Law and created a National Assistance Board to make payments to people who were not eligible for insurance payments for one reason or another. When it left office in 1951, the Labour Party had created the modern British welfare state, but there was no national minimum wage.[364]

It is easy to see, both from the official title of Beveridge's report and the ministry created to carry it into effect, that social insurance was felt to be the main pillar of social policy. Public assistance was necessary to make it work, by addressing poverty where and when insurance did not reach. The minimum wage had fallen completely off the table. The reforming stance had moved from a

---

363. Kenneth Morgan, *Labour in Power, 1945-51* (Oxford: Clarendon Press, 1984), 142.

364. The Trade Boards were renamed Wages Councils and some administrative tightening up was done. No major changes were adopted, though.

position of relying on a minimum wage and social insurance as its centerpieces to one leaning exclusively on social insurance and public assistance.

As in the United States, the hope and expectation of Beveridge and those who implemented his policies was that social insurance would grow in importance and public assistance would retreat to society's corners, if not vanish altogether. However, as happened in the United States, this prediction was wildly off base. In the 1930s social insurance payments constituted about 60 per cent of all social security expenditures. Beveridge believed that with his plan this percentage would grow steadily and public assistance payments would fall. "But this never happened. . . [T]he proportion of the population receiving means-tested Income Support has shot up since 1951. . . Social insurance appears simply to have broken down."[365] Payments followed the same trend. In 1993 payouts for public assistance exceeded those for all contributory social insurance schemes, a pattern not witnessed since the 1920s.

	Table 9-1 **Income Support Receipient Compared to Population, 1950-60 (U.K.)**	
	Number receiving income support (millions)	Population (millions)
1950	1.285	50.6
1960	1.857	53.0
1970	2.738	55.7
Source: Office of National Statistics		

Driven by the same types of ideological and social trends as in the United States, the taking of "benefits" became less damnable in the public mind. A "right" to welfare payments, with no real distinction drawn between national insurance and public assistance, seeped into the public consciousness. Reflecting that approach, the 1974 Labour manifesto called for "urgent action . . .

---

365. Josephine Webb, "Social Security," in A. H. Halsey and Josephine Webb, eds., *Twentieth Century British Social Trends* (London: Macmillan, 2000), 568-69.

to strike at the roots of the worst poverty." But then it called for heavy new expenditure programs (to be accompanied by price and rent controls and redistributive taxation).

In sum, social policy in Britain has gone through roughly the same three stages as in the United States. Finding an acceptable program of public assistance occupied policy makers until the late nineteenth century. Then, reformers turned to a combination of social insurance and a minimum wage. The flurry of reforms immediately prior to the First World War gave Britain an extensive social insurance system and the beginnings of a minimum wage. After the failure of the National Industrial Conference to secure a uniform national minimum wage, though, the burden of relieving poverty was left to the social insurance system. Overwhelmed by the unemployment of the 1920s and the 1930s, the government had to turn once again to public assistance. The minimum wage had by now fallen from view. The *Beveridge Report* based its hope on a strengthened social insurance system, but the new policies rather soon gave way to a renewed emphasis on public assistance.

In Britain, as in the United States, this phenomenon was not economically or politically sustainable.

CONCLUSION

The wreckage wrought by the unrelenting rise in the level of public assistance programs in both countries spurred calls for reform. Although the accent is somewhat different in each, the broad outlines of the reform agenda have been similar on both sides of the Atlantic. However, both countries have gone only halfway to welfare reform. Unearned cash payments have been cut, to be sure; but poverty and inequality remain facts of life in both societies, the former still stubbornly high and the latter actually increasing. We need to resurrect the living wage to complete the task, returning, ironically, to the heritage of the early twentieth century reformers.

10. Halfway to Welfare Reform

Both the United States and the United Kingdom enacted major reforms to their welfare policies in the 1990s. Despite the differences in political structure and the still important differences in approach to welfare state issues in general, the outcomes in both countries were broadly similar. The underlying theme in both was moving people off benefits paid by the state into work, preferably in the private sector. Measured by the numbers of people moved into jobs, the policy was a success on both sides of the Atlantic, and there has been no shortage of self-congratulations by many of those who drafted the policies. However, if we turn our attention to the incomes of those who have made the transition from welfare to work, the picture becomes bleak. Thus, we have come halfway to welfare reform. It was a good thing to take an ax to the dilapidated structure that was the means-tested programs of cash assistance. Emphasizing work carries benefits both to the individuals gainfully employed and for society at large. However, the original goals of the welfare state — fighting poverty and softening inequality — should not be tossed aside. We should not confuse the discarding of a failed method with policy success. We need a fresh approach to combating destitution and destructive inequalities, and the anchor of that approach should be a living wage.

Background

From one perspective, it is not surprising that efforts to reform welfare produced similar results in Britain and the United States. President Bill Clinton and Prime Minister Tony Blair were cut largely from the same political cloth. Both were men of the center-left, although where exactly that lies on the political spectrum is somewhat different in the two nations, and both argued, legitimately, that they were leading their respective political parties in a new direction. Clinton liked to talk about being a New Democrat, shedding the party's total embrace of traditional Democratic interest groups: unions, minorities, public servants, and environmentalists. For Blair, the label was New Labour, signaling a breaking away from the grip especially of the unions but also of the militant left in general. Both were influenced, they said, by The Third Way, a set of ideas popularized by the sociologist Anthony Giddens.[366] The values Giddens mapped out that are most germane to the present inquiry entailed respect for business and the marrying of rights to responsibilities.

The similar political approaches of Blair and Clinton were reinforced by their warm personal relationship and the close links forged between their policy teams. The sky between Washington and London was a busy place in those years.

Yet, as when writing any history, it is too easy to impose a pattern on events after the fact, to see what happened as all but foreordained. Indeed, Blair and Clinton were both driven by, or at the very least embraced, similar approaches to welfare policy. But each of them had to navigate within the institutional and political realities of his own political system. There was no guarantee either would make welfare reform a major part of their own political agendas, or, even if they did, that they could secure enough political backing to get their preferred policies written into law. Countless historical monographs about policy making in both countries tell the tales of failed initiatives. We easily could have had welfare reform in one but not the other, or indeed in neither.

In John Kingdon's formulation, issues get on the serious political agenda when the *problem*, *policy*, and *political* streams converge.[367] Welfare as a problem has long been on the general agenda, of course; it was always froth for a good

---

366. His best-known book is *The Third Way: The Renewal of Social Democracy* (Cambridge: Polity Press, 1998).

367. John Kingdon, *Agendas, Alternatives, and Public Policies*, 2nd ed. (New York: HarperCollins, 1995).

political speech anywhere. Hence it is a constant background factor. However, problems of welfare had become more pronounced by the early 1990s, as the number of people who were long-term recipients seemed to be steadily growing. The policy stream refers to the ideas that shape new policy proposals. In both countries, over the years powerful interests had obtained a more or less veto position on changes in the public assistance programs. Any proposed alteration that reduced benefits or imposed more stringent requirements on recipients would activate these veto groups, and it would slip into the political graveyard. It was very important that new thinking in the late 1980s and early 1990s widened the range of acceptable alternatives, providing policy makers a bit more room to maneuver. Finally, the vagaries of politics play a full-blown role: the outcome of elections, personal rivalries, bargaining over other policies, internal party politics, etc. In the end, though, even when all these factors favor change, the actual stance of a chief executive and his ability to convince others to go along with his ideas are absolutely critical. Take away either Blair's or Clinton's attachment to achieving welfare reform, and the outcome would undoubtedly have been different.

It is interesting that, in the whole debate over welfare reform on both sides of the Atlantic, it was only means-tested cash benefits that were discussed. Hardly a word surfaced over social insurance. It is proof that these latter programs have for many years now been detached, at least in the public debate, from discussions about the welfare state in general. In both countries, it is true also that the minimum wage was debated at the same time as welfare reform. In the United States, Congress passed a significant increase in the minimum wage in 1996; meanwhile parliament adopted Britain's first National Minimum Wage in 1998. In both cases, there was a nod or two to welfare reform when debates were held over the minimum wage, but only in the most tangential way. Minimum wage policies belonged largely to another sphere. Had the two been linked together, though, it would have been much healthier for everyone — and there is some chance we would not have gone only halfway to welfare reform.

WELFARE REFORM IN THE UNITED STATES

After the demise of Nixon's Family Assistance Plan, discussions of "welfare reform" continued. In part, this was because the AFDC program itself continued to grow, both in numbers of people it served and budgetary outlays. From 1960 to 1971 the number of participants increased from three million to 10.2 million, while the combined expenditures of federal and state governments grew over the same period from one billion dollars to $6.2 billion.[368]

"Welfare reform," of course, is a slippery phrase. In general, almost everyone agreed that it would be better to have two-parent households with at least one, if not both, of the adults holding steady, well-paying jobs in either the private or public sector, with both parents actively involved in raising their children in a responsible fashion. However, consensus broke down on how best to achieve that. Furthermore, the very design of the program made it inordinately difficult, politically or practically, to reform. In essence, policy makers faced three "traps."[369]

The first is the "dual clientele trap." The original ADC was established to serve children by allowing their mothers to stay home and care for them. Through the years, this justification continued to underpin the AFDC. Any funds to help children, though, have to be funneled through the parents. How do you ensure, then, that those monies will in fact be used for the children's welfare? It was blatantly obvious that many, but of course not all, of the parents, mostly mothers, who received the funds were not using them in the best interest of the children, and further were not making good choices for their children in general. However, any reduction in funds for AFDC, or any policy that made it harder to qualify for the program, would clearly push even more children into poverty, something no one wanted.

Second, there was the "money trap." Given the low educational levels and the general lack of job skills possessed by most welfare mothers, the practical reality was that any sensible work requirement was going to cost more money in the short run. Job training, placement services, counseling, and, of course, monitoring, were going to be costly. In the long run, of course, if the program worked, costs would decrease as wages replaced public assistance as the primary source of people's income. However, many felt that welfare reform should reduce costs, not increase them, even in the short run. Politicians, after all, cannot think too much about the long run, given the election cycle.

Finally, there was the "complexity trap." A number of other public assistance programs, such as food stamps, Medicaid, and housing benefit, had means-tested and work-related eligibility requirements. There was almost always a "notch" at which someone was actually going to be worse off by going to work and losing eligibility for some of these benefits. Another complicating

---

368. R. Kent Weaver, *Ending Welfare as We Knew It* (Washington: Brookings, 2000), 55.
369. I have taken these, but modified them somewhat, from Weaver, *Ending Welfare*, 43-53.

factor was the joint federal-state system of administration. In short, it was a morass.

The simple fact was that no one could come up with a program that could navigate all these traps. The range of what was acceptable to various interest groups, members of Congress, and the general public was severely constricted by the interaction of all three traps.

Jimmy Carter promised during his 1976 presidential campaign to "clean up the welfare mess." Following through, he sent Congress what he called the Program for Better Jobs and Incomes (PBJI). Under the plan, cash benefits were to be consolidated with food stamps into a single program. Recipients were to be divided into two groups, those who were expected to work and those exempt from work. Single parents with children under fourteen, incidentally, fell into the second category. A different guaranteed cash benefit was payable to each group, with a complicated phase-out formula for earned income. The federal government would assume a larger percentage of the welfare budget, to provide fiscal relief to the states. At the same time, public sector jobs at the minimum wage were to be created to employ those required to work. All this was scheduled to go into effect in 1981, largely so that the goal of a balanced budget could be met before then.

PBJI ran into immediate problems in Congress, as explained by R. Kent Weaver:

> There indeed was something in the PBJI that each element of a potential coalition for welfare reform disliked. Business groups were suspicious of a larger public sector jobs program, and labor unions strongly disliked the creation of a potentially large new public service work force competing with their members at much lower cost. . . . Congressional liberals and advocacy groups for the poor disliked the fact that benefit guarantees were far below the poverty line. States and localities were unenthusiastic about a package that did not offer fiscal relief until 1981. The congressional agriculture committees, which regarded food stamps as part of an important log-rolling coalition to gain critical urban support for their core commodity support programs, were reluctant to see them abolished as part of Carter's consolidation proposal.[370]

Despite Carter's best efforts, the proposal died in Congress. Efforts in the subsequent years of his presidency to revive portions of PBJI also fell by the wayside.

---

370. Weaver, *Ending Welfare*, 65.

President Reagan and most of his aides were instinctively hostile to public assistance programs, and were always on the lookout for domestic spending programs to submit to the budget knife. AFDC was, therefore, an easy target to select. Two significant changes to American welfare policy occurred during the Reagan presidency. The first was part of the administration's initial push for major new tax and spending policies in 1981. During this battle, several suggestions for restricting eligibility for AFDC emanated from the White House, some of which were ultimately adopted by Congress. At the same time, the president argued that states should have to impose work requirements on all able-bodied recipients. In the end, Congress balked, and only approved a measure *allowing* states to impose more stringent work requirements.

However, the most significant alteration to welfare policy during the eighties was what came to be known as the Family Support Act of 1988. Reagan recommended renewed attention to welfare reform in his State of the Union messages in 1986 and 1987, but failed to provide much in the way of specifics. The seeming success of "workfare" programs in several states combined with a renewed concern to track down absent parents (mostly fathers) and make them pay child support set the framework for the ensuing battles in Congress. After marathon sparring and lengthy negotiations, both houses of Congress finally produced a bill the president would sign. The most controversial provisions dealt, as usual, with work requirements. In essence, conservatives wanted more, liberals less. As part of the compromise, several new incentives aimed at encouraging work were included in the law. Some of the formulas on earnings disregards (how much a person could earn before benefit reduction set in) were adjusted to make work more attractive; modifications to Medicaid eligibility were made; and states were required to provide help with child care and transportation costs for those entering employment. The act also created the Jobs Opportunities and Basic Skills (JOBS) program. States were compelled to have a slowly increasing percentage (only reaching 20 per cent by 1995) of their caseloads enrolled in this state-operated effort. This entailed that all those enrolled in JOBS were slated to begin "work-related activities." These could include searching for a job, attending training classes, or performing community work. In short, it sounded a lot better than it was. Sending out a few resumes or enrolling in a class on building "self-esteem" would suffice. In hindsight, it represents an important shift, though, in that for the first time some recipients might actually have to do something in return for their benefits. A different path was being set for future reform.

In the late 1980s and early 1990s there was also some important intellectual ferment in the welfare policy field. Using the framework suggested above, these ideas contributed significantly to the *policy stream*. On the right, two writers had opened up important questions that needed to be addressed, even by those who disagreed with them. Charles Murray pointed to the problems of dependency that public assistance could generate. While he overstated his case in his book *Losing Ground*, he raised a serious issue.[371] Lawrence Mead took the position, especially in his *Beyond Entitlement*, that there was nothing inherently improper with requiring those who receive public assistance to agree to certain conditions.[372] These could quite legitimately take the form of a work requirement or the insistence on conforming to certain social norms.

But it was two other writers, positioned largely on the moderate left, who perhaps had the most impact. University of Chicago sociologist William Julius Wilson stressed the importance of work to healthy community life. His thesis, argued in two books, *The Truly Disadvantaged* and *When Work Disappears*, was that the disappearance of low-skill but relatively well-paid manufacturing jobs in central cities at the very moment African Americans were entering the work force in significant numbers was at the root of the problem of inner-city decline.[373] The resulting joblessness had led to the erosion of viable communities by spawning family breakdown (since few fully employed African-American males were available as marriage partners), cynicism about education, crime, and other pathologies. His acknowledged liberal credentials made his homage to the importance of work something liberals could not dismiss in a cavalier fashion. David Ellwood, a Harvard economist, had an equal impact with his book *Poor Support*.[374] Ellwood felt that low-income workers needed additional help through an enlarged Earned Income Tax Credit and a higher minimum wage. Those in need of temporary assistance could obtain cash payments. However, after a certain point, one would have to work at a minimum wage job (provided by government if need be) to keep receiving payments. The book not only stressed work, therefore, but broached the idea of setting time limits for the receipt of public assistance.

---

371. Charles Murray, *Losing Ground: American Social Policy, 1950-1980* (New York: Basic Books, 1984).

372. Lawrence Mead, *Beyond Entitlement: The Social Obligations of Citizenship* (New York: Free Press, 1986).

373. William Julius Wilson, *The Truly Disadvantaged: The Inner City, the Underclass and Public Policy* (Chicago: University of Chicago Press, 1987) and *When Work Disappears: The World of the Urban Poor* (New York: Knopf, 1996).

374. David Ellwood, *Poor Support: Poverty in the American Family* (New York: Basic Books, 1988).

In his 1992 campaign for the presidency, candidate Bill Clinton echoed Jimmy Carter by promising to "end welfare as we know it." Once in office, he was urged by many of his advisers to make welfare reform an early priority, but the president instead turned to health care reform. Nevertheless, he did create a sizeable task force to begin hammering out a welfare reform package stressing time limits, work, and responsibility. While the president was preoccupied with his ill-fated health care reform proposal, the task force began its deliberations. In June 1994, it laid out a package of recommendations under the title Work and Responsibility Act of 1994. Two events outside the administration's control, though, were about to influence the battle for welfare reform: an outpouring of innovation in the states and the dramatic election victory of congressional Republicans in 1994.

States had long chafed under the rigidities of the AFDC program's requirements, imposed by whatever majority in Congress enacted each new law. Technically, there was a procedure to request a waiver in some instances, but it was cumbersome and seldom used. President Reagan had appealed to Congress to make waivers easier to obtain, but had come up short. He had, however, managed to get the authority to approve waivers transferred to the executive branch. Little happened, though, until the first Bush presidency. The established rule had been that no waiver could be granted unless the program produced no increase in spending. Bush loosened this rule to one that said that a state could spend more money in the short run if the long-run costs would be lower. Moreover, Bush signaled governors that he would be receptive to waiver requests on a wide variety of fronts.

The upshot was that states began requesting and Washington approving waivers, a policy that continued after Clinton entered the White House. Realizing that they could claim political credit for innovation and at the same time could actually do something, several state leaders obtained waivers for a variety of purposes. Policies adopted by states such as Wisconsin, Michigan, New Jersey, and California caught the eye of other state policy makers, and then national politicians in Washington. Something approaching a policy bandwagon set in. Republican governors in particular pushed innovations, and in time came up with their own proposal for a national policy, the touchstone of which was further latitude for the states.

In 1994, the voters handed both the House of Representatives and the Senate to the GOP. Republicans had not controlled both houses of Congress since 1948. Before the election, Republican congressional candidates had put together a campaign document called the Contract with America, a brief section of which called for welfare reform. More detail was available in a proposed Personal Responsibility Act, drafted by think tank personnel with close links to the Republican House leadership.

With the administration's June 1994 proposals still technically on the table, there were now three reform blueprints in circulation. A delicate political dance was about to begin, with not only the substance of policy at stake, but also concerning who could take credit or perhaps be forced to accept blame for what. The House Ways and Means Committee was the site where the complex cobbling together of proposals began, but as usual the legislative process was long and exhausting to all concerned. Republican leaders in Congress were clearly in the driver's seat on their end of Pennsylvania Avenue. However, the veto pen that sat on the president's desk gave him and his people potent leverage. In fact, two preliminary versions of welfare reform were vetoed. In the end, though, Congress passed and Clinton signed what was called the Personal Responsibility and Work Opportunity Act (PRWOA) of 1996, the most far-reaching welfare reform package in at least a generation.

PRWOA was an enormously complex piece of legislation, and full of compromises of all kinds. Terminology, for starters, was important. Temporary Assistance for Needy Families (TANF) was to replace AFDC. Primarily, there are five provisions of the law that stand out:[375] the ending of entitlement, the shift to block grants, the establishing of looser requirements for state policies, the setting of time limits for receipt of public assistance, and the providing of modest help for child care. (Incidentally, the law provided that it needed to be reauthorized in 2002, but that has not been done as of this writing. Hence, it has merely been extended and remains in effect.)

AFDC had been an individual entitlement.[376] That is, if you met the stipulations of the law, you were legally entitled to the benefits. If you were denied them, you had a right to go to federal court and seek redress. Now, this right was abolished. States retained the authority to make their own programs a state entitlement if they wished, but this would limit an applicant's judicial relief to state courts.

Depending on a state's relative wealth, federal funding for AFDC had been between 50 per cent and 80 per cent of program costs in each state. Now, states

---

375. There was also an emphasis on encouraging marriage, but that is not directly relevant for present purposes.

376. Technically, the federal statute had always only made the program an entitlement for states, not individuals. However, beginning in the 1960s legal aid attorneys had succeeded in having entitlement status granted to individual recipients.

were to be given a block grant for public assistance. A set total was established, $16.5 billion, with each state's share based on a complex formula that tried to avoid penalizing states that had already reduced their caseloads. Future amounts were constant, which meant that they would lose real value because of inflation. (To date, since inflation has been relatively low, this has not posed a serious problem, however.) To maintain their levels of funding from this pie, states had to show progress toward directing certain percentages of their caseloads into work. By 2002, half of the 1996 caseload was supposed to be working.

In line with the block grants went new flexibility for state policy makers. They were now freer to determine who was eligible for benefits, what procedures applicants would have to follow, and what sanctions might be imposed on those who did not comply with the new guidelines.

Of special importance was the establishing of strict time limits for receipt of TANF. The benchmark was 60 months during one's lifetime, but states could reduce that if they so chose. On the other hand, states could also exempt 20% of their caseload from this requirement. And, of course, they were free to use their own funds to extend benefits for longer periods of time.

Finally, some added funding was set aside for child care, but there was no entitlement to such help.

In short, the central aim of the statute was to move as many people as possible from the public assistance rolls into work.

THE EFFECTS OF PRWOA

Without question, the welfare rolls have fallen dramatically. In 1995, the year before welfare reform, 4,963,000 families and 13,931,000 individuals were receiving AFDC. In March of 2003, that had fallen to 2,040,000 families and 4,964,000 individuals. Compared to August 1996, right before the new law went into effect, that represents a 59.5.7% drop for families and a 53.7% drop for individuals. As the data come out, there are usually laudatory statements from government officials. Secretary of Health and Human services Tommy Thompson noted when the March 2003 figures were released that "Americans are demonstrating that they want to be self-sufficient and economically independent for the benefit of themselves and their children."[377] There are, however, significant regional variations. Between March 2002 and March 2003,

---

377. Department of Health and Human Services, News Release, September 3, 2003.

for example, while the overall rolls were falling by 4.3% for families, Maine experienced a 41.8% growth but Illinois a 28.8% decline.

Table 10-1		
Decline in TANF Caseloads, 1993-2003		
(000s)		
Year	**Families**	**Individual recipients**
1993	4,963	14,115
1994	5,053	14,276
1995	4,963	13,931
1996	4,628	12,877
1997	4,114	11,423
1998	3,305	9,132
1999	2,734	7,455
2000	2,208	5,781
2001	2,103	5,343
2002	2,025	5,008
2003	2,040	4,964
Source: Department of Health and Human Services		

Moreover, the number of people who leave welfare for work and stay in the labor market is encouraging. For example, 60% of the leavers are employed one year after exiting the welfare system.[378] Looking at the two most comprehensive studies, covering Wisconsin and South Carolina, the detailed findings support this conclusion.[379] In Wisconsin administrative data were used to compare those leaving welfare in 1995 with those leaving in 1997. In South Carolina, a three-year study was done using surveys of leavers. Thus, the two are not strictly comparable, but nonetheless they point in the same direction.

In Wisconsin, 68.1 per cent of those who left in 1997 had some earnings in the fourth quarter after they left the program.[380] In South Carolina, 68 per cent of those off welfare were either working or living with an employed adult.[381]

Two caveats to this rosy picture can immediately be raised, and the jury is still out on how important they are. The first is that the most easily employed,

378. Courtney Jarchow, *Employment Experiences of Former TANF Recipients* (Denver: National Conference of State Legislatures, 2002), 1.
379. Maria Cancian, *et al., Before and After TANF: The Economic Well-Being of Women Leaving Welfare* (Madison, Wisconsin: Institute for Research on Poverty, 2002), Discussion Paper No. 1244-02 and Philip Richardson, *Three-Year Follow-Up Study of Welfare Leavers in South Carolina* (Prepared by Maximus for South Carolina Department of Social Services, December 2002).
380. Cancian, *Before and After TANF,* 11.
381. Richardson, *Three-Year Follow-Up,* ES-5.

those with the most skills and the fewest behavioral problems, such as addiction, are now off the rolls and the remainder will be much more difficult to place in the labor market. The other is that welfare reform coincided with a booming economy and a strong job market, and that recessions will be a serious barrier to more people leaving welfare, as well as possibly eroding some of the gains already made. There is some macro evidence that one or both of these factors may have come into play. Figure 10-1 depicts the status of former TANF recipients in two different years. In 2002, as the recession set in, fewer were working than in the boom year of 1999.

However, other data, more micro in character, cast some doubt on how salient either of these two factors really is. For example, Wisconsin began its compulsory work program before the 1996 law was passed. Therefore, those leaving welfare later should be the less employable. When the researchers examined data for those returning to welfare, though, they found the opposite result from what they expected: those leaving later were less likely to return to welfare than those who left in the earlier wave. "The relatively lower rate of returning to welfare in the second period is notable, given that a high proportion of cases leaving welfare in the second period included individuals with more substantial barriers to employment." [382] Then, if we look at unemployment and wage data for single mothers, the picture is not grim at all. True, in 2003 the unemployment rate among single mothers climbed two percentage points from seven to nine per cent.[383] Importantly though, in contrast, in late 1996, when welfare reform was adopted, it was 11 per cent in a booming economy. Furthermore, wages of single mothers have continued to go up, even during the recession. From late 2001 to late 2002, in the heart of the recession, their wages grew three per cent after inflation, with an even higher growth rate recorded among low-wage single mothers.

Interestingly, too, given the fact that most of these jobs are in the low-wage service sector, welfare leavers report a good bit of satisfaction with their positions. Table 10-2 reports the results from studies of job satisfaction done in four states.

Moreover, there does not seem to be any harm done to children from welfare recipients going to work. A detailed study of preschoolers and adolescents in low-income families by four university researchers reached rather definite conclusions.

---

382. Cancian, *Before and After TANF*, 19.

383. These and the following data are from *Single Mothers Retain Nearly All Their Employment and Wage Gains in the Current Economic Slowdown*, Urban Institute Monitor, January, 2003.

Figure 10-1

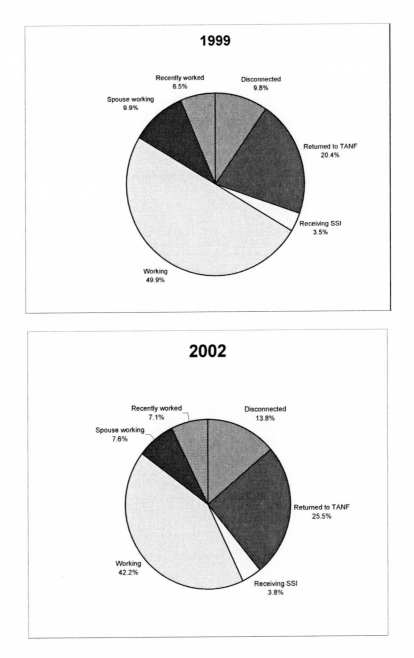

Table 10-2
Job Satisfaction of TANF Leavers

State	Per Cent Who Report Being Satisfied or Very Satisfied with Carrent Job
Illinois	79
Kentucky	78
New Mexico	58
North Carolina	81

Source: National Conference of State Legislatures

[N]o significant associations with mothers' welfare and employment transitions were found for preschoolers, and the dominant pattern was also of few statistically significant associations for adolescents. The associations that did occur provided slight evidence that mothers' entry into the labor force was related to improvements in adolescents' mental health, whereas exits from employment were linked with teenagers' increased behavior problems.[384]

In part, this may be because former welfare recipients feel better about themselves. In the South Carolina study, over 81 per cent said that being off welfare made them feel better about themselves.[385]

At the same time, while the record is somewhat mixed, many of the leavers are staying off welfare. Eleven different studies conclude that around one-fourth to one-third of welfare leavers return.[386] A major explanatory factor is the reason for leaving welfare in the first place. Those who left to pursue earnings are much less likely to return than those who were sanctioned or whose time expired. Another important factor, which is closely tied to the first, is how good a job, defined primarily by the level of compensation, a person obtains when he or she leaves welfare. And, of course, the better the initial job, the more likely the person is to stay with that job. This, in turn, leads to greater personal stability,

---

384. P. Lindsay Chase-Lansdale, *et al.*, "Mothers' Transitions from Welfare to Work and the Well-Being of Preschoolers and Adolescents," *Science*, March 7, 2003, 1548.

385. Richardson, *Three-Year Follow-Up*, ES-11.

386. Pamela Loprest, *Who Returns to Welfare?* Urban Institute Series on New Federalism, Paper Number B-49, September 2002.

better long-run promotion possibilities, and even better pay. In New Mexico, for instance, among those who began earning at least $4,000 per quarter, 66 per cent were employed all four quarters after they left welfare.[387] However, this dropped to 43 per cent for those earning between $1,500 and $3,000. Regarding job continuity, "Leavers in Iowa who were employed consistently had average quarterly earnings that were more than 100 per cent greater than those who were employed for only some time after exit."[388]

Two additional points need to be made before we turn to the downside. First, a significant number of those leaving TANF continue to receive means-tested government benefits. In 2002, 35.4 per cent continued to receive food stamps and 54.3 per cent utilized Medicaid for children.[389] Second, if we look at return rates, three very important variables stand out: child care, health insurance, and job training. In 2002, 19.5 per cent of the leavers receiving help with child care returned to welfare in the first three months whereas 27.7 per cent of those without such assistance did so. As for government funded health insurance, 21.7 per cent of those with it returned to welfare compared to 32.0 per cent of those lacking it. Help with job search and job training, though, was the other way around. Those receiving this kind of help returned to welfare at a 33.7 per cent rate, but those without it had only a 25 per cent return rate.[390] Clearly, people need help with child care and health insurance but, seemingly, are wise to avoid "help" in searching for or training for a job.

All is not rosy, however. In 2002, the median wage for *all* welfare leavers, regardless of how long they had been off the program, was $8.06 per hour.[391] Furthermore, a third of these people were only working part-time (35 hours a week or less). To document the obvious, incomes have not risen much. The Wisconsin study used three measures of income: the person's earnings, the person's own income (including such items as food stamps), and total family income. The unpleasant fact is that "42 percent of leavers were better off [after leaving welfare] using our measure of family income compared to only 32 percent using our measure of own income. However, nearly half of leavers are worse off than they were before leaving welfare, according to all the income-based measures."[392] In South Carolina, only 38 per cent "enjoyed" earnings of $15,000

---

387. Jarchow, *Employment Experiences*, 11.

388. Jarchow, *Employment Experiences*, 11.

389. Pamela Loprest, *Use of Government Benefits Increases among Families Leaving Welfare* (Washington: Urban Institute, 2002), 3.

390. Loprest, *Use of Government Benefits*, 3.

391. Pamela Loprest, *Fewer Welfare Leavers Employed in Weak Economy*, Urban Institute, 2003, 1.

392. Cancian, *Before and After TANF*, 24.

or more annually, while 22 per cent earned less than $9,000.[393] Perhaps this would not be so bad if these people had realistic prospects of significant wage increases — if, as the employers of low-wage workers like to say so often, these really were "entry-level jobs." However, the data from South Carolina confirm what most people would suspect. Average earnings rise somewhat in the first year of a person's employment, then stabilize. In other words, you get the raise for sticking it out six months at the fast food restaurant or the motel, then you get no more.

Measured by even the paltry official federal poverty level, the economic fortunes of these families can only be described as dismal. In Wisconsin, 69 per cent of the welfare leavers were in poverty if we use total family income (including that from other means-tested benefits); if we used after-tax earnings alone, as we should, then 80 per cent fall below the federal poverty level.[394] Likewise, in South Carolina, based on total family income, 62 per cent were below the poverty level.

In sum, we have come halfway to welfare reform. We have reduced the rolls dramatically and moved substantial numbers of these people into work. Even with the recession, the jobs are not disappearing, and they are holding on to them at significant rates. The former welfare recipients feel better about themselves; further, their children's well-being, what so many people fretted about, has not been adversely affected. It may even have been helped. However, we must remember the goals of the original welfare state, of which the public assistance programs were only a part: to lift people out of poverty and make them productive citizens of a democratic society. In this, we still fall far short. The route to that goal is to keep moving people off public assistance into jobs, but into jobs that pay well. Child care, medical care, and transportation remain critical needs (but not more government-run job training programs). However, what is needed most of all is a living wage. When people move off welfare and can support themselves on their earnings, we will have completed the task of welfare reform, but only then.

WELFARE REFORM IN BRITAIN

It is interesting that even though British welfare policy during the postwar years differed rather sharply from that in the United States, both countries

---

393. Richardson, *Three-Year Follow-Up Study*, ES-7.
394. Cancian, *Before and After TANF*, 24.

entered the twenty-first century with quite similar policy kits. Furthermore, it seems clear that much that happened in Britain drew its inspiration from policies pioneered in the United States.[395]

Although the Conservative Party generally opposed the adoption of Labour's welfare state policies in the 1940s, the opposition was short-lived. Quite soon, a consensus set in regarding social insurance, public assistance, and the direct provision of health services.[396] To be sure, the Conservatives argued that they could administer the welfare state's apparatus more efficiently than Labour, but no prominent politician talked about rolling back, much less dismantling, the programs. For its part, Labour argued for a little higher benefits and a slightly less restrictive set of criteria for eligibility. Overall, though, these were placid years in British social policy.

Moreover, there was never any real concern about the lack of work effort on the part of recipients, nor for the fact that lone parents stayed home to care for their children rather than entering the labor market. The blurring of the line between unemployment insurance and the dole in the 1920s and the 1930s was still too fresh in the collective memory for fingers to be pointed at those on public assistance. Plus, the fact that some programs, such as child benefit, were universal muted the political opposition to public assistance.

It was not until Mrs. Thatcher assumed office that any serious rethinking about welfare state policies took place. Enthralled with neoliberal approaches to public policy, Mrs. Thatcher and her advisers worried both about the size of the state's budget and the lack of flexibility in labor markets, especially low-wage labor markets.[397] A variety of policies were adopted that were designed to push the young especially off benefits and into paid work. Thus, expenditures could be lowered and people pushed into private sector employment at the same time.

Inspired to a large degree by the ideas of Americans Charles Murray and Lawrence Mead, popularized in Britain by two think tanks, the Institute of Economic Affairs and the Adam Smith Institute, John Major's government continued the policy direction set by Mrs. Thatcher. A new Jobseekers Allowance, established in 1996 to combine job placement help with benefits,

---

395. See Alan Deacon, "Learning from the USA? The Influence of American Ideas on New Labour Thinking on Welfare Reform, *Policy and Politics* 28 (2000), 5-18. However, European influences were not absent. See Claire Annesley, "Americanized and Europeanized: UK Social Policy since 1997," *British Journal of Politics and International Relations* 5 (2003), 143-65.

396. The best analysis of these years remains Samuel Beer, *British Politics in the Collectivist Age* (New York: Knopf, 1965).

397. The literature on Mrs. Thatcher's period in office is legion. A good introduction is Dennis Kavanagh, *Thatcherism and British Politics*, 2nd ed. (Oxford: Oxford University Press, 1990).

compelled recipients to sign a contract laying out the precise steps they were using to locate a job. Additionally, those 18- to 24-year-olds who had been unemployed for more than two years were required to enroll in a special employment plan. Rising numbers of lone parents, along with disturbing evidence on the nonpayment of child support, led the government to create new policies for enforcing child support payments (although the implementation of this scheme proved unsuccessful) and tinker with the way benefits were calculated. The thrust of the latter was to disregard a certain portion of earnings, hoping to make work more attractive. Nevertheless, there was never any serious talk of making work compulsory for lone parents.

The Labour Party suffered horrendous defeats in 1983 and 1987, humiliations that forced a rethinking of party ideology. Only narrowly defeated in 1992, the party continued to make adjustments in its policy thinking (and its organizational structure as well). What is called New Labour emerged, under its *nom de guerre*, The Third Way.

The sociologist Anthony Giddens, often referred to as Tony Blair's favorite intellectual, has written the most widely read book on The Third Way. Although his ideas range over several fronts, Giddens has much to say about welfare issues. Whereas, he says, the old left looked on benefits as individual rights, the Third Way takes as its "prime motto" that there are *"no rights without responsibilities."*[398] Accordingly, those who draw funds from the public purse may be expected to work, and also fulfill certain behavioral expectations. Tony Blair's close political ally Gordon Brown, who was to become Chancellor of the Exchequer and has been immensely influential in crafting New Labour's welfare policies, has had a passion about the virtue of work. He has always spoken about it forthrightly: "To the unemployed who can work, we will meet our responsibility to ensure that there are job opportunities and the chance to learn new skills. You must now meet your responsibility — to earn a wage."[399]

Two years before he took power, Blair echoed these thoughts.

> A society geared to extending opportunity is one then able to demand responsibility with some realistic prospect of it being given. It allows us to be much tougher and hard headed in the rules we apply, and how we apply them.[400]

---

398. Giddens, *The Third Way*, 65. Emphasis in original.
399. Quoted in Mike Brewer, Tom Clark, and Matthew Wakefield, "Social Security in the UK under New Labour: What did the Third Way Mean for Welfare Reform?" *Fiscal Studies* 23 (2002), 509.

Furthermore, for the first time in 50 years, the Labour Party's manifesto in 1997 promised to address welfare reform.

Winning landslide elections in 1997 and 2001, the Labour Party has been able to reconstruct British welfare policy along their preferred lines. Given the dominance a winning party enjoys under the British parliamentary system, there has been no need to compromise with opposition political leaders. Of course, there always has to be some accommodation made to political factions within the governing party, but if the leadership is committed to a particular course of action, they can almost always carry the day. In 1998, the government produced a Green Paper on welfare reform which used the phrase *Work as the Best Form of Welfare* as one of its descriptive subtitles.[401] In short, the government left little doubt about where policy was headed. According to Robert Walker and Michael Wiseman, Labour has pursued a four-pronged strategy in social policy: making work pay, welfare to work, ending child poverty, and fighting social exclusion. The third and fourth of these were mentioned earlier; the first and second are the more germane here, and the ones where the parallels with American policy are the most pronounced.[402] The centerpiece of New Labour's social policy is its New Deals, of which there are several: one for 18- 24-year-olds, one for the long-term unemployed, one for those over 50, one for the disabled, and so forth. Of primary concern here are the youth and lone parent New Deals, since they cover the most important segments of the population on the receiving end of social policy.

The New Deal for Young People (NDYP), adopted in 1998, is designed for those 18 to 24 years of age who have been unemployed for six months or more. Enrollment in the program is compulsory for those wishing to continue receiving public assistance. A variety of benefits are available to those in the program (such as the Jobseekers Allowance), but the central pillar of the program is the assignment of a personal adviser (PA) to each recipient. The PA tailors a program (which may include training) that attempts to move the young person into a permanent job and then provides encouragement along the way. Most young people in the program reported that their PAs were helpful, and the PAs, by all accounts, record significant satisfaction with their jobs.[403] Naturally, the

---

400. Quoted in Alan Deacon, "The British Perspective on Reform: Transfers from, and a Lesson for, the US," in Robert Walker and Michael Wiseman, eds., *The Welfare We Want: The British Challenge for American Reform* (Bristol: Policy Press, 2003), 69.

401. Department of Social Security, *New Ambitions for Our Country: A New Contract for Welfare* (London: HMSO, 1998). Green Paper.

402. Robert Walker and Michael Wiseman, "Sharing Ideas on Welfare," in Walker and Wiseman, *The Welfare We Want*, 17.

success or failure of those in the program has depended heavily on the relationship they build with their PA.

The New Deal for Lone Parents (NDLP), the closest British approximation to TANF, is somewhat similar. The chief difference is that NDLP is voluntary, although the level of coaxing has increased. Initially, no one was coerced into even hearing about the details of the program. Then, in 2000, three areas were selected for a pilot program requiring at least a meeting with a PA. PAs were then supposed to encourage entry into the NDLP, but it was not mandatory. In 2001, a meeting with a PA was prescribed nationally for all those with children over 13, and beginning in 2004 all lone parent Income Support (the current name for public assistance, adopted in 1988) recipients will have to meet with a PA. Nevertheless, there is still no compulsion to join the NDLP after the meeting. According to the latest study, under 10% of those on Income Support have entered NDLP.[404]

While verbally urging lone parents to enter the work force via the system of PAs, the government has also attempted to make work more attractive financially. New help with child care and a working tax credit (which can have a substantial "top up" effect on income) have been put in place, for instance. Also, there have been increased "earnings disregards" in calculating benefits. The government has set a goal of 70 per cent of all lone parents working by 2010, which would be an increase of 16 percentage points from the 54 per cent working in 2002.

Effects of the New Deals for Young People and Lone Parents

If you surf to the webpage of the NDYP, you will find heartwarming stories of people who have been helped, such as Paul.

> My personal adviser was really nice. I told her what I wanted to do and she pulled out all the local jobs in printing. . . I've changed a lot since I've been at Brikenhead Press. I've grown up a lot. Being in work makes a big difference — actually having a job gives you a boost.[405]

---

403. See the summaries on the Joseph Rowntree Foundations' website: http://www. jrf. org. uk/ knowledge/findings/socialpolicy/740. asp

404. Martin Evans, *et al.*, *New Deal for Lone Parents: Second Synthesis Report of the National Evaluation* (Bristol: Centre for Analysis of Social Policy, 2003), 18.

405. http://www. newdeal. gov. uk

There are also testimonials from PAs about the rewards the work offers as well as from employers regarding the benefits they have reaped from participating in the New Deal.

Government spokespeople, of course, are quick to tout the program's success. Desmond Browne, the Minister for Work, told the House of Commons on November 17, 2003:

> Along with our other welfare-to-work policies, the new deal has helped reduce youth unemployment to around its lowest level since the mid-1970s and has virtually eradicated long-term youth unemployment. The new deal for young people has been a great success. . . [S]ince 1997, [youth unemployment] has been reduced by 40 per cent.[406]

Data released in February 2004, detailing all activity through December 2003, indicate that many people have in fact benefited from the program. A total of 479,660 youths have been moved into jobs, 380,260 lasting at least 13 weeks ("sustained" jobs). Altogether 1,081,680 people started the NDYP, and only 86,390 remained by the end of 2003. Of those leaving, 39 per cent were in sustained jobs, but 12 per cent moved to other benefit programs. The others left for various known reasons or simply dropped out. Overall, the government can take justifiable pride in this program.

The NDLP has also been rather successful, in a sense. Because the program is voluntary, however, it is likely that those most likely to seek employment anyway have enrolled. Plus, there is evidently some confusion among lone parents on Income Support. In one survey, half thought that their second interview with a PA meant that they were in the NDLP. In any event, through December 2003, 459,070 individuals (94% of whom were women) passed through the program. Of these, 54 per cent, 247,310 had found jobs. Moreover, it appears that sustainability is high, standing at 85 per cent.[407] Some jobs paid so little, though, or the hours worked were so few that a number stay on Income Support. Overall, 54 per cent of those who have left NDLP also left Income Support. Looked at from another angle, one analysis found that with a matched set of participants and non-participants (that is, they shared all relevant traits except program participation), after nine months the employment rate for those on NDLP was 41 per cent whereas it was only 15 per cent for the non-participants.[408] Nevertheless, 29 per cent of those who leave Income Support return.

---

406. Hansard, November 17, 2003, p. 138642.
407. Evans, *New Deal for Lone Parents*, 81.
408. Evans, *New Deal for Lone Parents*, Table 5. 2, 75.

Other data tend to support the conclusion that the message is getting through. For example, the total caseload of lone parents on Income Support has continued to fall, as shown in Figure 10-2. (The total number of claimants for Income Support, however, has not fallen much, if any.[409]) Further, the employment rate among lone parents, even those with very young children has grown significantly. Therefore, more lone parents must be supporting themselves through paid work than before.

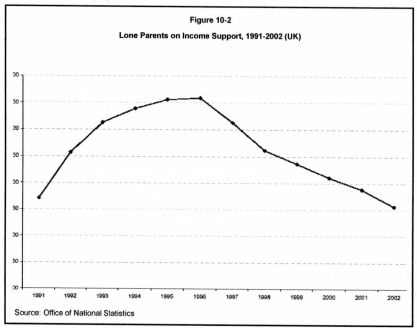

Figure 10-2

Lone Parents on Income Support, 1991-2002 (UK)

Source: Office of National Statistics

It is not clear what the escape rate from poverty is, as there are no survey studies such as those done in the United States. Some signs are encouraging, though. For example, as reported in Chapter 4, under Labour incomes in the lower deciles have grown slightly faster than those in the top reaches. Furthermore, the Child Tax Credit and Working Tax Credit, both of which are more generous than their American counterparts, can often lift someone who works enough hours, even at a low-wage job, out of poverty. However, there is no guarantee that the take up rate for these programs is 100 per cent, and they are still payments from the public purse. Indicative of these facts, perhaps, some data tell a different story. In 1994-95, 14 per cent of the working age population

---

409. Office of National Statistics, Department of Work and Pensions Statistical Summary, March 2004, 2.

Table 10-3		
Lone Percent Employment Rate (UK)		
Lone Percent's Youngest Child's Age	**1992**	**2002**
Under 5	22%	35%
5 to 10	44%	56%
11 to 15	62%	66%
Over 16	67%	75%
All lone parents	41%	54%

Source: Martin Evans, et al., New Deal for Lone Parents: Second Synthesis Report of the National Evaluation, p. 9.

was in poverty on a BHC basis and 20 per cent on an AHC basis. In 2002-03, the comparable percentages were 14 and 19. So, more young people and lone parents may be working, but they are not better off, at least relative to the rest of the population (recall that Britain measures poverty as 60 per cent of median income).[410]

Indeed, Martin Evans and his colleagues, authors of the major study evaluating the NDLP, concluded:

> Finally, the strong work-first orientation of current policy could be re-considered to widen the focus from transition into work to trajectories in work. One of the main concerns about this employment-based strategy for lone parents is that it risks locking them into low-paid work, from which it is difficult to escape and improve their situations. Helping lone parents increase their chances of obtaining better-paid and more secure employment is an even tougher challenge than getting lone parents into paid work, *but essential if the government also wants to achieve its target of creating a fairer and more inclusive society, including the elimination of child poverty.*[411] (Emphasis added.)

It will only be when a living wage job awaits those leaving NDYP and NDLP will reform be complete, and Mr. Browne or his successor be able to crow that there is truly a new day.

---

410. Office of National Statistics, *Households on Below Average Income Statistics, First Release*, March 2004, Table 4.1.

411. Evans, *New Deal for Lone Parents*, 109.

11. CONCLUSION

Marlene Mendoza is a waitress at Los Angeles International Airport. Before her city's living-wage ordinance, she made $5.50 an hour. With two children, she had to put in 80 hours a week to make ends meet. When the living wage passed, she jumped over the $7.00 per hour level, and could cut back to "only" 50 to 60 hours a week. "I work a lot less," she reported, and can now spend more time with her children. Kebede Woldesenbet, a 72-year-old parking attendant in Alexandria, Virginia, praised that city's living wage. Before, he made $6.50 an hour, afterward a little over $10.00. "I can't tell you how much we were suffering, and now, we're getting better.[412] Claudia Arevalo, a 37-year-old home health care worker in San Francisco, was able to give up her second job as a janitor when that city's living wage law went into effect. She now earns $10.00 an hour at her primary job. Diane Cunningham, a home health worker in Chicago, managed to buy a modest home when she went from $5.30 an hour to $7.60 an hour, thanks to the windy city's 1998 living wage policy.[413] Undoubtedly, these stories could be multiplied many times.

How much better would these people's lives be if we had a national living wage along the lines laid out in Chapter 5? They would not have to wear themselves out physically; they could have a better family life; they could save a little something for a rainy day; more of them could buy homes; they might could even take a small vacation. Their jobs would be no less unpleasant than they are

---

412. Both these examples are from Stephanie Armour, "Living-Wage Movement Takes Root Across Nation," *USA Today*, July 23, 2002.

413. Jane Tanner, "Living Wage Movement," *The CQ Researcher*, September 27, 2002, 781.

now, but the higher compensation would mean they could walk down the street and look anyone in the eye. They could walk with the self-confidence that only dignity gives. They could, whatever else, feel that they belong.

Welfare reform was a major political accomplishment. The welfare state had become crusty, inefficient, and counterproductive. The problem is that we have lost our way concerning the political theory of the welfare state. The right was correct to emphasize work. Only work can provide the dignity needed by every adult citizen. But the right has been shamefully unconcerned about what that work pays. We hear nothing but paeans to the free market and its wonders. However, when no one will work for the wages some firms are willing to pay, we get lectures on how we must open up the borders to allow more people in "who will take the low-wage jobs our people do not want." If the right were truly committed to the market, they would say that the shortage of dishwashers, gardeners, and cleaners should drive up the pay. On a recent television spot on President Bush's proposal to admit more foreign workers, the owner of a San Diego restaurant said that no American had ever applied for his dishwashing jobs and he therefore needed immigrants. I would be willing to bet that if the wage were high enough, any number of Americans would apply. The situation is the same in Britain, as the immigrant dominated portrait of low-wage workers given by Polly Toynbee attests. Of course, most Americans and Britons do not want to wash dishes or scrub floors for the minimum wage. But if the right were serious about markets, they would simply say to business owners, "up the wage."

The traditional left, on the other hand, has often devoted its energies to defending the indefensible: the right to public benefits without making any contribution. By adopting this stance, they have simply surrendered the battlefield to the right. The left needs to defend work as ardently as the right. Then it can unabashedly insist that work should pay adequately. It should pay enough, that is, to enable a person to live a decent life — without any fancy jury-rigging from the government such as the Earned Income Tax Credit or the Working Families Tax Credit. These programs are merely benefits by another name. They are tied to work, to be sure, and they are handled through the tax code, partly hiding their true character. But these payments are, quite simply, cash benefits from the state. They are a subsidy from the taxpayers which enables businesses and other employers to pay less than a living wage. Why not require the payment of a living wage in the first place and let the economic readjustments work themselves out? Of course, there would be some businesses that would face declines in profitability, but there would be others that would gain. I suspect, for example, that restaurants would face a profit squeeze. But if more people ate at home there would be more business for grocery stores. And so on. We should always remember that consumers are going to spend their money somewhere; it does not just dry up.

Anthony Giddens' idea of *The Third Way* provides a good start towards erecting a new political theory of the welfare state, one that stresses work and responsibility.[414] However, he does not, in my view, go far enough. A revitalized theory of the welfare state should rest on three basic propositions.

First, there should be a minimum standard of living below which no citizen will ever be allowed to fall. The definition of this standard will be subject to modifications as living standards increase. What it must *not* be is a poverty standard. It will be a "decent living" standard. Of course, it will be difficult to calculate and adjust, but the concept needs to be firmly planted. If you are a citizen, you are entitled to that standard of living.

Second, no cash benefits (or cash like items, such as vouchers) will be provided to anyone, except in rare instances, except as payment for work. There would have to be some exceptions, first, for those with certain types of disabilities. Second, social insurance programs — workmen's compensation, unemployment insurance, and old age pensions, for example — would continue in place. These are all work related, and therefore legitimate. Any other item the public deemed necessary for a decent life (such as health care or education) would be provided by public institutions. All such services would be available to everyone free of charge at point of service.[415] The general principle of no cash without work would always guide policy. This would mean, of course, that everyone who wanted to work would be guaranteed a job.

Thirdly, anyone who works full time, year round should earn enough to maintain a decent life style. The problems discussed in Chapter 5 will always be with us. There is no magic measuring rod. However, the general principle is crucially important: a full-time job will always allow you to meet the minimum standard.

A political theory of the welfare state erected around these three principles would achieve three ends. First, it would virtually eliminate poverty (I say virtually because there will always be people who, perhaps for reasons of mental illness, will reject the chance to work)[416] and go some distance toward softening inequality. Second, it would restore a sense of common citizenship. The ethos to

---

414. Anthony Giddens, *The Third Way* (Cambridge, UK: Polity Press, 1999).

415. No one should be compelled to use the public facilities. If someone wanted to attend a private school or obtain private health care, then that would be his/her choice. But no state funds should ever be used to pay for such private services.

be engrained in all would be twofold. You must make a contribution to society through work; such work will be adequately rewarded. Thus, no one would ever have his or her status as citizen questioned. (I expect that this would lead to increased participation in civic life, also.) Third, it would rebuild public support for the welfare state. The welfare state's critics won the war for public opinion in the 1990s because the left ceded it. They retreated to a decrepit citadel with multiple holes in the walls. The American and the British public both support welfare state policies, but they will not support them if they are not coupled to work. Through the living wage, there is therefore an opportunity to recover the initiative for decency.

Ironically, constructing this type of political theory would not be novel. It would merely be returning the welfare state to its origins. In both the United States and Britain, the minimum wage, aimed at being a living wage, was a cornerstone of the early reform movements. Its backers were motivated, to be sure, by a combination of civic republican and religious ideals, with somewhat different emphases in the two countries. But the connection between work and just compensation was central to them all. Modern support for a rejuvenated welfare state based on the living wage can also flow from several streams, as elaborated in Chapters 2 and 3. What is critical, though, is for there to be an indissoluble link forged between the obligation to work and the right to receive a living wage.

It would be a magnificent achievement if no one could ever write another book like either *Nickel and Dimed* or *Hard Work*. A universal living wage is the surest, most practical, and most widely supported path to that end.

---

416. In my view, they should be cared for in humane institutions and given the minimum standard there.

SELECTED BIBLIOGRAPHY

Ackerman, Bruce and Anne Alstott. *The Stakeholder Society*. New Haven, CT: Yale University Press, 1998.

Appleby, Joyce. *Liberalism and Republicanism in the Historical Imagination*. Cambridge, MA: Harvard University Press, 1992.

Armstrong, Barbara. *Insuring the Essentials: Minimum Wage Plus Social Insurance*. New York: Macmillan, 1932.

Atkinson, A.B. "The Case for a Participation Income." *Political Quarterly* 67 (1996), 67-70.

Banning, Lance. *The Jeffersonian Persuasion: Evolution of a Party Ideology*. Ithaca, NY: Cornell University Press, 1978.

_____. *The Sacred Fire of Liberty: James Madison and the Founding of the Federal Republic*. Ithaca, NY: Cornell University Press, 1995.

Bernstein, Jared, Chauna Brocht, and Maggie Spade-Aguilar. *How Much is Enough? Basic Budgets for Working Families*. Washington: Economic Policy Institute, 2000.

_____ and John Schmitt, *Making Work Pay: The Impact of the 1996-97 Minimum Wage Increase*. Washington: Economic Policy Institute, 1998.

Blackburn, Sheila. "Ideology and Social Policy: The Origins of the Trade Boards Act." *Historical Journal* 34 (1991), 43-64.

Blank, Rebecca. *It Takes a Nation: A New Agenda for Fighting Poverty*. Princeton, NJ: Princeton University Press, 1997.

Blitzer, Charles. *The Political Writings of James Harrington*. New Haven, CT: Yale University Press, 1960.

Card, David and Richard Krueger. *Myth and Measurement: The New Economics of the Minimum Wage.* Princeton, NJ: Princeton University Press, 1995.

Citro, Constance and Robert Michael. Editors. *Measuring Poverty: A New Approach.* Washington: National Academy Press, 1995.

Cole, G.D.H. *A History of the Labour Party from 1914.* New York: Augustus Kelley, 1949.

Dagger, Richard. *Civic Virtues: Rights, Citizenship and Republican Liberalism.* New York: Oxford University Press, 1997.

De Vries, Barend. *Champions of the Poor: The Economic Consequences of Judeo-Christian Values.* Washington: Georgetown University Press, 1998.

Dorrien, Gary. *The Making of American Liberal Theology: Idealism, Realism, and Modernity.* Louisville: Westminster John Knox Press, 2003.

Ehrenreich, Barbara. *Nickel and Dimed: On (Not) Getting by in America.* New York: Metropolitan Books, 2001.

Ellwood, David. *Poor Support: Poverty in the American Family.* New York: Basic Books, 1988.

Employment Policies Institute. *Living Wage Policy: The Basics.* Washington: Employment Policies Institute, 2000.

Epstein, Steven. "The Theory and Practice of the Just Wage." *Journal of Medieval History* 17 (1991), 53-71.

Evans, Christopher. Editor. *The Social Gospel Today.* Louisville: Westminster John Knox Press, 2001.

Evans, Martin, et al. *New Deal for Lone Parents: Second Synthesis Report of the National Evaluation.* Bristol, UK: Centre for Analysis of Social Policy, 2003.

Fraser, Derek. *The Evolution of the British Welfare State.* London: Macmillan, 1973.

Friedman, Milton. *Capitalism and Freedom.* Chicago: University of Chicago Press, 1962.

Gay, Craig. *With Liberty and Justice for Whom? The Recent Evangelical Debate over Capitalism.* Grand Rapids, MI: Eerdmans, 1991.

Giddens, Anthony. *The Third Way: The Renewal of Social Democracy.* Cambridge, UK: Polity Press, 1998.

Gilbert, Bentley. *British Social Policy, 1914-1939.* Ithaca, NY: Cornell University Press, 1970.

Glennerster, Howard. *British Social Policy since 1945.* Oxford, UK: Blackwell, 1995.

Glickman, Lawrence. *A Living Wage: American Workers and the Making of a Consumer Society.* Ithaca, NY: Cornell University Press, 1997.

Goodman, Alissa, Paul Johnson and Steven Webb. *Inequality in the U.K.* New York: Oxford University Press, 1997.

_____ and Andrew Shephard. *Inequality and Living Standards in Great Britain: Some Facts.* London: Institute for Fiscal Studies, 2002.

Greenstein, Robert and Isaac Shapiro. *The New, Definitive CBO Data on Income and Tax Trends.* Washington: Center on Budget and Policy Priorities, 2003.

Hammond, Matthew. "The Minimum Wage in Great Britain and Australia." *Annals of the American Academy of Political Science* 48 (1913), 22-36.

Harris, Jose. *William Beveridge: A Biography.* New York: Oxford University Press, 1977.

Hart, Vivien. *Bound by Our Constitution: Women, Workers, and the Minimum Wage.* Princeton, NJ: Princeton University Press, 1994.

Hicks, Douglas. *Inequality and Christian Ethics.* New York: Cambridge University Press, 2000.

Hohman, Helen Fisher. *The Development of Social Insurance and Minimum Wage Legislation in Great Britain.* Boston: Houghton Mifflin, 1933.

Keister, Lisa. *Wealth in America: Trends in Wealth Inequality.* New York: Cambridge University Press, 2000.

Levine, Aaron. *Economic Public Policy and Jewish Law.* New York: Yeshiva University Press, 1993.

Lowe, Rodney. "The Erosion of State Intervention in Britain, 1917-24." *Economic History Review* 31 (1978), 270-286.

Marshall, T.H. *Citizenship and Social Class.* Cambridge, UK: Cambridge University Press, 1950.

Mishell, Lawrence, Jared Bernstein, and Heather Boushey. *The State of Working America, 2002-2003.* Ithaca, NY: Cornell University Press, 2003.

Morris, Jenny. *Women Workers and the Sweated Trades: The Origins of Minimum Wage Legislation.* Aldershot, UK: Gower, 1986.

Moynihan, Daniel Patrick. *The Politics of a Guaranteed Income: The Nixon Administration and the Family Assistance Plan.* New York: Random House, 1973.

Neusner, Jacob. *The Economics of the Mishnah.* Chicago: University of Chicago Press, 1990.

Noble, Charles. *Welfare as We Knew It: A Political History of the American Welfare State.* New York: Oxford University Press, 1996.

Noell, Edd. "In Pursuit of the Just Wage: A Comparison of Reformation and Counter Reformation Economic Thought." *Journal of the History of Economic Thought* 23 (2001), 467-489.

Nordlund, Willis. *The Quest for a Living Wage: A History of the Federal Minimum Wage Program.* Westport, CT: Greenwood Press, 1997.

Oldfield, Adrian. *Citizenship and Community: Civic Republicanism in the Modern World.* London: Routledge, 1990.

Palmer, Guy, *et al. Monitoring Poverty and Social Exclusion 2003.* London: Joseph Rowntree Foundation, 2003.

Park, Alison, *et al. British Social Attitudes: The 20th Report.* London: Sage, 2003.

Piven, Frances Fox and Richard Cloward. *Regulating the Poor: The Functions of Public Welfare.* New York: Vintage, 1971.

Paulsen, George. *A Living Wage for the Forgotten Man: The Quest for Fair Labor Standards, 1933-41.* Selingsgrove, PA: Susquehanna University Press, 1996.

Petit, Philip. *Republicanism: A Theory of Freedom and Government.* New York: Oxford University Press, 1997.

Phelps, Edmund. *Rewarding Work: How to Restore Participation and Self-Support to Free Enterprise.* Cambridge, MA: Harvard University Press, 1997.

Phillips, Paul. *A Kingdom on Earth: Anglo-American Social Christianity, 1880-1940.* University Park: Pennsylvania State University Press, 1996.

Pollin, Robert and Stephanie Luce. *The Living Wage.* New York: New Press, 1998.

Quigley, William. *Ending Poverty as We Know It: Guaranteeing a Right to a Job at a Living Wage.* Philadelphia: Temple University Press, 2003.

Rackman, Emanuel. *Modern Halakhah for Our Times.* Hoboken, NJ: KTAV Publishing House, 1995.

Rauschenbush, Walter. *Christianity and the Social Crisis.* New York: Macmillan, 1907.

Ruggles, Patricia. *Drawing the Line: Alternative Poverty Measures and Their Implications for Public Policy.* Washington: Urban Institute Press, 1990.

Ryan, John A. *The Living Wage: Its Ethical and Economic Aspects.* New York: Macmillan, 1906.

Sen, Amartya. *Commodities and Capabilities.* Amsterdam: North Holland, 1985.

Shephard, Andrew. *Inequality Under the Labour Government.* London: Institute for Fiscal Studies, 2003.

Sider, Ronald. *Just Generosity: A New Vision for Overcoming Poverty in America.* Grand Rapids, MI: Baker Books, 1999.

Sklar, Holly, Laryssa Mykytz, and Susan Wefald. *Raising the Floor: Wages and Policies that Work for All of Us.* Boston: South End Press, 2001.

Smith, Adam. *The Wealth of Nations.* London: Methuen, 1911. Originally published 1776.

Tanner, Jane. "The Living Wage Movement." *Congressional Quarterly Researcher*, September 27, 2002.

Thiemann, Ronald. *Religion in Public Life: A Dilemma for Democracy.* Washington: Georgetown University Press, 1996.

Toynbee, Polly. *Hard Work: Life in Low-Pay Britain.* London: Bloomsbury, 2003.

Trattner, Walter. *From Poor Law to Welfare State: A History of Social Welfare in America*, 5th edition. New York: Basic Books, 1994.

Van der Veen, Robert and Loek Goot. Editors. *Basic Income on the Agenda: Objectives and Political Choices.* Amsterdam: Amsterdam University Press, 2000.

Walker, Robert and Michael Wiseman. Editors. *The Welfare We Want: The British Challenge for American Reform.* Bristol, UK: Policy Press, 2003.

Waltman, Jerold. *The Politics of the Minimum Wage.* Urbana: University of Illinois Press, 2000.

Weaver, R. Kent. *Ending Welfare as We Knew It.* Washington: Brookings, 2000.

Webb, Sidney and Beatrice Webb. *Industrial Democracy.* London: Longmans, 1897.

Wilson, William Julius. *When Work Disappears.* New York: Knopf, 1997.

Wolfe, Alan. "The Moral Meanings of Work." *American Prospect*, October 1997.

Wolff, Edward. *Recent Trends in Wealth Ownership, 1983-1998.* Annandale-on-Hudson, NY: Jerome Levy Institute, 2000.

Wuthnow, Robert. *Poor Richard's Principle: Rediscovering the American Dream Through the Moral Dimensions of Work, Business, and Money.* Princeton, NJ: Princeton University Press, 1996.

Zweig, Michael. Editor. *Religion and Economic Justice.* Philadelphia: Temple University Press, 1991.

INDEX